praise

You Are Never Alone

"I have spent the greater part of my adult life spiritually seeking answers and guidance on a very complex life path. The loss of my only son over twelve years ago plunged me into a depth of depression that was often unbearable—until I discovered through *You Are Never Alone* that the signs from my beautiful Guardian Angel were always there to see. In my view, Judith Turner is a gift to mankind. Her books on birthdays and relationships are treasured resources in my library, used constantly by me and close friends. Judith Turner is the real deal; her intuitive interpretation is matched by very few spiritual consultants."

—**Joe Cicio**, fashion retail CEO, environmental designer, creative consultant, author of *Friends**Bearing Gifts*

"In the midst of your chaos, Judith gives answers in finding peace with Guardian Angels and guides, one story at a time."

—**Gila Seliktar**, The Feminine Channel

"Seven out of ten people believe they have a Guardian Angel. I am one of them. I feel the presence of my grandfather every day as he guides and protects me through life. In this book, Judith does a wonderful job decoding hundreds of stories into messages that help us relate and understand the energy we all receive from Heaven."

—**Tiqui Atencio Demirdjian**, author and philanthropist

"I have known Judith Turner for decades, and she has been a trusted confidant. As loss started to become overwhelming, she helped me recognize the signs that surround me. Whenever I find a dime, am visited by a fly, or encounter any other signs I've come to recognize, I have Judith to thank for the interpretations. She is always spot-on—an amazing resource. I believe in this book because others who are feeling the pain of loss can be comforted by these stories, just as I am."

—**Michele Litzky,** Litzky Public Relations

"A friend and advisor for over thirty years, I've always said I don't need a shrink because I have Judith Turner. Her insight and messages have always comforted and educated me, providing meaning and profound wisdom beyond measure."

—**Wendy Federman**, sixteen-time Tony Award–winning Broadway producer

"Judith Turner is a renowned psychic. She has written for *BC the Mag* for many years, and her abilities are known throughout the area. She has truly given her clients amazing insights into their lives and passed along many thoughts from relatives or friends from the beyond. She is truly amazing!"

—**Sharon Goldstein**, copublisher *BC the Mag*

"Judith Turner is a spot-on psychic medium, my experiences with her have been spiritual and enlightening. She is the perfect author to write *You Are Never Alone*."

—**Kim D**, *Real Housewives of New Jersey,* author of *My Life with the Big Boys*

"Judith Turner amazes me with her accuracy and precise predictions each time I have had the pleasure of being in her presence. Her books are a must read. The knowledge that she puts forward in regard to birthdays and zodiac signs blows you away. Judith has withstood the test of time with her spiritual gift of connecting to the afterlife and forwarding the information in a clear, concise manner."

— **Connie Panicucci,** TikTok influencer @napolipizzalodi and cohost of *Connie & Tyra's Diner Podcast*

"With intuition, insight, and her magical powers of common sense, Judith will bring these messages and their meanings to you all wrapped up in a bow. If I were you, I'd listen."

— **Ally Walker,** writer, director, actress, and author of *The Light Runner*

You Are Never Alone

Hugs from Heaven

A JOURNAL OF LOVE & INSIGHT

JUDITH TURNER

Foreword by Tommy Hilfiger

Artist: Susanne Nothdurft
Editor: Elizabeth Waters Murray

Heavenly Wishes LLC

Published by Heavenly Wishes LLC

Produced by GMK Writing and Editing, Inc.
Managing Editor: Katie Benoit
Copyedited by Kelly Nutter Clody
Proofread by Elizabeth Crooks
Cover design by Vicky Vaughn Shea
Text design and composition by Libby Kingsbury

Printed by IngramSpark

Print ISBN: 978-1-966981-11-4
Ebook EISN: 978-1-966981-12-1

Visit the author at www.judith-turner.com

This work was written, designed, and produced without the use of AI (Artificial Intelligence). Human creativity and intelligence may not be perfect, but they are far better than anything artificial.

Note: *This publication is presented solely for informational, educational, and entertainment purposes. It is not intended to provide personal, relationship, legal, business, financial, or other advice and should not be relied upon as such. If expert assistance is required, the services of a professional should be sought. The producer and the author and their affiliated entities and individuals do not make any guarantees or other promises as to any results that may be obtained from using the content of this book. To the maximum extent permitted by law, the producer and the author and their affiliated entities and individuals disclaim any and all liability in the event any information contained in this book proves to be inaccurate, incomplete, or unreliable, or results in any harm or loss. You, the reader, are responsible for your own choices, actions, and results.*

Dedication

**In Memory to Honor
Kevin Turen**

Thank you to the one who encouraged me to pick up a pen and rediscover my voice as an author.

You believed in this book along with my ability to write something that could captivate any audience. Your faith and support meant everything.

You were an Earthly Angel that has become a Guardian Angel, watching over me and so many others.

Truly loved and never forgotten.

The Eagle Has Landed!

My Honors Through My Journey of Love & Insight

JERI TURNER SINNIG

My Earthly Angel,
Who shows up in silence,
Fighting the battles of life today, yet never giving
    up on me, all while being my biggest cheer-
    leader, my sister, my friend, and, of course,
    my courage.

You share every part of my life: my joy, my
    sorrows, my strength, my weaknesses.
You share your thoughts but keep your own burdens quiet,
    never wanting to burden others.
You have reason to walk with paralyzed fear, yet carry quick
    wit, a sense of humor, and boundless love for those you hold
    dear.
You move through this world with a pure heart and soul, always
    finding a way to pay it forward when and where you can.
You are a giver who leads with her head, yet always with her
    heart.
My earthly message back to you:
I am never me without you.
You are Never Alone; I am always here for you.
You always make me know I am Never Alone either.
Thank you, my girl!

Campbell, Hadleigh, & Babies to Come

My purest souls, my Earthly Angels who recharge and revitalize
my heart and soul with every smile. With every hug you give, you
bring me so much joy!

Walter "Sparky" Deptuch

If I didn't love you, I would always like you! Thank you for being you! You're the best there is! I Love and Appreciate You Always! XO

Walter "Wojo" Deptuch

The man of few words, who says so much in silence. Then comes law, comedy, football, and, of course, giving encouraging advice. You believed in me finding my path and I did.

Brianne Deptuch Kuder

The kindest and most generous soul! You are more than the glue that holds me and so many together. One amazing person. So glad you picked me!

Alexandria Deptuch

You lead with your heart, while you keep mine beating. You're still too young to realize how "Gucci" a person you truly are!

John Kuder, Bonus Son

The perfect pitch, and you landed into our family. How lucky are we? The perfect fit!

Ricky Sinnig

Everything you build in life takes a great contractor. You are ours for our family. The fixer of all things wonderful.

Joanne & Dave Connelly

Always showing up at the right time on the right day! In the absolute right way! No coincidence.

Andrew (Runt) & Debora Turner

Always showing up in ways you think don't matter, yet they matter the most.

Mommy & Daddy

Thank you, my Angels, for helping me through each project. Every day, I realize more and more how amazing you are. I carry your footprints in my heart always.

A very special thank-you to all my Guardians who joined me in writing this book, who brought forth the words and answers we all need.

acknowledgments

Elizabeth Waters Murray, Editor: There is no other explanation for how I was lucky enough to work on this project with you — God decided one Tuesday at noon. I am forever grateful to have had you as my editor and, more importantly, as my friend on this journey. Your passion to understand my vision has been unwavering, and your kindness, boundless. I will never forget this all-encompassing project and your relentless efforts from day one. I hope this journey continues, as work has never been so fun! Beyond Blessed!

Susanne Nothdurft, Artist: The most incredible visionary in the art world, if you ask me. This was a dream — one that came together beautifully. There's no other artist I would have wanted to embark on this with — plus, they wouldn't have brought chocolates! Thank you beyond words, my dear Miss Susanne.

Jennifer Connelly, Communications Director: TikTok, Instagram, and everything in between — you did it all! You were the butcher, the baker, and the candlestick maker. Your ideas, thoughts, and input were invaluable. It was such a pleasure working with you on this project. You are a true complement to everything you touch.

Walter J. Deptuch, Esq., Quiet Support Staff: It's always the quiet ones who make the greatest impact. Thank you for your impeccable timing and your incredible encouragement.

Robert Metzdorf: The best at giving advice by refraining from giving advice. I love you for that. A girl's best friend.

Debbie Reilly: As always, your efforts and support make everything I do that much easier. Thank you!

Joe Ciccio: You are a rock star and always will be. Your unwavering support has been truly unbelievable. To have the backing of such a creative director, with so many accomplishments under your belt, is something a girl could only dream of. Thank you for everything. You are The Man!

Jan Turen: Thank you for keeping the pen in my hand with your stories, for picking up where Kevin left off, encouraging *You Are Never Alone: Hugs from Heaven*, and believing in both his vision and mine.

Gary M. Krebs: Thank you for believing in me and in this project. I'm incredibly grateful for the faith you've always shown in me.

Patricia "Squires" Lindemann: Thank you for your help and support, Cuz!

Bob Murray: Thank you for all your support — namely Staples and Sear!

Liz Kall: From eight grade to eighty, I could Kall on you! Walking through life one step at a time.

Carol Sahagian: Walk and talk.

Melinda Daley: The gift! The book!

Susan Monaghan: Encouraging, always.

Janice Meyer: Just in case girl.

Rhonda Charles: Cheerleader.

Alicia Metzdorf: Director of input.

Donna Lanza: No coincidence, 217.

Elena Cioffi-Williams: You're my Guardian Angel stories Earthly Angel.

Elaine & Lauren LoConte: Thank you both for being on this journey with me.

Lily Beahm: Thank you for your incredible creativity and support to help kickstart this project.

Bruce Fischer: For being an incredible sponsor and champion behind this book.

Lindsay Tesher: You are both a blue rose and a rock.

Paul Tong: Thank you for hosting a wonderful evening. Those Angels must have had a plan when we met in 8th grade.

Jill Sedley: Everything happens for a reason, and I never imagined one of those reasons would be you hosting a party for this book. Thank you for your enthusiasm and for calling the book "spectacular."

To All the Contributors: Grateful and blessed for all the slices of life you've shared along with your Guardian Angels and for participating in this journey to create this platform for others to accept what they feel, what they see, and what they know. These are messages that matter!

Thank you for bringing comfort through libations and sustenance in our time of need, along with all of your support:

- Dimora #1 of Norwood, New Jersey
- Sear of Closter, New Jersey
- Mimi's Plates of Tappan, New York (Karen & the girls)
- JK Ryan's of Tappan, New York (Neal & Amy)

Contents

Foreword

by Tommy Hilfiger

Why should you read this book?

When you know someone is going to write a great book long before they do!

"When you know, you know."

That's what this book is all about!

Congratulations, Judith!

I always knew you were going to write an incredible book! I cannot wait!

I am so happy for you.

You are a very special person!

X Tommy

Tommy Hilfiger

preface

A Journey Guided by Guardian Angels

I have been writing this book my whole life without even realizing it, one Guardian Angel story at a time. A wink, a nod, a recurring number on a clock, or a penny found on the street are all subtle signs from beyond.

For years, I searched for the right way to bring this book to life, not just to validate my own experiences but to affirm the experiences of others. Then, one afternoon, I had a conversation with my friend Kevin Turen, a highly successful Hollywood producer. Somehow, the idea for this book came up, a collection of Guardian Angel stories with a twist—not just the stories themselves, but insights into their meaning. Kevin loved it. He said, "Wow, this could be so much more—not just a book, but a podcast, a TV show, even woven into movies and other mediums."

His excitement was contagious. It is rare to find someone who believes in your passion as much as you do. Inspired, I set a deadline to organize my vision and gather enough stories to share with him. We brainstormed titles, and his last words to me on the subject were: "I love this title for the book, *You Are Never Alone: Hugs from Heaven.*"

Two days later, Kevin tragically passed away at the age of forty-four.

Looking back, I don't see our conversation as mere coincidence. We had been talking about hugs from Heaven, and now, he had become the one sending them. That realization made me even more determined to bring this book to life, knowing that Kevin's belief in it was his final gift to me.

Throughout this book, you'll find stories about Kevin, but his presence isn't the only one guiding me. Since his passing, other Hollywood legends have unknowingly encouraged me by sharing their own Guardian Angel experiences. Here are some stories, revealed through various media, that perfectly align with the message of this book, and their stories help validate why I'm writing this book.

- In December 2023, Anderson Cooper's podcast episode with Stephen Colbert, titled "Grateful for Grief," was a profound reveal for dealing with grief and touched me personally.

- Alan Hamel, husband of Suzanne Somers, shared with *People* magazine in January 2024 that signs and strange occurrences happened after his beloved wife passed away.

- In a May 2024 interview, Carol Burnett shared that receiving the gift of bird of paradise flowers was a loving message from her daughter.

- In May 2024, Courteney Cox spoke about getting a little help from her guides, meaning Matthew Perry and her parents.

This book was meant to give ordinary people a platform to share their stories, only for me to discover that even the most extraordinary people experience the same signs and the same messages from beyond. Their messages have fallen in my footsteps for a reason. When I needed inspiration after Kevin's passing, I was looking for a significant sign to motivate me to move forward with this book. I look at all these words from Hollywood icons as guidance and Kevin's hugs from Heaven.

Introduction

After many years as an intuitive consultant and writer, I have discovered that we all share something profound in common, though we don't always speak about it—the presence of Guardian Angels.

Everyone has a story they hesitate to tell, fearing it might sound unbelievable. Yet, these very stories are what bring us hope, reassurance, and a sense of connection. They remind us that we are never truly alone. God watches over us, as do our loved ones and those who guide us from beyond. Miracles—both big and small—happen every day, and the signs we receive from our Guardian Angels are often the subtle yet powerful moments that bring us comfort and direction.

Signs can be as simple as finding a penny in an old pocketbook that causes just enough delay to prevent an accident or receiving a phone call at the exact moment we need it most. These moments hold deeper meaning, guiding us through life's challenges and celebrations alike.

In this book, each story is paired with *"Judith's Insight,"* an intuitive interpretation that helps uncover the significance of the signs and symbols within each experience. Some stories may be brief, while others span several pages, but each holds a unique and meaningful message. Readers may connect with different elements of every story, depending on their own life experiences. For instance, while multiple stories may involve cardinals, each carries its own distinct meaning and interpretation.

There is something extraordinary about receiving the perfect sign at a wedding, a funeral, or during a moment of uncertainty. Many people experience these signs but hesitate to share them. I believe that everyone, at some point, has encountered them.

Some recognize their Guardian Angels in loved ones who have passed or even in animals, while others may see them as divine messages. Whether it's a song that strikes an emotional chord or a number that repeatedly appears, these moments are not coincidences. A blue jay, dragonfly, or butterfly might arrive just when we need a reminder that those who have passed are at peace, sending us love and reassurance. Even dreams can be a way for our loved ones to bring guidance and comfort.

Through these stories, I hope you will see how connected we all are when it comes to receiving signs from Heaven. Each experience shared here is a testament to the hope, comfort, and presence of our Guardian Angels. Remember, the profound and sometimes inexplicable experiences we encounter are real for us, offering solace and inspiration; an ever-present reminder that you are never alone.

REFLECTION 1

Heavenly

*When the unexplainable can only be explained by knowing
you have a Guardian Angel.*

—Judith Turner

Broken People Need More Than Glue

Jan Turen

Life's journey can bring more pain and grief than one could ever imagine enduring. Why do I want to tell this story? Because you are reading it. What I once believed was the greatest tragedy of my life was losing my first son, Scott. To this day, the circumstances of his death remain an incredible mystery. He was a young father with two small children, his whole future ahead of him. I'm still not sure how I survived that loss—but somehow, I did.

Scott once said, "Broken people need more than glue." Those words became my lifeline. Every day, I searched for what I needed to hold myself together. I clung to every sign he sent me, watching football games as if he were still beside me, sometimes even feeling as if he were one of the players on the field. I reflected on his deep love for politics and history, remembering the memorabilia and collectibles he couldn't resist. But the greatest gift, the one that truly kept me going, was the bond I shared with his two amazing boys. Day after day, year after year, they gave me another reason to live.

Of course, my other children, Kevin and Ashley, were my anchors. Kevin did everything he could to help me heal, always keeping me engaged with stories about his latest Hollywood project, a last-minute trip to a film festival, or a new creative venture. He and his wife, Evelina, blessed me with two more incredible boys. Their home was always filled with warmth, love, and laughter, and they made sure I felt included at every moment. Life was beginning to move forward again. Then, my daughter Ashley gave me the most unexpected gift—a grandson, Luca. A beautiful surprise. A blessing. A hidden prayer answered. I felt as if Scott knew exactly what I needed and had sent me an Earthly Angel. Talk about a Heavenly hug.

But just as I started to believe I had found solid ground again, the unimaginable happened. Kevin—my rock, my light—died suddenly while driving with his son. My ten-year-old grandson, with an instinct far beyond his years, took the wheel, pulled the car to safety, and called 911 to try to save his father's life. But Kevin was gone.

The grief was beyond comprehension. There are no words that could adequately describe the numbness, the pain, the anger, the frustration—the absolute devastation. Another son. Another shattered heart. I didn't believe I would ever recover.

Yet, in the depths of my despair, Kevin sent me signs just as Scott had. At his funeral, thousands of people gathered. Every A-lister in Hollywood was there, sharing stories of his kindness, his generosity, his brilliance. But what comforted me most wasn't the accolades. It was the messages Kevin sent. The hawk. The eagle. The producer.

He produced more than films, he produced hope, love, family, and even small miracles. And he continued to do so, even after he was gone. Not just for me, but for his wife, his children, and his friends. One by one, stories poured in. Signs appeared.

In an ironic twist of fate, Kevin had been working with my dear friend Judith on an entertainment package for a book and podcast. Their last conversation took place two days before he died. They had been brainstorming titles, searching for the perfect one. No coincidence, Kevin's final words to Judith about the project were: "Miss you! I love the title *You Are Never Alone: Hugs from Heaven*. I can't wait to read it, and I'll send it around." I was speechless.

And then, just yesterday, I was speaking with my daughter-in-law. She told me that Kevin's son, Jack, had come to her and said, "Dad came to me and told me to ask you if you're okay." She responded gently, "Yes, Jack, I'm okay. What did it feel like?" Jack's answer? "It feels like he's giving me hugs." (Hugs from Heaven.)

Judith's Insight:

This reads like a movie, because, in a way, it is. And behind it all was one hell of a producer. A great film captures the full spectrum of human emotion: heartbreak, pain, love, loss, and the glue that holds it all together. They say what doesn't kill you makes you stronger. But sometimes, it feels like it just might kill you.

In your story, your boys found a way to help you—not just in life, but in loss. Not only did they prepare you for the unimaginable, but they continue to hold your hand through both the pain and the healing.

Scott laid the blueprint, giving you the foundation to find your way through his absence. Then Kevin, the ultimate producer, filled in the scenes—adding the bells and whistles, the first takes, the second takes, and even the outtakes. He created an incredible legacy, one that now allows you to not only cherish every moment of his life but also to move forward with your own.

Life is a journey of footprints and blueprints: a story filled with hidden signs, like a scavenger hunt sent from those we've lost. We climb mountains, struggle through valleys, and find healing in the ocean's waves. We need every part of it—the challenges, the beauty, and the messages from beyond—because they remind us that love doesn't end, even when life does.

We need to tell our stories, no matter how bizarre or unexplainable they may seem. We shouldn't question the signs that touch our hearts or the feelings we can't quite define. If it means something to us, that's all that matters. There is no right or wrong. How beautiful is it to know that someone, somewhere, is still looking out for us; sending a sign, a nod, a wink, a hug, a hello, or simply whispering, "I got you."

So, walk forward, knowing that no explanations are needed. No definitions are required. Just hold on to this truth: You are never alone. And embrace the hugs from Heaven.

Evelina's Story

Jan Turen

The battles of grief and loss are deeply real, especially following the recent loss of my son, Kevin. As you can imagine, we've all been on high alert, looking for signs and messages from him. I have been lucky enough to have had my own winks and nods. Kevin's soul connection with my daughter-in-law, Evelina, has been a source of incredible comfort. Since his passing, she has received constant guidance and messages from Kevin. Their bond is extraordinary, and together they leave no stone unturned in their passionate and consistent efforts to communicate heart to heart.

For weeks, Evelina had been asking Kevin to send her a "colorful butterfly." Yes, for weeks. She would share how prompt Kevin had been with her requests since his passing. But despite her repeated requests, the butterfly hadn't appeared. Frustrated, she asked again, pouring out her feelings and expectations, knowing this time would be significant. This wouldn't be just any butterfly. No, it had to be something extraordinary.

Around this time, Evelina's friend Harrison, who had a brotherly bond with Kevin, had been trying for weeks to give her a gift for from his mother. Harrison and Kevin had shared a special connection, something that felt almost like fate. Kevin had always felt blessed to have such a close-knit circle of friends. So, when the gift arrived, it turned out to be the most magnificent, colorful butterfly. It glistened like a star in the night sky, or like a diamond catching the sun.

When we saw it, we all knew this was Kevin's way of sending the butterfly through Harrison and his amazing mother— like a carrier pigeon bringing a sign of love and connection. The signs and even the smallest nods have been ways Evelina has been able to communicate and feel Kevin's love from the other side. The butterfly and other messages and gifts are how we breathe when tomorrow comes and Kevin's not here!

Judith's Insight:

Every answer comes with its own perfect timing, and though we often look for reasonable and rational responses, our guides don't always follow those rules. Like the stories of Guardian Angels, the answers often reveal themselves in unexpected, sometimes thrilling ways. Expect the unexpected.

This butterfly, full of serenity and hope, is just the beginning of an incredible story. It teaches us that even when we ask for signs, we may not receive them exactly as we expect. We often envision how things should unfold, how our requests should be answered, even imagining what the response might look like. Sometimes, it happens just as we expect. Other times, the answer arrives with a twist, offering a deeper and more loving meaning.

Kevin's message: "I am here, listening, even when you think I am not." The response may not always come in real time, but it will come. When you think I'm not answering, remember, I may be using others—my family, my village of brothers—to help me communicate what I can't.

This story mirrors the journey of a butterfly: the egg, the caterpillar, the waiting, the frustration, and then the butterfly—finally, the answer. The most exquisite, colorful butterfly you could ever receive.

The ultimate message: You Are Never Alone. I left you with my heart, a village of family and friends, and my brothers, who will continue to be my shadow and hold your hand, along with your heart, so you are never alone. Even though you may not always see me the way you want or feel me, know that I will always find ways to send you a hug from Heaven.

Crossing Over Angel

Elizabeth Waters Murray

There is never a good day when your hero dies. When the man who walked this earth holding your hand dies way too young, having so much life ahead of him. His passing didn't just take my breath away, it paralyzed me. It took Heaven and earth for me to move forward after his death.

One year to gate, that's Heaven's gate, he was fighting esophageal cancer, enduring surgery after surgery, test after test. With every prod, every poke, I felt his pain as if it were my own. But not him. He took it all like a champ. My father, the big, burly fireman, was larger than life not only to me but to so many; he carried himself with strength and pride. He walked through our community with purpose, with heart. Watching him struggle day by day was unbearable, yet even then, he made it all look so easy. Dad carried the heavy weight of his journey with the same grace, courage, and faith that he carried everything else. My champ. My hero. Although I had three very young children, I lived just around the corner, which became the ultimate Godsend during his last days. With the unwavering love and support of my husband Bob, our close proximity allowed me to be there for my dad.

The last few days of his life were the hardest. But my faith in God and Angels is what saved me. I knew he wouldn't go alone. I knew there would be so many to take his hand—family, friends, even passersby. And I knew in my heart that when he left me, he would somehow find his way back to me to hold my hand and walk in the sand at the beach again.

And he has. He walks beside me in ways only I can feel. In the sight of his badge number, 60, appearing in unexpected places. In the days I spend at the beach with my feet in the sand, where I feel closest to him. In the rainbows that seem to follow me. In the words of others, spoken at just the right moment, as if he's sending me messages through them. In sermons at church, in songs I hear on the radio, and those sung by friends and family.

Dad was a man who never gave up. And he still hasn't. He is my Guardian Angel. I know it. I live it. I feel it. I can't forget those pennies from Heaven.

Judith's Insight:

Your father knew your love. He felt it in every moment you cared for him; in every second you sat by his side. He also felt your pain, the way your heart broke as you watched him struggle. But his journey was his own, and even though your love was undeniable, he carried his own burdens as he faced the inevitable.

Some people choose to pass alone, while others welcome the presence of those who have gone before them. No matter the path, no one ever crosses over by themselves. There are always Crossing Over Angels—whether they are loved ones, spirits, or guiding energies—who come to help.

You were meant to be there at that moment. It wasn't an accident, nor was it coincidence. You were a part of his journey, a witness to his transition, and that is no small thing. Being present for someone's crossing is, in fact, a gift. Earthly Angels are chosen to be there, just as those crossing over are chosen to receive them. It is a sacred exchange.

Many people who are nearing the end begin to see and speak to those who have already passed. They might call out to their parents, spouses, or long-lost friends, sometimes even holding full conversations with those we cannot see. These aren't hallucinations. They are glimpses into something beyond this world, a final reunion before the journey home. In those final days and moments, their lives replay like a story unfolding one last time. Memories surface—some long forgotten, some crystal clear. It's as if their spirit is performing its final act, retelling the moments that mattered most before they step into the unknown.

Sometimes we can feel the presence of others as someone crosses over—like my mother did, calling out to my dad, whose name was Bobby, and to her mother, whom she called Mama. Being present as the soul lifts brings peace as you feel they are now in Heaven. Heaven's gate is not a cross to bear alone. Some spirits struggle to find peace in their passing, feeling the weight of unfinished business or the pain of leaving loved ones behind. Crossing Over Angels ease that burden, offering comfort and guidance. They ensure that the journey is made not in fear, but in love.

Just as a newborn intuitively knows its mother's heartbeat, there is a sacred knowledge that comes with death. Some people seem to choose the moment they pass, holding on until the right person is there, or slipping away when they feel it is time. There is a destiny in it, a knowing that is beyond explanation.

The final moments of a person's life, their Last Act, hold the essence of everything they were: the love they gave, the struggles they endured, the people they cherished. It all converges in those last breaths, in that quiet space between two worlds. And for those who are present, for those who bear witness, it is both heartbreaking and beautiful. Because in that space, love doesn't end. It transforms. It lingers, it whispers, it waits to be recognized. And if you listen closely, you'll hear it. Always.

Picture This

Lindsay Tesher

I have been incredibly lucky to be close to all my grandparents. However, I had a very special bond with my grandpa Sidney, whom I called Pop Pop. He lived into his nineties and was the kind of guy who felt like he would live forever. As I grew older, I made sure to spend plenty of time with him. He was a true New

Yorker, and our usual activity involved eating food from diners, delis, or pizza parlors. One day, after one of our excursions to order a slice of his favorite pesto pizza, I was walking him back to his apartment. Suddenly, I felt the need to take his picture. He had lived in his building for over sixty years, and it felt so right to encapsulate the moment. As he walked away, I yelled, "Turn around and wave." I took a picture and immediately added it to my photo folder in my phone.

A few years later, his health started to decline. My dad, who had moved away, was struggling with the possibility of losing his father. I sensed he needed something from his father to hold on to. I remembered the picture and felt it was the perfect item to send my dad to give him some comfort. I had the photo printed on canvas and shipped it to his house. One week later, as my dad was opening the package with the picture in it, he received a call from the hospital that his father had just passed away. He was actually opening the picture of his father waving goodbye at that exact moment. That day, Pop Pop was waving goodbye to my dad.

Judith's Insight:

"Picture this." That's exactly what you do as you read this story — fragments of life coming together to form a complete picture. Sometimes, what seems like a simple moment turns into something far greater, revealing the hidden connections between this world and the next.

This Guardian Angel began his work long before he left. Before he ever earned his wings, he was already proving himself as an Earthly Angel. And when the time came for him to move on, his role simply shifted. They do that, you know. They don't leave us; they just change form. As time passes, you'll likely notice more pictures, more signs, and more of those unforgettable Heavenly hints that whisper messages of love when you need them most.

Then there's your dad's story, a perfectly timed gift, arriving within minutes of his father's passing. He lived too far away to be there, never knowing how quickly his father would be gone. And yet, a simple, thoughtful gesture from his daughter became something extraordinary, something priceless. That picture, the wave, the unspoken goodbye, it wasn't just a memory. It was a bridge between worlds. The father found a way to say goodbye, and the son received the message. Now that's peace.

Photographs, pictures, and videos—these are the ways we pay it forward for the days when we need them most. They become signs from our Guardian Angels when we least expect them, but most need them.

So, if you've ever searched for a sign, go ahead, I dare you. Reach into that old box of photos. Pick one. Hold it. Let it speak to you. No, it's not magic, but something magical will happen. Angels are always trying to reach us. A picture is never just a picture. It's a message. A moment frozen in time. A hug from Heaven. All you have to do is hold it close and listen, feel, and "Picture this."

'Twas the Night Before Christmas
Karen Laggner

Every Christmas Eve, my dad gathered all his grandchildren around and read *'Twas the Night Before Christmas* to them. After he passed away, we felt it was only fitting that the book be placed in his coffin. Unfortunately, no one was able to locate the book. While I was writing his eulogy, I heard a loud crash by the front door and ran over to see what had happened. Everything looked in order until I opened the coat closet. There on the floor was the lost book, *'Twas the Night Before Christmas*. My dad had to show me where it was!

During a funeral or wake, those who have passed sometimes find ways to interfere or interrupt—gentle nudges to remind us they're still near. A flickering light. A butterfly landing at just the right moment. A sudden movement. Uncontrollable laughter in the midst of grief. A bird soaring overhead. A single raindrop falling as if on cue. The list goes on, but the message is always the same: "I'm here."

It was never about taking the book with him; it was about leaving behind the tradition. He was more than happy to carry a piece of all of you, along with the memories you shared. Your dad is your Guardian Angel, and he wasted no time letting you know he would always be by your side, especially every time you hear or read *'Twas the Night Before Christmas*. And if you ever find yourself spotting that book on a shelf, in a store, or tucked away in a forgotten corner of your home, know that he is still sending you a message.

Traditions are like etched footprints on our souls, creating sacred spaces in our hearts where memories are stored. We may not think of them every day, but then—out of nowhere—a trigger brings them rushing back. A sound, a smell, a simple moment. A fast recall of something that once warmed our souls. And just like that, yesterday reaches out to help us through tomorrow. Guardian Angels truly do work in mysterious ways. And if you're paying attention, you'll always know, they never really leave.

The Day My Heart Broke
Elaine LoConte

On June 13, 2021, I received a phone call that forever changed my life. I was called by the police department to come to the station immediately. My day started out normally, as my sister Jackie and I were cleaning out our beach house because we had just sold it. My husband was at work. It was a beautiful day. There wasn't a cloud in the sky, or so I thought. I met my husband at the police station thinking we may be in a little trouble because one of my pit bulls may have caused a problem with a neighbor. I couldn't have been more wrong. I didn't know I was moments away from completely losing my mind.

The officer sat my husband and I down and proceeded to tell us that our daughter, Lauren, was dead. Tears flowed and my heart raced. I thought I was going to die myself. At one point, I think I left my body because I just couldn't handle the pain. The police officer continued to tell us that Lauren and her boyfriend apparently received a "bad batch" of something from a dealer on the street. Lauren was found dead on the floor in her apartment. Her boyfriend, Alex, survived, as he happened to have only one dose of Narcan, which he decided to administer to himself. Even after he realized he was okay and my daughter was unconscious on the floor, he still did not call 911. He waited. Then, he went across the hall to the neighbor's apartment while Lauren was lying on the floor dying. As I heard the recap of her death, it only compounded my hysterical reaction. The pain to hear that he could have had a chance to save her life, but chose not to, was unbearable. From that day forward, every waking hour was a nightmare of pain, confusion, anger, and suffering.

Over the next few months, it became harder and harder to cope with the grief and handle my own anger. In my eyes, Alex always claimed to love my daughter, yet he allowed her to die so callously and selfishly. I believed he was the one who gave her the drugs that wound up killing her. I'm not proud of this, but I prayed to God to please take this monster. For months I would encounter people who told me that Lauren was with me. They told me to pay attention to the signs from her because they were all around me. They told me that she would come to me in my dreams. To this day, I wait for Lauren to find me in my dreams.

One day, Lauren sent me a message while I was wide awake. "Mommy, please, you will have peace. Alex will meet his own burdens in his life. It's going to be okay, Mommy." Almost two years to the date of Lauren's death, I received a call from one of Lauren's friends. As I picked up the phone, I heard the words, "The monster is dead, the monster is dead." At that moment, I found myself relieved, not because I wanted him dead. I was relieved that what happened to my dear Lauren would never happen to anyone else. I never wanted to hear that another person died at the hands of this awful person. I must say, it gave me peace knowing that others were saved, even though Lauren was not.

Judith's Insight:

Though grief still holds you tightly, Lauren's message has offered you a glimpse of peace and hope. Your Angel daughter has been reaching out, hoping you would trust in her words and understand that her passing was not in vain. She has never left you — not through the unbearable burden of losing a child, not through the profound powerlessness and pain that followed.

To you, the reasons behind her passing may never fully make sense. But her message was never about predicting more loss, it was about easing your suffering. Angels don't come to foretell the future; they come to protect, to guide, and to hold us steady when we can no longer stand on our own. Lauren's death, while an unimaginable tragedy, became a catalyst for change.

It shed light on the importance of trust and the dangers of drugs, ultimately saving lives and teaching invaluable lessons in its wake. Her legacy is not one of loss, but of hope, transformation, and love that endures beyond this world.

Grief—especially the kind that comes with shocking tragedy—steals your heart, beats it to a pulp, and then steps on it. There is no logic, no reason that can make sense of it. The weight of such loss is too much for one soul to carry alone. It takes an army of Angels, maybe even the Army of Angels — or perhaps the borrowed strength of others' Angels to help you through.

Grief has no timeline, and no one should ever question its length. It unfolds in its own way, on its own terms. And then, somewhere in the midst of the sorrow, a new form of oxygen starts to breathe life back into your soul.

Is it a cure for loss? No. Is is a way to move on with the ultimate understanding that although they have moved to the other side, you now get to embrace the messages and signs as a way to live with them, instead of focusing on living without them.

The Love of My Life
Jan Turen

I share this story on behalf of my daughter-in-law, Evelina, who experienced the profound loss of my son. When your true love dies, and the pain is so overwhelming that it feels like you can't breathe, it's hard to imagine how you will ever live, walk, talk, or simply exist again. I know she found herself wondering if she would ever feel his presence, hear his voice, or know every time he would be reaching out to her. Yet, it immediately began to happen. My son was the love of her life who passed away suddenly at forty-four, a shock so deep it seemed it would never leave any of us. I constantly questioned when the tears would stop and when we all would be able to breathe freely again.

I believe she feels that the most beautiful part of their love was the way that they cherished their children. They meant more to them than life itself. They were committed to bettering themselves and growing as individuals so that they could be better parents. I love the effort they put into raising their children as a team. Their love was genuine, their conversations always seemed heartfelt, and you could see how they embraced each other even through the challenges life had thrown their way. They lived as though their relationship was one that you expected to last forever. Every disagreement only led them to a deeper understanding and a stronger bond, always with the promise of a shared tomorrow. The greatest gift I saw them treasure together was every minute they spent with their two boys. They always seemed to strive to create a nurturing environment for them, always kept an active involvement in their lives, and I know that was their greatest priority.

One night Evelina revealed a story to me. This is my version of the story, and it goes something like this. "My son sat on my lap, his heart beating close to mine. As I closed my eyes, I wasn't dreaming but rather experiencing a profound connection. Our breaths were synchronized, and I could hear my love's voice, though I chose to keep his words private. I felt his presence and a comforting peace that washed over me. It was as if he was embracing me, holding my hand and heart with unwavering strength. I knew at that moment that his presence was meant to give me solace and courage. I grappled with whether to share the exact words he spoke to me, until I spoke with his mother, who had received the very same message."

It was truly uncanny that I had heard the same words Kevin spoke to Evelina. Kevin's death had a bigger purpose than any of us know.

Judith's Insight:

This is not just a story of a Hollywood romance; it is the story of a profound soulmate connection. Not everyone is fortunate enough to find their one true love, but for those who do, it is a rare and extraordinary gift. No marriage is without its struggles; love is never just roses and butterflies. It is more like a diamond in the rough—one that, through time and endurance, is polished into something brilliant, something unbreakable.

Losing such a love, especially in an untimely way, is a grief beyond words. Yet, the connection your son and daughter-in-law shared was so extraordinary that it went beyond spoken language. They didn't just communicate with words, they communicated through thoughts, through energy, through the very rhythm of their heartbeats. That kind of connection is rare, reserved for those whose souls are truly intertwined.

And then came the sign. The same message, delivered in a different way, to her and to you, his mother. His way of ensuring that she knew his love had reached her. That his presence was still near. That his message had been received. This synchronicity was no coincidence, it was confirmation. They were not just partners in life; they were soulmates and twin flames, bound by a love that transcends time, space, and the physical world.

We all witness grief in different ways. Some become paralyzed by it, unable to move forward. Others struggle to navigate the loss, trying to find their place within the shared sorrow. When someone we love passes, the hearts left behind become the most important part of the story.

Grief is like a scale—each person carries their own weight of loss, yet no two burdens are exactly the same. The pyramid of loss stretches endlessly, affecting friends, family, colleagues, and communities in different ways. When someone larger than life is lost, the ripple effect is immeasurable. Some will receive signs in different ways. Some will see the same sign at the same time. And some days, those signs will feel like a shot heard around the world. When a soul who touched so many is taken too soon, expect endless stories. Expect endless hearts left broken.

Expect endless love. And among all the lives they touched, there will always be one—the love of their life—who feels it the deepest. But even in loss, true love doesn't evaporate. It will find its way to say: "I am still here, sometimes using words."

My Guardian Angel's Love Story

Judith Turner

My mom was in the hospital for weeks, and each time her doctor scheduled her discharge, it was postponed. To my dismay, this happened multiple times. One night, before she received any diagnosis, I had a vivid dream that I was in my mom's kitchen. Even though my dad had already passed away, I saw him walk out of the bathroom. He was wearing a blue-and-white-striped collared shirt and a pair of blue jeans. I asked him where he had been, but he didn't answer. He simply walked toward me, and the closer he got, the more I wondered about his whereabouts.

"I have missed you," I said. "Where were you?" He didn't respond to my questions; instead, he extended his arms to hug me. Overcome with emotion, I began to cry. He said, "I am so sorry. I am so very sorry." My sobs grew uncontrollable, and my husband, sensing my distress, woke me up.

"Judi, what is it? What's wrong?" he asked. Through my tears, I told him that my dad had visited me in my dream. My husband inquired why I was crying, and I replied, "Because he told me he's sorry!" I then told him that I felt something was going to happen to my mom.

The next day, I visited my mom in the hospital. When I arrived, her doctor was in her room, and I asked him if he had checked for cancer. His response was shocking: "No! Why? Do you want her to have cancer?" I was taken aback and told him that my mom had been in the hospital for over a month without a diagnosis, and I was deeply concerned. After he left, I said to my mom, "He's an ass! He has no idea how much you are loved and needed!" She agreed that his response was awful but added, "He may never know how much I am loved, but I certainly do!"

A few days later, my mom was diagnosed with pancreatic cancer. My dad's words of apology continued to echo in my mind.

About a year later, my mother was staying with me, and we had just returned from my nephew Ricky's eighth-grade fashion show. We were both asleep in the family room when my mom suddenly began to scream my dad's name, "Bobby! Bobby!" I rushed to her side. She was shouting, "Bobby, don't you dare! Don't you dare!" Then she said to me, "Judi, I have to go now. I am going to die. Daddy's here."

I cried out, "No, Bobby! No Dad, not tonight! Joanne, Jeri, and Andrew will be so upset if they don't get to say goodbye. Please, please, stay!" I called 911, and my mom was taken to the hospital.

A few weeks later, she passed away in the night with my siblings and me by her side. Her final spoken words were "Bobby" and then "Mama! Mama!" before she left us. Then I felt her energy lift from her body as we held on to her hands. When we told the nurse she had passed she said, "No, she has not left us yet." But I said to her, "Yes, she did, because I felt it.' The nurse left the room, checked the monitors, and came back and said, "Yes, you are right. She did pass."

Judith's Insight:

My dad is one of my Guardian Angels. During a time of deep distress, he visited me in a dream, offering his protection and comfort. Dreams often serve as a direct channel for important messages, especially when the need is greatest. I believe he was deeply concerned about how shocking and overwhelming the news of my mother's illness would be for us. While he may not have been able to find the words to ease our grief, his love was unmistakable. He came to me, embraced me, and in that silent gesture, I understood everything he wanted to say.

His visit wasn't just about comforting me, it was also his way of reassuring me that he would be there for my mother, too. Even as she faced her own struggle, he let me know he would continue to support her, just as he had always done in life. Their love story began when they were just twelve years old, a bond that lasted a lifetime. A love like that doesn't simply end; it transcends time, moving beyond the physical world into the spiritual realm.

Now, both of my parents stand beside me as my Guardian Angels, their love forever intertwined, their presence still guiding me. I feel their warmth in the quiet moments, their support in my hardest days. They remind me that true love does not disappear, it evolves, expands, and continues to surround us in unseen ways.

And if our souls know, then we will know. Not just me—but even you. We have a million dreams in our lifetime, but some linger longer, carrying a message, a meaning, or a feeling of connection to the other side. These dreams are not just dreams, they are visits. They come to comfort us, to guide us, to prepare us.

Some dreams are warnings. Others feel like déjà vu, suddenly making sense only when life catches up to them. And then, there are those dreams that are touched by an Angel.

These dreams are not coincidences. They are gifts, helping us handle the hardest parts of our journey—softening the blow, protecting our hearts, and reminding us that even in loss, we are never truly alone. Remember, when you feel their support and warmth in every step you take, that presence is a constant reminder of the enduring love that transcends this world.

Angel Sign
Michelle Goffredo

Moving from Englewood, New Jersey, to Tennessee was a very scary idea. It was so far from everything we had ever known. But somehow, deep in my heart, I thought it was the right thing to do. During the process of looking for houses, I asked for many Heavenly signs along the way to help me solidify that I was making the right move with my family.

I went down to Tennessee alone to meet a realtor to look at different homes in various towns. My realtor and I made a stop to look at a home in Alexandria, Tennessee, which is a rural area with less than 1,000 people. I loved the house. It was perfect. But I kept wondering if I could really do this. I asked my realtor to give me a moment. I went to the porch and as soon as I closed the front door, I smelled "Angel," the perfume my mom always wore. I burst into tears and said, "Thank you, Mommy."

When I went inside, my realtor said, "Michelle, you smell so good!" I do not wear perfume. We moved to Tennessee.

Judith's Insight:

Scents are one of the most subtle yet profound ways a Guardian Angel can reach out to us. We often underestimate how deeply we are connected to smell memories, yet they have the power to transport us instantly to moments long past, awakening emotions we thought were buried. It is an incredible gift, one that bridges the senses and the presence of those we love.

Your mother's scent was significant for two reasons: It was her favorite fragrance, and it was called "Angel." This was no coincidence. It was a message—one layered with meaning. She wanted you to feel reassured that you had chosen the right house, but more importantly, she wanted you to know that you had truly found home—a place infused with her love, where her presence still lingers.

Guardian Angels often use scents to communicate. Sometimes it's a fleeting moment, like the whisper of a cool breeze carrying an unexpected fragrance. Other times, it's a familiar perfume drifting through the air with no explanation. Many wonder if these experiences are real. They are. These olfactory signals are not random, they are deliberate signs, a way for our loved ones to capture our attention and remind us that they are near.

Magical triggers from Guardian Angels are meant to bring joy, comfort, and reassurance. When you catch a scent that stirs something deep within you, pause. Take a breath. Absorb the moment. Read the room. Look around. Because in that moment, something is being revealed.

Let go of the past, release the anxiety of the unknown, and step boldly into the future knowing that you are never alone. Love lingers, in whispers, in scents, and in the quietest moments. And when you recognize it, you will know.

My Journey of Loss
Sandy K.

I have felt several instances of Guardian Angels in my life, specifically from my son Blake and my nephew Paul, who have both passed away. My son Blake passed away tragically in his early thirties, and since then, he has shown up several times as my Guardian Angel. I am tortured by the death of my son, crying every day over his loss, and I feel that I will never fully mend from this heartbreak.

On the anniversary of Blake's second year in Heaven, I asked him to send me a sign that he is with me, and a cardinal appeared. It sat on the tree branch in front of me for twenty minutes. Another time, I was watering Blake's garden in the early morning light. There was an Angel statue in the garden, and as I stood there speaking aloud to my son, the light in the statue began blinking in and out. Later, while lying on a raft in my pool, talking to my son again, I expressed how it had been over two years without any new signs from him, wondering if he had left me forever. Suddenly, a cardinal flew into the yard and landed on the tree before taking off in flight.

Another time, I was with my grandniece Cali, who was two

years old at the time. She suddenly said she could see a man by the door, though no one was there. I was curious, so I asked her to describe the invisible man, and she said, "He's a big man." My nephew Paul, Cali's uncle, had lived with Cali and her mother before his untimely death, and Cali's description of the man by the door could only have been him.

These signs, but especially the signs from Blake, provide me with moments of comfort amidst the ongoing pain of their absence, though the weight of their loss remains a profound burden on my heart.

Judith's Insight:

Blake speaks loudly, clearly, and often — just the way most people wish to hear from their Guardian Angels. There's no mystery or puzzle in his messages. He wants you to know he is at peace. His soul is no longer tortured. And most of all, he wants you to feel his presence, his gratitude, and his love.

Those gentle pats on the back, the whispered "I love you, Mom" — they are his way of showing that he understands everything you did for him. And now, it's his turn to return the favor.

Blake continues to give you the same love, support, and guidance that you gave him throughout his life. You'll find yourself asking for a sign, and suddenly, there it is. A song, a number, a sudden feeling of warmth. He is working hard to ease your loneliness, surrounding you with people who love and support you. Reminding you, in every way possible, that you are never truly alone.

Even Paul showed up to let you know he's with Blake. And the number two keeps appearing, carrying a message of its own. Two stories, both connected to second anniversaries. A quiet confirmation that they are together. Pay attention, you may start noticing the number two more often, or see things in pairs: birds, cars, bicycles, motorcycles riding side by side. It's their way of showing you they've ridden off into the sunset together.

Even your little niece is part of this message. Children speak the truth without filters and when they say something that makes you do a double take, listen closely. Blake is speaking through them, too.

Guardian Angels don't always have an easy job delivering their messages. Sometimes, it takes a village to get through to us.

Some of us are skeptical, stubborn, or too caught up in the noise of life to notice the winks, the nudges, the gentle handholding, or the playful tugs at our hair. For some, a simple sign won't do. So, the Angels build them a rainbow, inch by inch.

Not everyone gets a burst of sunshine after the storm. Some need a sky filled with words, a sign so big they can't ignore it. Some will trip over a reminder right in their own driveway. And for others, their Angel will orchestrate an entire parade of memories—a grand display, impossible to overlook—just to make sure the message is heard. Your Guardian Angel is doing that and is not going anywhere.

A Christmas Like No Other
Judith Turner

Some days blur into each other, but tonight was supposed to be different. My husband Sparky and I had plans to attend a glamorous dinner party at Tommy Hilfiger's house, and we were both excited. Christmas week always carried a touch of magic. In past years, we would have been at Disney, soaking in the holiday spirit. I'm not sure why we didn't go this year, but as this story unfolds, you'll see how being in the right place at the right time can change everything.

I was sitting in the living room, facing the stairs, when I glanced up and saw my husband coming down. Something was off. I asked if he was feeling okay. "Why wouldn't I be?" he responded. His answer was dismissive, but something about him didn't look right. He brushed it off, blaming it on indigestion. I walked away, heading to the bathroom, and that's when it happened. I saw my dad's face. He didn't speak. He just appeared in my vision. A warning.

A surge of urgency rushed through me. I quickly left the bathroom and told my husband, "We need to go to the hospital." He insisted he was fine, just feeling a little off. At that point, I hadn't mentioned seeing my dad, but the vision made me more insistent. I knew—deep in my bones—that something was wrong. Even though Sparky wasn't complaining much, he admitted he felt uncomfortable. To convince him, I suggested that if everything checked out fine, we'd be back in an hour and could still make it to the party. Reluctantly, he agreed.

I called my neighbor, Debbie, and asked her to come watch our kids. Quietly, I confided in her: "I think Sparky might be having a heart attack." Sparky asked if we should call an ambulance. I knew we didn't have time for a debate, so I grabbed my keys and drove him to the hospital myself.

At the hospital, while I was handling the paperwork, the medical staff took him in for evaluation. Moments later, as I walked toward the triage area, a nurse rushed out and said: "Judith, your husband is having a heart attack!"

My heart sank. "Right now?" I asked.

"Right now," she said. In that instant, the urgency of my dad's warning became crystal clear, and I was overwhelmingly grateful that I had listened.

Judith's Insight:

Seeing my dad's face didn't just change my day, it changed the entire course of our lives. That fleeting but vivid image was the spark that ignited my urgency to get my husband to the hospital. Without that divine intervention, I can only shudder to think of what might have happened.

I never take these messages lightly. In that instant, an unshakable certainty gripped me, as if to say, "Help is on the way." That vision didn't just alert me — it gave me the push to act.

Intuition is real. A revelation, a gut feeling, an unexplainable urgency — these moments have a way of awakening something deep inside us. I had felt my dad's presence before, but never like this. This time was different. His face wasn't just a memory; it was a message. A beacon. A call to action. His influence was unmistakable, and I felt his guidance at every step.

The lesson? Listen to your gut. When someone doesn't seem right, say something. Advocate for yourself. Advocate for others. Take charge of the moment. Send that text to your friend who's been on your mind. Call your sister and tell her to get checked out. Be the nudge that someone needs. No, you don't want to be a nag, a nuisance, or come off as overbearing. But you will feel prouder for speaking up than for staying silent. And when you feel that inner voice pushing you forward, realize it's not just you. Someone is giving you the nudge.

I Listened and Lived

Joanie Heaney Connelly

In 1994, I was pregnant with my daughter. I was driving on Route 5, by the car wash in Palisades Park, New Jersey. I was in the left lane heading toward Edgewater when I suddenly heard this loud, deep man's voice that said to get over to the right lane, "Now!" I was alone in the car with the windows up. Scared, I immediately pulled over to the right lane. A second later, a car came around the turn into the same lane I was just in. When I got around the bend, there was a big truck that had broken down. I would have been in a head-on collision if I had not listened to "the voice." It was my Guardian Angel who saved me and my baby.

Judith's Insight:

This is exactly why I am writing this book. Few would believe a story like this—unless they've experienced something equally extraordinary. And yet, countless individuals share similar experiences, unprovable, yet profoundly real. This is a true Guardian Angel moment, with an outcome that feels nothing short of miraculous.

You didn't imagine it. You didn't fabricate it. In moments like these, the voice of reason often defies conventional logic. And yet, the truth remains: They lived happily ever after. Why? Because you had a Guardian Angel.

It's stories like these—unexplainable yet undeniable—that turn skeptics into believers. While some may dismiss them as coincidence, faith asks us to embrace the messages that go beyond common sense. Many readers will recognize pieces of their own experiences in these pages—the sudden, unexplained intervention, the intuitive warning, the overwhelming sense of protection.

Whether one believes in God, Guardian Angels, or a higher power, one thing becomes clear: Something greater was at play. Many have found themselves in life-threatening situations, only to be pulled back from the brink, certain that an unseen force intervened to save them.

Sometimes, we question ourselves. Other times, we question what just happened. But in the end, the outcome speaks for itself.

Near-death experiences are more than just real, they are proof that some things cannot be explained, only felt. Surviving a moment like that is never accidental; it is help from a friend. Whether that friend is God, a Guardian Angel, or a spiritual guide, one truth remains: It wasn't your time. And that, in itself, is divine intervention. Because something—or someone—saved you, you have a purpose.

Help From Heaven

Marie S.

My daughter was on a recruiting trip at a college near Atlantic City, New Jersey. My husband and I drove her down and decided to wait at the casino for her call to pick her up. We did not have money to gamble but walked around the casino while waiting.

I was moving around when my beloved late mother-in-law suddenly appeared and started walking quickly through the crowd of people. I had taken my mother-in-law to the casino many times, so somehow her appearance in this setting made sense to me. I followed her as she weaved in between the slot machines, which were so crowded that it was impossible to get near one. I had to run to keep up with her as she headed toward an empty quarter machine. She remained with me as I sat down to rest. She whispered words encouraging me to play. I put in the maximum three quarters, pulled the lever, and hit the jackpot of $1,199! My husband and I had just finished saying, "Where are we going to get the $1,200 deposit the school wanted to hold for our daughter's admission?" I had $1.00 left in my wallet. I cried knowing my mother-in-law had led me to that slot machine at the exact right moment.

Judith's Insight:

Angels are always working to help us in ways we may not immediately recognize. Their presence is often woven subtly into the fabric of our lives, gently guiding us, nudging us, and responding to our unspoken prayers. Many times, we don't even realize how much we are reaching out to them — or just how deeply they are reaching back.

That's what makes your experience so extraordinary. Not only did you feel your mother-in-law's presence, but you saw her. Witnessing a Guardian Angel in corporeal form is incredibly rare, a gift that few ever receive. You are truly blessed to have had that moment.

It seems your mother-in-law, the adventurer, with a gambler's spirit, saw an opportunity that day. And in true fashion, she solved a problem in the most unexpected way. By dropping a few coins in your path, she orchestrated a little magic. Or, as I see it, she answered your prayer, wrapped you in a comforting embrace, and sent you on your way with a smile.

Sometimes, signs come as whispers, as thoughts that suddenly pop into our heads, or as a chance encounter that leads us exactly where we need to be. Sometimes, it's a stranger who unknowingly delivers a message, or an instinct we follow without quite knowing why.

What seems small and ordinary often holds the key to something extraordinary—the beautiful and mysterious ways our prayers are answered and our dreams come to life.

Seeing your mother-in-law's image wasn't just a sign. It was a reminder, a profound one, of the incredible ways our Guardian Angels touch our lives.

In life, patterns emerge, little coincidences that shift the outcome just when we need it most. And when they do, we know love was at the heart of it.

If life were a recipe, it would be made of simple ingredients—a stove, vegetables from the garden, meat from the store, bread from the bakery, a little salt and pepper. But the most important ingredient? A dash of love. And that's what we look for in every story. In every sign. In every message from beyond. The unmistakable touch of love that stops by to remind us to keep looking and not give up.

REFLECTION 2

Believe

*Be grateful for the friends in your life—both old and new.
The ones you share memories with. The ones you talk to
every day. The ones you rarely speak to but
always carry in your heart.*

*Cherish the friends who have become family, the ones who
were there in your youth, the ones who have seen your
struggles, and the ones who simply love to see you happy.
Treasure those you met just yesterday and those
who have been by your side for years.*

*Hold close to the friends who are still here and honor the
ones who have left you. Their presence, whether near or
far, remains a part of you always. Just believe.*

—Judith Turner

Man's Best Friend
Vicki D'Auria

I couldn't sleep last night. I was awake at 1:00 a.m., thinking of my friend who also lost her son and the hard time she was having at the moment. I turned my thoughts to my son Brian, and I asked him to let me feel his presence. I sat there quietly and just embraced what I was feeling. Suddenly, my dog got up from the other room and went into the kitchen. I have never heard or seen her do that before during the night. She came out of the kitchen with the toy my son gave her and brought it straight to me! Now that was a special delivery. I miss my Brian so much.

Judith's Insight:
You wrote this story on October 20, and I am responding with this interpretation on November 11, a date often regarded as Angel's Day. Receiving this message on such a day is more than a coincidence; it is a beautiful sign of love from above.

Dogs are known as man's best friend, not only because of their loyalty but because of their intuitive nature. They sense what we feel, understand what we need, and sometimes, they serve as messengers between this world and the next. In this instance, it seems your dog was more than just a companion—he was embodying the role of man's best friend, reaching out to you with a heartfelt message.

Though Brian may no longer be physically present, his love remains woven into the fabric of your life, and in this moment, his presence was felt through the actions of your loyal companion.

Messages from beyond come in many forms, and dogs often play a role in delivering them. In your story, you were seeking solace and comfort in the familiar space of your home. That setting, that moment, paints a vivid picture of what the message truly meant: It was about bringing you comfort, laughter, and hope.

The toy your dog brought to you was not just a playful gesture but a symbol. A reminder to smile. A small but powerful sign that love transcends space and time. Your dog's actions were a warm hug from Brian, letting you know that while he may not be there in body, his spirit is always with you.

We often say that dogs matter. Cats matter. If you have a turtle, a bird, a rabbit—they matter, too. Every pet, every companion, leaves their imprint on our hearts. Paws in the sand of life are more than just footprints; they are symbols of love, hope, and infinite guidance. A man's best friend is not just his dog; it is any creature whose love becomes intertwined with his own. What truly matters in this story is the unbreakable bond between a soul and the pet it welcomes into its family. Unlike human relationships, this connection begins with one simple but profound choice: The moment you choose them, they choose you back. And that bond? It lasts into infinity and beyond!

Butterflies to Give Me Peace
Lisa Warner Jansen

I was the caretaker for my good friend's property when he passed away suddenly. I remember every time I went to check on the house after his passing, I was always greeted by butterflies.

Judith's Insight:
Butterflies are timeless symbols of serenity and peace, appearing as reminders that the love and comfort we once shared with someone still extend beyond this world. Their presence is not just a fleeting sign but a profound emblem of the tranquility and harmony you brought to your loved one during their lifetime. In their graceful flight, butterflies carry a message of deep connection, a silent whisper of the love and serenity you both cherished.

In nature, butterflies undergo a remarkable transformation, from a grounded caterpillar to a creature of breathtaking beauty. Life mirrors this journey. We begin in our caterpillar phase, growing, evolving, and navigating life's challenges. Then comes the chrysalis—a quiet and mysterious transition—death, the veil between two worlds. But in the afterlife, we emerge as butterflies, Angels in their most ethereal form.

When a butterfly graces you with its presence, it is more than coincidence. It is a tender, celestial kiss from an Angel, a delicate but powerful affirmation that their love is still with you, their presence ever near.

And sometimes, in the mystery of the afterlife, the roles of caregiver and cared-for are reversed. If you were the one who provided comfort and care, now it is their turn. Now, they take care of you.

Through small but meaningful signs—a butterfly, a whisper on the wind, a sudden feeling of warmth—they let you know: "It's your turn to be taken care of now." Just in case you're wondering, someone out there has your back.

Wish

Judith Turner

When I was about three years old, my baby brother Richard was born. To my small, innocent eyes, it seemed he never stopped crying. The house carried a weight of sadness that I couldn't quite understand but deeply felt. My mother's tear-filled eyes, the frequent hospital visits, the quiet tension in our home— it all left an imprint on me, even at such a young age.

In 1963, parents rarely discussed their struggles with their children, yet I could sense that something was terribly wrong. One day, while Richard was in the hospital, my aunt took me to the park. The grass was scattered with dandelions, their delicate white seeds drifting in the breeze. My aunt told me they were called "wishes." I didn't know their real name, but I understood that if I caught one, I could make a wish.

From that moment on, I chased those floating seeds, wishing for Richard to stop crying and to get better.

But time passed, and Richard's illness took him from us. I remember the day he left us with piercing clarity. My cousin Jay had come over to babysit, and we were still living at 38 Post Ave. The sadness in the house deepened. My father, whom I had never seen cry before, sat in the living room, tears streaming down his face. Easter baskets in the house suggested that it must have been around that time of year.

That summer — or maybe the next — my mother took us to the park again. I told her I was going to catch "wishes" for Richard. I explained that I had wished for him to come back so everyone would stop crying, so our house could be filled with happiness again.

Years later, on a sunlit afternoon in Cape Cod, my mother and I sat together, reminiscing. She told me she had never forgotten that day, the day I ran, gathering wishes for Richard. Every time she saw those white, floating seeds, she thought of him.

I reassured her: "Mommy, in your heart, he never left. He's always letting us know he's okay." Tears welled in her eyes as she nodded in agreement.

Since my mother's passing, whenever I see those wishes, those delicate, drifting seeds, I still make wishes. For her. For Dad. For Richard. It's my way of keeping them close. Each floating seed feels like a sign, a gentle reminder that they are together, watching over me, sending their love on the whisper of the wind.

Judith's Insight:
Sometimes, it takes years before we fully understand the meaning of a sign or why something resonates so deeply with us. Even

as a child, I sensed that the dandelion held something more than its fragile seeds. It wasn't just a fleeting puff carried away by the wind—it became a symbol of Richard's presence, of hope, of an unbreakable bond that even death could not sever.

As children, we don't always grasp the significance of the moments we cling to, but looking back, I know now that every dandelion was a silent message. A gentle hug from Richard. A promise that he was still with us.

Who would have thought that something as simple as a dandelion could carry such profound meaning? And yet, it did.

Flowers, like signs, find us in the most unexpected ways. They appear on birthdays, in our gardens, at funerals, in grocery store aisles, on our tables, as opening night bouquets. We pass them in the park, admire them in the hands of strangers, or notice them blooming unexpectedly in places where we least expect them. Each flower tells its own story. Each one has its journey. And just like the people we love, each one touches a different heart.

Our guides plant these flowers along our paths, not just to bring beauty, but to awaken memories, emotions, and connections that never fade. Yes, sometimes they bring tears. And that's okay. But if today you see a flower—or a dandelion—that makes you pause, makes you look twice, know this: It is a sign. A message that whispers, "You are loved." A gentle reminder: "I heard you. I am here."

A Kiss from Beyond

Deborah M. Light

The other day I walked by my husband's dresser and was completely overwhelmed. I could smell his aftershave. It was so strong. Since he passed away, I have walked by this dresser every day, multiple times a day, and this has never happened before. I looked inside the dresser thinking maybe something had spilled. All the contents of the drawers were intact. In the past, my husband would shave, put on his aftershave, then come and give me a kiss. I stood there for several minutes. I knew he was letting me know he was there.

Judith's Insight:

When we catch a familiar scent that once belonged to someone who has passed, it feels as though they are reaching out—a deliberate, loving gesture from beyond. It's truly awe-inspiring.

Imagine the profound sense of connection you felt when that fragrance filled the air. Though you may not have seen him, I bet you felt his presence, as if he were standing right beside you. These moments are nothing short of miracles. They gently touch our hearts, offering the quiet reassurance that our loved ones are never as far away as we think.

His scent wasn't just a fragrance; it was a message. A tender kiss from the other side.

It's remarkable to consider how your husband, in a seemingly ordinary moment, managed to conjure that specific aftershave, a scent so unmistakably his. This wasn't a coincidence. It was intentional. A sign. A promise.

His mission is clear: to remain by your side. To guide you. To comfort you. To remind you that even though he no longer walks this earth, his love is still very much alive. Each time you experience that familiar scent, it's his way of saying, "I'm here."

These experiences are like whispers from the universe, quiet affirmations that love transcends time and space. It's in these beautiful, unexpected moments that we realize just how deeply connected we are to those who have gone before us.

For some, the connection goes even further. The "aftervisit" can be as real as real gets. Many have shared stories of seeing, touching, feeling—even dreaming of sleeping beside—their loved ones after they've passed. Their presence becomes their present.

The scent of a fragrance, cologne, or aftershave, it's more than just a smell. It's a memory, a message, a gift.

Our loved ones work in mysterious ways. And that's exactly what's happening here. So, keep paying attention. Keep sniffing around. Keep looking for the signs. Because when something fills your heart, when it brings warmth and peace, that's not just a memory. That's love. And that, my friend, is healing.

Hidden Hugs

Rachel Zitomer

I have heard of finding pennies from Heaven, but this was incredible. I was cleaning out my closet and found an old purse that I rarely used. Tucked inside was a crisp $100 bill and my grandpa's funeral Mass card. This was not random luck or coincidence; it was a clear spiritual sign. Angels will usually toss down coins to get our attention or because they really miss us. Anyone who knew my grandpa knows that he was larger than life. A little pocket change would not have been enough for him. My grandpa was always grumpy yet loving and charming all at the same time. In no particular order, he loved his family, Ford Motor Company, Frank Sinatra, golf, and shellfish. Most importantly, his grandkids meant everything to him. I feel very lucky to have been his granddaughter! He was always very generous to me. Whether it was my birthday, a significant milestone, or just a Tuesday, he always gave me $100.

Recently I have become fascinated by numerology. Angel number 100 is a very powerful number. It is a sign from your Angels to trust their guidance and your own intuition as you follow your spiritual path. This Angel number is generally associated with the achievement of goals and celebration. My grandpa passed away right before I got married and never got to meet my daughter Jolie. By showing me the number 100, I think he was saying that he sees what I have accomplished and is still here supporting and loving me from Heaven. If you notice certain numbers popping up in your life do not ignore them. I urge you to look them up and see what message the Angels have waiting for you.

Judith's Insight:

Numbers are a powerful way for Guardian Angels to communicate, often appearing in unexpected places—clocks, license plates, receipts, or even cash. When you come across 100, it's not just a random moment; it's a clear Angel number, carrying deep significance.

Seeing 100 is more than mere coincidence; it's a divine nudge that there's a message being sent to you. It's a signal that you're on the right path, that your prayers or thoughts are being acknowledged.

In your case, finding the $100 alongside the Mass card was a profound example of a "combination message." A combination message happens when two signs align, forming a complete story or a more detailed message. The Mass card represents a prayer or a request from your grandfather, while the $100 is an affirmation that you are indeed heading in the right direction.

By bringing these two signs together, your grandfather is delivering a clear and encouraging message—you are being guided, supported, and reassured. When we look at signs holistically, they begin to weave together a more meaningful and powerful message.

Money always makes us stop and think. Whether it's a found bill, a lucky scratch-off, or a surprise cash prize, there's something magical about it. No one finds money and doesn't take a second to appreciate it.

The phrase "pennies from Heaven" is universal, but in truth, any amount of money found unexpectedly can be a sign. Whether it's a penny, a dollar, or even winning at a tricky tray or lottery, it's often a message from your loved ones or Guardian Angels, letting you know they are easing your burdens. Maybe not immediately, but in a broader sense, they are sending you luck, encouragement, and support.

So, the next time you find a penny, pick it up. Because all day long, your Guardian Angel is trying to lift you up and bring you luck. Love those Angels!

A Mother's Day Gift
Jan Turen

The past few years have presented me with an incredibly difficult journey. The loss of my son was a heart-wrenching blow, one that no parent should ever have to endure. The pain of losing a child is beyond words; it feels as if the very fabric of reality has been torn apart. The weight of this sorrow is something that never fully heals. I find solace in focusing on my remaining children and the young grandchildren my son left behind, who carry their own profound sadness.

My husband and our children—my son, who was a father of two, and my daughter, who is unmarried and without children—were all equally devastated by this loss. In the midst of this grief, I clung to the precious blessings still in my life, doing my best to cherish every moment. My sister "C" became my pillar of strength. She was someone who loved my son as much as I did, and reminiscing with her provided a bittersweet comfort. I sought out signs from my son, my departed parents, and my Heavenly Guardian Angels every day. These signs appeared in various forms—birds, rainbows, football games, music, or even words on a page. Recognizing these signs became a vital part of my coping process.

The pain deepened with the heartbreaking loss of my sister. She was my confidante, my morning coffee buddy, and the person with whom I shared every detail of my life. She was the keeper of my secrets and always had my back. We shared a unique bond being Roll Tide University of Alabama girls who felt connected to each other no matter where we were watching the game. Losing her was a profound blow, and the sorrow was compounded by the deaths of other loved ones, including a best friend and our beloved dogs. These losses pushed me to my limits, and few can truly understand the depth of my grief.

This past Mother's Day brought an unexpected twist of joy amidst the ongoing heartache. My daughter woke up feeling unwell and given that someone we had recently been with had contracted COVID, we both decided to get tested. At the urgent care, we saw our favorite physician's assistant, Brie. I shared with her the signs I had been receiving from my Guardian Angels — rainbows, coins, two birds outside my window, and even my son's name in a newspaper headline. After the routine COVID and flu tests, Brie conducted an additional test on my daughter, one I hadn't anticipated given her age and single status. As I sat there, I reflected on how strange it was to spend Mother's Day in an urgent care, worrying about COVID results. But then Brie walked in with a smile and said, "Yes, the test is positive. Positive for pregnancy, that is." In that moment, I felt a surge of joy and connection to my Guardian Angels that I hadn't experienced in years. It was an unexpected and beautiful piece of news that seemed like a miraculous gift from above.

What started as a challenging Mother's Day ended up being one of the happiest days of my life. My daughter is going to be a mother, and this news was the greatest gift of all. I believe that all my Guardian Angels played a part in bringing this miracle to fruition. Happy Mother's Day to me!

Judith's Insight:

Your Guardian Angels have been working tirelessly, reshaping the landscape of pain and loss that has surrounded your life. They have gone above and beyond to ensure you noticed their presence, sending an array of undeniable signs—nudges from beyond—to capture your attention and guide you through your darkest moments. It's as if they were orchestrating something greater, preparing you for the incredible blessing that was on its way.

Babies are powerful symbols of hope and new beginnings—pure reminders that life continues, love endures, and joy can still bloom even in the midst of sorrow.

Even though your journey has been marked by heartache, your Angels have never left your side. They have been guiding you, whispering reassurance, and laying the groundwork for divine intervention. They have wrapped you in signs—rainbows, coins, serendipitous moments—each one a symbolic hug reminding you that you are never alone.

These signs are their way of enveloping you in a cocoon of love and protection, urging you to trust in the journey and find comfort in their presence.

And now, this new life—this precious baby—stands as a living testament to the unwavering love and guidance of your Guardian Angels. This child is not just a new beginning but a tangible reminder that strength, love, and hope are always within reach.

Sometimes, the arrival of a new soul is exactly what is needed to bring light into the shadows. This child brings a reason to smile again, a beacon of hope to illuminate your healing journey.

Angels bring Angels. Some are passing Angels—one leaving just as another arrives, their souls meeting in a sacred exchange. Those who leave and those who come within a short window of time are Sharing Angels, souls that are naturally connected, eternally bonded.

Sometimes, one soul departs as another is born. Other times, one arrives as another prepares to go. Either way, it doesn't matter. These two souls are not replacements for one another. They are simply Unity Angels, souls who share a sacred connection across time and space, whose presence in your life is part of something far greater than we can understand.

When an Angel arrives, take notice of who has left. They are not gone. They are simply watching from the other side.

Taking a Lunch Break
Judith Turner

Some days begin with a gentle nudge of optimism, and this was one of those mornings. I woke up to a breathtaking rainbow stretching across the sky, a vibrant reminder that something special was on the horizon. As I moved through my morning routine, a small gold bag tumbled unexpectedly from my closet. Inside, I discovered a collection of half dollars and assorted coins—a charming surprise that I didn't immediately recognize as a sign.

In the weeks leading up to this moment, my life had been a whirlwind of uncertainty. I had lost over 25 percent of my vision, and the looming fear of blindness had consumed me. For weeks, I had bounced between doctors, endured countless tests, and clung to the hope that someone—anyone—could provide answers. The emotional toll was overwhelming.

Then came the day of reckoning—my long-awaited specialist appointment. After a thorough series of tests, the doctor delivered news that felt nothing short of miraculous, my vision had improved. The relief was immeasurable. After a series of inconclusive blood tests, I posed a question that had been nagging at me for months: Could my eye condition be connected to the concussion I suffered in February?

The doctor paused, then nodded. "You're probably right."

It was a validation of something I had intuitively felt all along. Sometimes, we know our bodies better than any test ever could. That day was better than winning any lottery.

As I left the doctor's office, I was overwhelmed with gratitude—so much so that I found myself stopping at the desk of Erica, one of the assistants. Without hesitation, I placed a generous sum of money on her desk and told her to treat the entire staff to lunch.

Erica ran after me, bewildered. "Why? What is this for?"

I smiled and said, "Because today, for the first time, I'm walking out of here with joy instead of tears." I wanted to share that joy, to pass along the light that had just been given to me.

Later that evening, I received another stunning surprise—I had won $900. I was floored. At that moment, I could feel my Guardian Angels wrapping their arms around me, not just with comfort, but with a celebration of faith, generosity, and resilience.

And if that wasn't enough, right in the middle of my health struggles, my dryer broke down—only to be replaced with a brand-new one the very next day.

A simple act of kindness can brighten your day. But sometimes, the universe finds a way to return the favor in ways beyond our imagination.

Judith's Insight :

Our Guardian Angels have a way of adapting their methods of communication to make sure we take notice. Rainbows, for instance, are never just rainbows. They hold layers of meaning, appearing at just the right moment to remind us that nothing is random.

Other times, our Angels choose unconventional ways to reach us—a social media post that stops us mid-scroll, a headline that feels eerily personal, a song on the radio that echoes exactly what we need to hear. If something catches your attention, it's not by accident.

Looking back on my journey, it feels as though I was walking a long road, searching for answers, much like chasing a rainbow to find its pot of gold. The bag of coins that fell from my closet was a prelude, a whisper of what was coming. Paying it forward with lunch? A ripple effect. Winning $900? A divine wink and nod from my Angels, a way of saying, "We see you. We've got you."

This experience was a tapestry of signs, each one woven with purpose and reassurance. The doctor's words were exactly what I had been praying for. The sequence of events proved what I already knew deep down—that while fear can paralyze, faith has the power to heal.

Life has a way of throwing us into unexpected storms—a hospital stay, a job loss, a sudden divorce, the rug being pulled out from under us when we least expect it. In those moments, we find ourselves searching desperately for someone, somewhere to say something that will magically make it better.

But here's the thing: We don't know what we need to hear—until someone says it. Maybe it's a headline you see as you walk past a newsstand. Maybe it's a billboard on the highway that suddenly feels meant just for you. Maybe it's a line from a TV show, or a phone call from an old friend, out of the blue. This is about words. Words matter. Words happen. So today, pay attention. To what you read. To what you see. To what you hear. It's okay to be skeptical, until you're not.

Best Friends Always

Donna Marie

My best friend Susan and I are extremely spiritual. We always promised each other that whoever passed first would visit the other and show signs. Susan passed unexpectedly on January 16, 2020. I am still devastated and speak to her every day. She visited me in dreams several times, which was very comforting and brought me joy. But then her visits stopped. I would pray to her every night to show me a sign she was still with me. I knew she was but just could not understand why the signs and dream visitations stopped. After her passing, I put a shrine together for her on the ledge of my kitchen sink. I felt comfort looking at her picture and the figurines of Angels surrounding it.

On her second anniversary, January 16, 2022, I begged her to show me she was with me. I told her my heart was breaking. We had a pact, and I could not understand why she wasn't fulfilling it. The day came and went. I was sad and somewhat confused.

The next evening, my boyfriend and I were watching TV in the family room, which is adjacent to the kitchen and is separated by a half wall. We heard a crash. I went into the kitchen and found the small Angel figurine had fallen off the shelf onto the kitchen counter! I have no doubt that it was my Susan! It took a long time, but she eventually answered my prayers!

Judith's Insight:

This story holds deep meaning and resonance for several reasons. When our departed loved ones attempt to reach us, they often adjust their methods to ensure we notice. Susan, in her own unique way, may have needed to create a memorable moment — like the Angel figurine falling over — to make sure her presence was acknowledged.

In life, we often have preconceived notions about how signs will appear. We look for familiar patterns, and in doing so, we might overlook the quieter messages. It's possible that Susan has been reaching out in ways that were more subtle, ways that perhaps went unnoticed because you weren't in the right mindset to receive them or were expecting something different.

The figurine falling could be seen as a dramatic gesture, a "big bang" moment — a way to break through the noise and ensure you recognized her presence. This unexpected event was more than coincidence; it was a powerful reminder that she is with you.

Beyond simply making her presence known, Susan's message may be one of love, reassurance, and approval, letting you know that she sees the joy you're finding in your new relationship. Perhaps she wants you to know she supports the happiness you've rediscovered in simple, heartfelt moments: watching television, holding hands, sharing laughter.

As you continue on your journey, keep your heart open to the unexpected. These signs are tokens of love, reminders that the ones we cherish are never truly gone.

Guardian Angels, guides, protectors—or as some call them, lifesavers—can take many forms. They may be someone you have met on your journey of life, but they can also be someone you've never met: a grandparent who passed before you were born, an aunt or uncle whose name you carry, or a kindred soul who, for reasons beyond our understanding, has chosen to connect with yours.

On any given day, in any given way, a special Angel could be showing up for you. Keep asking. Keep inviting them in. And when you do—you'll see the signs. Then, like so many before you, you'll have stories to tell, moments to share, and proof that love never disappears—it takes on a new journey.

The Watch: A Daughter's Love Never Ends

Elaine LoConte

It has been nearly a year since my beautiful daughter Lauren passed away. Throughout this time, I have encountered many signs that I believe come from her. Each of these signs, whether through photographs, songs, or unsolicited messages, has brought me a step closer to finding my peace. More importantly, these signs make me feel that Lauren is finding her peace as well. While the comforting words from others have been invaluable, I still find myself in tears more often than not. It's as if the ache of her absence is a constant companion.

One story stands out as a profound reminder that Lauren is watching over me. I was backing out of my driveway one day when a man suddenly tapped on my window. I had no idea where he had come from, he seemed to have appeared out of thin air. His unexpected appearance startled me, and I felt a surge of nervousness. I rolled down the window, and he said, "I think this belongs to your daughter." As I looked at him, I felt a sense of déjà vu; he seemed vaguely familiar, but I couldn't place him. He was someone I'd seen around town but had never encountered in my neighborhood.

My confusion was evident as I stammered, "Umm, what?" The man then produced a watch from his pocket and handed it to me. "I believe this is your daughter's," he said. My heart sank as I replied, "My daughter passed away." The man simply nodded and continued to offer me the watch. Tears welled up in my eyes as I took the watch in my hands. I was speechless. When I went to say thank you, he was gone as quickly as he arrived.

Judith's Insight:

It was Lauren's watch, a piece of her you didn't even know existed. It was as if she had orchestrated this moment as a chance to send you a gift of comfort. This unexpected encounter was a precious reminder that gifts can come from anywhere.

The watch you received is overflowing with meaning—a profound message from your daughter, a tangible reminder that she is always with you. This watch is more than just an object; it's a symbol of her continued presence and the unique way she communicates with you.

Time itself holds messages. Pay attention to numbers, especially those that appear on clocks or in unexpected places. They are clues, gentle nudges from her spirit, reminding you that she is watching over you.

The man who returned the watch is more than just a messenger; he represents the people and connections from your daughter's life. His unexpected appearance serves as a powerful reminder that those who knew and loved her will continue to bring you moments of comfort, warmth, and even joy.

Just as your daughter was cherished by many, this man's presence is a testament to the enduring impact of her love. He is part of the beautiful ripple effect she left behind, a reminder that her influence continues to touch lives in unexpected ways. The way this man appeared—seemingly out of nowhere—is a reflection of how your daughter chooses to make her presence known. She was spontaneous, free-spirited, full of surprises. And that hasn't changed.

This experience is her way of saying she is still here—still playful, still full of love, still finding ways to keep you on your toes.

With this Guardian Angel, expect the unexpected. She will continue to show up in unconventional ways, bringing signs that are uniquely her.

The tears you shed are a reflection of the unbreakable bond you shared, a bond that no passage of time can weaken. Her memory will always bring laughter, warmth, and joy, just as much as it brings longing. This story is a perfect example of her unique, spirited way of reminding you that she is never truly gone.

Sometimes, signs from our loved ones come in surprising, even tangible ways—a check in the mail, an unexpected inheritance, a forgotten piece of jewelry, or a painting with newfound significance.

Other times, the gifts are simply an old set of dishes, a handwritten note, or something seemingly ordinary. But the real gift isn't in the object itself. It's in the love behind it. And that love? It never fades. It will always find new ways to reach you.

My Father's Visit

Judith Turner

I often find myself dreaming of my parents who have passed away, and their presence is always so vivid. A few months ago, I had a particularly striking dream where I sensed that something was amiss. My dad appeared with a powerful presence, and when he embraced me, I couldn't hold back my tears. It felt as though he had come to offer a warning about what was to come. Since that dream, my life has been a whirlwind of challenges — my husband has undergone four surgeries, and I've faced a series of health issues ranging from minor to major. Yet, the greatest heartache has been the news of my sister's cancer diagnosis.

My sister is my soulmate, my confidante, the peanut butter to my jelly. I have come to understand that my dad's hug was his way of preparing me for the trials ahead, particularly for supporting my sister through her tough journey. I firmly believe that both my parents have been sending her their own signs of comfort and are with her, holding her hand each day.

Despite the turbulence, my faith remains my anchor. I strive to stand firm in my belief, knowing that while faith might not alter the course of my journey, it will certainly provide the strength I need to navigate it. I am deeply thankful for the preemptive embrace from my dad. I know that both my parents are sending my sister signs to give her strength and help her "get her spaghetti ready," as there's more joy to come than sorrow.

Judith's Insight:
Dreams about life and love act as beacons of light, guiding us

through our waking days. While I may not recall every dream with perfect clarity, there are certain ones that stand apart — dreams so vivid, so profound, that they feel like visits rather than mere imaginings. These dreams bring love, reassurance, and sometimes even gentle warnings about challenges ahead. They serve as Guardian Angel signs, illuminating our darkest moments and providing a glimmer of sunshine before dawn.

Dreams are often the most accessible way for our loved ones to reach out to us. They step through the veil in the quiet hours of the night, whispering messages that can linger in our hearts long after we wake.

Many people wonder: Are these real visits, or are they simply creations of our subconscious? The answer often reveals itself in time. The unfolding of events in our lives can confirm the authenticity of these dreams. Think about it, how many times have you dreamed of something, only to realize later that it carried a deeper meaning? Ask yourself: Did the dream deliver a message with unusual clarity? Did something in the dream later manifest in real life? Was there an element of coincidence that felt too profound to ignore? If the answer is yes to any of these, even if not immediately, then the realization dawns: Someone I cherish found their way into my dreams.

Some dreams arrive wrapped in warmth, filled with the presence of a loved one's laughter, familiar touch, or comforting embrace. Others come as whispers of intuition, urging us to pay attention, to prepare, to trust in something unseen. Guardian Angels and departed loved ones use dreams as doorways, finding ways to offer us the insight, love, and reassurance we need — even before we realize we need it. So, the next time you wake with a lingering feeling, a message imprinted on your heart, pay attention. It may be more than just a dream. It may be a visit. Once you recognize they are visits, you will always feel grateful.

165th Street

Elaine LoConte

My daughter Lauren passed away about a year ago, and each day I actively seek out signs from her. A friend of mine repeatedly mentioned that, for some inexplicable reason, she felt Lauren's presence at the corner of 165th Street in New York City. This was particularly curious to me, as I had no reason to visit that area, especially given that it's the location of Columbia Presbyterian Hospital.

Then, as fate would have it, I began experiencing significant issues with my eye and needed to consult a specialist. Almost a year to the day after Lauren's passing, I found myself standing precisely at that very corner of 165th Street, heading to the eye specialist's office. The timing of this moment left me stunned, almost numb, and all I could think of was Lauren.

Judith's Insight:

I know you felt as though your daughter was guiding you, reminding you of her presence and love in a way only she could. Time to thank your Lauren!

Signs have a way of manifesting not just before an event, but also during and after, weaving their presence into our lives. In this instance, the message about that specific street was delivered ahead of time—a deliberate and profound way for your daughter to make sure you would recognize that she was with you on that day.

It wasn't just a coincidence. It was her way of holding your hand through the fear and uncertainty you faced. Our guides and loved ones often appear at the exact moments we need them most, offering support, protection, and reassurance as we navigate life's challenges. By giving you this early sign, Lauren was doing more than just preparing you—she was initiating healing before you even knew you needed it.

This foresight allowed you to feel her presence before the moment arrived, experience her comforting hugs in advance, and understand, in the depths of your heart, that her love and guidance would always be with you. Sometimes, getting a sign in advance is what makes the moment even more meaningful. It gives you that second glance, that double take—the moment where your head spins because you can't believe what's happening.

These experiences are gut-wrenching in their intensity; the way they unfold is almost too surreal to grasp. And yet, the comfort they bring is immeasurable. The kind of "wow factor" that only an Angel can deliver. It's like watching an acrobat leap from a rooftop, only to land precisely on a penny on the ground in front of you. Unbelievably captivating. Impossible—yet real.

This message, like so many signs from our loved ones, was orchestrated with love, precision, and purpose. Because some signs aren't meant to be subtle. Some signs are meant to take your breath away.

No Coincidence
Jill Castaldo Stewart

Today was an emotional day as I took my beloved Valentino to his vet appointment with Dr. Bloom, a veterinarian I hold in high regard. The day was June 13, a date that holds deep significance for me. I don't know what came over me, but as I sat in Dr. Bloom's office, I found myself overwhelmed with emotion. I expressed to her my desire to have Valentino recognized as an emotional support animal, explaining how much I relied on his companionship, especially with the worries about his illness.

As I spoke, tears streamed down my face. I shared with Dr.

Bloom that my cousin Lauren, who had named Valentino and was his godmother, had passed away on June 13 of the previous year. The coincidence of the date felt like a heavy weight on my heart. Dr. Bloom, with her comforting presence, reminded me that not all events on June 13 are negative. I responded, acknowledging that the number also marks my birthday and my anniversary, signifying moments of joy in my life.

Dr. Bloom then shared a personal connection, revealing that her son's birthday is also on June 13. This heartfelt revelation brought an immediate sense of comfort and reassurance. In that moment, I felt a profound sense of relief, as if Lauren's presence was being reaffirmed through Dr. Bloom's kind words and actions. This is the same vet who had saved my precious Valentino, and although I deeply appreciate her role, in my heart, I felt that Lauren had played a significant part in Valentino's healing, guiding and supporting us both through this difficult time.

Judith's Insight:

This story is truly extraordinary! The depth of your grief over Lauren's passing was already immense, but the added heartache of Valentino's illness, who was like a child to you, made your struggle even heavier. During this incredibly difficult time, you turned to Lauren, hoping for a sign, guidance, and reassurance.

And then, it happened. The coincidence of the date aligning with your vet appointment was more than just a chance occurrence, it was clear confirmation that Lauren was listening. It felt as though she was reaching out, wrapping you in her love, acknowledging your pain, and offering you the comfort you needed most.

And then, there was Dr. Bloom. Her role was significant not just because she helped heal Valentino, but because she became a direct link between your hope and Lauren's presence. Her words, her care, her connection, they were all part of something greater. And then, yet another sign appeared. The revelation that

Dr. Bloom's son shares his birthday with the day of Lauren's passing added an unexpected, yet undeniable, layer of meaning to this experience.

This wasn't just a random alignment of dates. This was Lauren's way of orchestrating a connection—one that would bring you peace, reassurance, and the strength to keep going. At one of the most trying times in your life, she made sure you knew: She was there. Coincidence? Or something more? Some might call moments like these coincidences. But are they, really?

I say no. Guardian Angels have a way of helping, revealing, and nudging us toward clarity. Your own story may not mirror this one exactly, but if you felt something stir within you while reading this, then perhaps it's not just about this story. Perhaps it's about you.

Because sometimes, the signs we're searching for are already here waiting for us to recognize them.

St Patrick!

Judith Turner

Last night, I had a vivid dream, one that felt more like a visit than a mere dream. In it, I was contacted by the mother of an old friend, Patrick—a woman I had only spoken with a handful of times, back when phone calls meant navigating through parents to reach our friends. Despite the years and the distance, her presence in the dream was clear and urgent.

She called me and said, "Hi, I'm very worried about Patrick. Can you please check on him for me?" Without hesitation, I responded, "Of course!" She continued, "I sense him feeling alone." I assured her I would reach out. The last thing she said before our conversation ended was, "Please do!" Then, as I hung up the phone in the dream, a thought crossed my mind: Do I even have his number?

When I woke up early the next morning, the dream was still fresh in my mind. It had felt so real that I found myself debating whether I should actually reach out to Patrick. I mentioned the dream to my husband, expecting skepticism, but instead, he encouraged me to make the call. His support surprised me but also reassured me. So, I did. I reached out to Patrick and told him about the dream—how his mother had appeared to me, worried and asking me to check on him.

What he told me next left me speechless. Patrick was dealing with serious medical issues. His doctors had found a mass, and he was in the midst of pre-op preparations for surgery. I asked if my reaching out had startled him or brought him comfort. At first, he admitted it shook him. But ultimately, it was reassuring to know his mother was still watching over him—just as she had in life.

As if the dream and its timing weren't already powerful enough, I soon realized the significance of the day. It was St. Patrick's Day—a day that carried deep personal meaning for him. Not only was it an Irish holiday, but for Patrick, it was his name day—one he had always celebrated as an extra birthday. When I wished him a "Happy St. Patrick's Day" on the phone, his response gave me chills. "Those were my father's words," he said.

At that moment, it became clear that Patrick wasn't just receiving a message from his mother—his father was present too. The timing of the dream, the call, and the significance of the date layered this connection with even more meaning. I reminded Patrick that while his mother had expressed concern about him feeling alone, he could now take comfort in knowing he was far from it. His parents were with him, guiding him and protecting him.

Judith's Insigh:

Guardian Angels often communicate through dreams—offering guidance, preparing us for what's ahead, or, in this case, delivering a message to someone who might not recognize the signs on their own. It's natural to second-guess these experiences. To wonder: Was it just a dream? Did it really mean something? Could it have been my imagination? But this was a gift—not just for Patrick, who received his mother's message, but also for me, the messenger.

Sometimes, when someone isn't a believer in signs—or may be reluctant to accept them—their Guardian Angel will seek out someone who does believe to deliver the message. That's why, if you ever receive a message in a dream about someone else, trust it. It may be a sign that it's time to check in, despite the years, the distance, or the circumstances. In this case, my dream became a bridge between the divine and the earthly. By being willing to accept and relay the message, I played a small but meaningful role in making a huge difference in Patrick's life. The clarity and urgency of the dream revealed how Guardian Angels work through us, ensuring that we never have to face our challenges alone.

This experience was a reminder of how these moments bring comfort, validation, and a deeper connection between the seen and unseen. There's a reason for our past connections. People don't just come and go, they leave imprints on our lives, even if we don't see the full picture right away. Think about it: Sometimes you meet a stranger at a doctor's office who later becomes a close friend; you stand in line at the Department of Motor Vehicles and strike up a conversation, only to realize they knew your deceased mother; or a long-lost connection unexpectedly resurfaces, delivering a piece of wisdom just when you need it.

The last pieces of a puzzle often come together when a Guardian Angel steps in to deliver them. They remind us that nothing is random — everything is connected. When those pieces finally fall into place, we gain a clearer view of the whole picture, allowing us to see the complete puzzle.

Today as I sit here, I learned that Patrick has passed away and has become a Guardian Angel to many. I am thankful to have been the messenger to bring him peace before he found the ultimate peace. Rest in peace, Patrick.

REFLECTION 3

Angels

There are Angels among us! Take a moment to find the Angel in your day.

At some point, you'll experience an AM—an "Angel Moment." It won't be hard to recognize. Maybe it's a few words from a stranger, a message on the radio, or a line on television that speaks directly to your heart— just when you need it most.

Here's to someone looking out for you—and to you noticing you have an Angel.

—Judith Turner

Finally, a Sign from My Sister

S. V.

One day I was hanging out with a close friend and the topic of my sister came up (my sister passed away when I was ten years old). As I was sharing, I became a bit emotional and was missing her. After the conversation finished, I heard my friend start singing "Finally, it's happened to me," lyrics from the song "Finally" by CeCe Peniston, which coincidently is the song that reminds me of my sister. I asked my friend how she knew that "Finally" was the song that reminded me of my sister. My friend said she had no idea, the song just popped into her head. I felt that it was a sign from my sister telling me she was still with me. I then felt a nudge to look into an old book that my sister used to own. As I examined the book, I noticed some new information about the high school she went to (which I had not known about before). I plan to research that information some more because I think it will lead me to something important.

Judith's Insight:

I absolutely love this. Every time you hear the word "Finally," it's as though your sister is reaching out, holding your hand through life. The lyrics aren't just words; they are a gentle nudge—a reminder to pay attention, to heal, to feel her presence. You might not even realize you were carrying pain, but whether you were aware of it or not, she knew. And because she loves you, she found a way to be there.

For her, "Finally" represents peace and resolution. It's her way of saying, "I'm here. I see you. I'm with you." She adores you deeply, and the messages you're receiving are reminders that there is still so much ahead of you.

This book—your story—is about moving forward, embracing

the future, and stepping into the next chapter. Your Guardian Angel isn't just sending you comfort; she's sending you affirmation. The road ahead is filled with promise.

Sometimes, we think we've been waiting years, even a lifetime, for a sign from someone who has passed. Until suddenly, it hits you right in the face. That's when the reflection game begins. You start to look back and realize that the signs were always there; they just didn't look the way you expected.

Maybe someone was watching over you when you needed it most. Maybe that friendship that fell apart was actually making space for the people who were meant to stay. Maybe the detour, the heartbreak, the unexpected shift—all of it—was leading you somewhere better.

The truth is that every sign, moment, and shift in your path has been guiding you here. Sometimes, when we recognize a sign, our reaction is simply, "Finally!"

I'm Alright

Vicki D'Auria

I lost my son and only child on April 6, 2022. Brian was just twenty-six years old. I was home alone on this particular day, one year after he passed. I started to talk to him. I told Brian that I wanted to know if he was okay. Afterward, I went and took a nap. When I woke up, I reached for and opened his iPad. I received a Snapchat notification that read, "3 years ago, Today." When I opened the notification, it was a selfie of Brian with the words "I'm alright."

Judith's Insight:

Timing can be remarkably uncanny. Your son wanted to let you know he hears you and is doing alright, and he has chosen unique ways to reach out to you. One of these ways is through electronics—think flickering lights, computers, phones, and emails. These can be subtle yet meaningful signs. Additionally, words might appear out of nowhere, or you might notice any combination of the numbers four, six, and two. These numbers hold significance, especially since he was also twenty-six years old at the time of his passing.

The date on which you saw this sign is also significant. It's a reminder that your son is aware of your moments of need and is making sure his messages come through when they matter most. Your son is always finding ways to send you messages, making sure they come through loud and clear. When you ask a Guardian Angel to show up, they often do. While it might not always be through a computer or a device, unexpected coincidences can occur—moments that seem too perfect to be mere chance. Your son was spontaneous, and his messages to you will feel the same, much like a jack-in-the-box, popping out of nowhere to show you he's there. These experiences are your son's way of letting you know he is looking out for you, reinforcing that his presence and care continue even from afar.

If you're someone who experiences unexpected moments, they may not always come with a dramatic entrance. Instead, they might appear as a sudden phone call, a random text, or an unexpected message on Facebook or Instagram.

Even if the message itself doesn't seem significant at first, take a closer look. Check the date, the time, and the numbers involved. Those small details might hold the deeper meaning you've been searching for, helping you understand not just how—but why—it all makes better sense.

Daddy's Girl

Judith Turner

My dad passed away unexpectedly on December 7, 1998, leaving me completely overwhelmed by the sudden loss. Just a few days later, I was supposed to leave for the premiere of my first book, *The Hidden World of Birthdays*, at the grand opening of the Atlantis Resort in the Bahamas. Atlantis had purchased over 25,000 copies of my book for their launch, and I was expected to attend a series of events, from meet-and-greets to book signings, alongside A-listers like Michael Jackson and Oprah. The publisher had covered all my travel expenses, making it a significant professional commitment.

Amidst my grief, which weighed heavily on my mom and siblings as well, all I could think about was my father's funeral the next day. The idea of leaving for the Bahamas seemed impossible. My mom, however, was firm. "You have to go on Friday," she insisted. "Daddy would want you to go. He wouldn't want you to miss this event. Besides, if you stay home, you'd be backing out of a commitment. You have a fully paid trip with your assistant. This is work, and you must go."

After the funeral, I still couldn't bring myself to pack. That evening, my mom asked, "Did you pack?" I shook my head. "No! I can't. I can't leave you. That would be terrible," I said. "Bury Daddy today and go to Atlantis tomorrow? It's not happening! Besides, I don't even know where my passport is."

That night, after an emotionally exhausting day, I fell into a deep sleep. In my dream, my dad appeared to me. His message was clear. "Stop making excuses," he said. "Don't let me be an excuse. Don't let the passport be an excuse. I'll tell you where it is." He described its exact location: on the miniature desk in my room, in the top left drawer, standing up on its side next to the wall of the drawer. He also mentioned that my aunt would be at the airport. Before he left, he added something that stayed with me: sometimes, what you think is right may not actually be right.

I woke up with a mix of disbelief and curiosity. Could I really have had a conversation with my dad in my dream? I walked to my desk, opened the top left drawer, and to my amazement, my passport was exactly where he said it would be.

I shared the story with my husband, who responded, "I hope this means you're going." I then called my mom and told her about the dream and how I had found my passport. "I know it was Daddy," she said. "He wants you to go. He would be so upset if you didn't. It's the weekend now, and everyone is here to support me. Please go."

Though I felt broken, with my mom's encouragement and my dad's unwavering presence, I went to the Atlantis opening to promote my book. It was undeniably a once-in-a-lifetime experience, even though it was hard to fully embrace so soon after my dad's passing. Throughout the trip, I felt him with me. When I landed back home, my husband picked me up at the airport and told me he had just dropped off my aunt, who had changed her flight and airport to leave at the exact time I was arriving. The timing was perfect.

Judith's Insight:

Sometimes, when grief feels so heavy that you can't lift your head from the pillow, all it takes is the right dream to give you the strength to rise.

Writing *The Hidden World of Birthdays* was one thing, but the title itself seems to connect to something much deeper—the hidden world of our Guardian Angels. The book's name now feels like a reflection of my father's presence. He was always direct, never one to sugarcoat his words, so it makes sense that he chose the most straightforward way to reach me. He didn't leave subtle signs that could be overlooked. Instead, he appeared in a way that mirrored how he was in life—firm, clear, and to the point.

This moment with my book and the Bahamas trip represents not just a milestone in my career but also a legacy of my father's love and guidance. Even in death, he made sure I didn't let my grief hold me back. His visit in my dream reassured me that he was still here, still showing up when I needed him most.

The timing of everything, from my passport's location to my aunt's flight, was orchestrated so perfectly that it left no doubt in my mind. My dad was making sure I followed through, not just for myself but as a reminder that life continues, even after loss.

The involvement of my family in this experience speaks volumes about the love my father had for all of us. He was a man who valued family above all else, someone who made sure that even in his absence, none of us would feel abandoned. His presence remains, and this was the first of many times he would reach out to remind me of that.

Books, like dreams, have a way of bringing comfort. They offer knowledge, entertainment, an escape, or even a form of meditation that transports us beyond everyday life. If you don't find solace in reading, try writing. There are hidden answers in both, waiting to be revealed—perhaps even a message from a Guardian Angel you weren't expecting.

Ladybugs

Donna Lanza

As the one-year anniversary of my mother's passing approaches on February 17, I've noticed something unusual: ladybugs. So many of them are appearing in my home, showing up repeatedly. I can't help but wonder, is she reaching out?

Judith's Insight:

Left wondering—this is how so many of us spend our time: contemplating what just happened, what it meant, and whether we should even say it aloud. You're not alone in asking, "Is this real? Am I imagining it?" The truth is this reaction is common when faced with something sacred, mysterious, and unexplainable. Perhaps you couldn't sleep or felt a sudden touch when no one was there. That's not crazy; that's a visit.

Many people experience these fleeting, blink-and-you'll-miss-it moments where they feel a presence, hear a whisper, or sense a shift in the air. It's often the soul of someone you love, stopping by to let you know they're near.

You've likely called out to her in your grief—especially around this anniversary—wondering if she's okay, wondering if she hears you. And then, the ladybugs come.

When this happens, the most important question is: What do I feel this is? More often than not, your instincts are right. While it may never be "proven," that doesn't matter—not when your soul knows. Your soul has a direct line to the universe, to the Heavens, and it often understands what your mind can't explain.

So let me say this: It's okay to believe in the things that bring you peace. It's okay to trust the signs that bring you comfort. It's okay to accept the touches, the visits, the whispers—even if they can't be measured or explained.

You've been touched.

And today? Lucky be this lady. Those ladybugs are anointing your home with love, comfort, and yes—with a little extra luck.

Ladybugs, like four-leaf clovers, have always been symbols of blessing and fortune. But when they appear this often, it's more than coincidence. It's a celebration, a signal, a spiritual moment with all hands on deck.

Your mother isn't just sending a sign—she's arriving in full force, like a gentle cavalry of wings, reminding you that she's here as this special date approaches: February 17, a day she knows lives in your heart.

Ladybugs and celebrations go hand-in-hand. They're heaven's way of saying: "Keep going. Good things are coming." They're her way of saying: "I see you. I'm proud of you. I'm with you."

So next time you see a ladybug, let it spark joy. Let it bring you back to appreciation. Let it serve as a reminder: You are lucky. You are loved. You are being pushed forward with encouragement.

Stars and Hearts

Elaine LoConte

I am incredibly fortunate to have been blessed with two wonderful children. When my daughter was born, I chose the middle name Stark for her, meaning "star." From the very first moment I gazed into her eyes, she captivated my heart completely. She arrived over thirty years ago, at a time when unique names were far from the norm, especially in our Italian family. Tragically, my beloved daughter, Lauren, passed away at the tender age of thirty-two. The depth of my grief is immeasurable, and it feels as though she has taken a piece of each of our hearts with her.

In the wake of her passing, as I sifted through her journals, Instagram pictures, and countless doodles, a poignant pattern emerged: Stars and hearts were everywhere. These doodles, scattered across her notebooks and on the margins of her papers, were not just random scribbles. They were her way of leaving behind subtle messages, signs of her presence and love. Each star and heart she drew seemed to take on a new significance, as if she was trying to tell us that her spirit is still very much alive.

Since Lauren's departure, I've been blessed with videos capturing her youthful exuberance—whether she was performing as a little rock star, belting out songs with a stage-worthy presence, or making grand entrances down our staircase. The songs she sang often spoke of the heart, and every word she sang reverberates through every chamber of my own heart.

Judith's Insight:

The signs you receive from your daughter, now a Heavenly Guardian Angel, come in the form of hearts, stars, and melodies. These signs offer you a sense of peace, a constant reminder that she remains with you, guiding and comforting you even from afar.

Our lives are intricately woven together long before we take our first breath. We don't simply cross paths with one another by chance; every connection is part of a larger, meaningful design. Naming her Stark was an intuitive recognition of her destined role as a guiding light. She entered this world as a beacon, illuminating every space she touched and creating her own unique stages.

The doodles she left behind, filled with stars and hearts, are more than simple decorations. They are messages, small but powerful reminders that her love continues beyond time and space. The music she cherished and that still plays today serves as a bridge, carrying pieces of her essence and echoing her spirit in the moments you need it most.

Lauren will always find ways to communicate with you. Her presence will remain steady in your life, appearing in subtle but unmistakable ways. A familiar song playing at just the right moment, a star shining unusually bright in the night sky, or a heart-shaped symbol appearing when you least expect it but need it the most—these are not coincidences. They are her way of reminding you that she is still with you, lighting your way and filling your heart with her love.

We all hold on to things that move us, that bring us a sense of comfort—like the rhythm of a song. Why do certain songs speak to us while others fade into the background? Is it the melody, the lyrics, or the emotions they stir? Some songs stay with us word for word, while others slip away no matter how many times we hear them. Some lyrics feel like answers, others are simply there because they make us feel something. Some songs resonate because they are tied to a memory, while others appear out of nowhere, playing at just the right moment—because an Angel wanted you to hear them today.

The Last Ride

Ed Tesher

The night before my father's funeral, I was having a particularly terrible night's sleep for obvious reasons. I was still in the depths of deep loss and mourning, feeling almost inconsolable. Instead of staying in New Jersey where the funeral home and my family were located, I chose to stay by LaGuardia Airport in my hometown of Queens, New York, to be closer to the cemetery on Long Island.

The morning came and we had to be at the cemetery early. I proceeded to get into the car earlier than necessary because I just didn't know what else to do. A flood of life's memories, love, and joy came over me. My father was an incredibly powerful spirit, loved and admired by a legion of friends, family, neighbors, and all who were lucky enough to cross his path.

Thirty minutes into my drive on the Long Island Expressway, one of the busiest highways in the United States, I looked to my right and saw my dear friend—the funeral director who had taken care of all the arrangements for my father—driving the hearse carrying my father right next to us.

I was absolutely shaken. There he was, right next to me, with no other explanation other than him saying, "It's okay, follow me, we're in this together." Out of the thousands and thousands of cars that travel that highway, what are the odds?

Judith's Insight:

Wow, talk about a lasting impression on the expressway. That day as you were driving, your dad wanted to guide you one last time, performing his final fatherly duty. He was passing the torch, leaving you to take the wheel, trusting that you would now be the one to keep the family together. This was his way of showing his faith in you, knowing that you were ready to step into the role he once played.

Your dad made sure that the two of you traveled the last mile together so that you would never doubt his presence. No matter where life takes you, he will always find a way to be with you. It may not always be on the road, but in moments when you need clarity, or when an unexpected thought or realization suddenly shifts your perspective.

This journey was unlike any other, an experience that will be etched into your soul forever. It was so significant that it didn't need words, only the unmistakable message of a father's love. It provided answers to the unspoken questions in your heart, confirming what you already knew deep down—he is with you, watching over you.

A man's best friend is often his son, even when he has more than one. A daughter, if he has one, steals his heart and never gives it back. No matter where your path leads, keep your eyes on the road and your hands on the wheel. He will continue to guide you, leaving signs along the way to remind you of his presence. Pay attention not just to the journey but to the messages hidden in the details—the cars traveling beside you, the places you pass, and even the literal road signs. Stop. Detour. U-turn. Caution. And perhaps most important of all, Slow Down.

What a tangled web we can weave while rolling down the highway. But in this story, there is no confusion—it is as clear as a bright blue sky. It may seem like an unusual way to deliver a message on the way to a funeral, but moments like these are so uncanny that they defy logic. This is when the unexplainable can only be understood by accepting the presence of a Guardian Angel, the one who continues to ride with you every step of the way. You may think it's a coincidence, but certainly not this time.

Nancy

Elissa Cahn

Yesterday, on my walk, I was thinking of the women who influenced me as a mother and as a person. One of my most positive influences was my mom's best friend, whom I called Aunt Nancy. When my mom went back to work, Aunt Nancy took care of me. Some of my fondest childhood memories are of snuggling on her lap while she read me *The Little Engine That*

Could. I should mention that Aunt Nancy had six children of her own, and as they grew, she became known as Grancy to her many grandchildren and great-grandchildren.

This morning, as I was walking to meet my mom and sister for breakfast, I saw a car with a personalized license plate, GRANCY#1, from the state where Aunt Nancy retired. I know that Aunt Nancy is still looking out for me and sending me many blessings, on this, her first Mother's Day in Heaven.

Judith's Insight:

This is a beautiful example of what I like to call the "name game," a way for messages—whether they come as love, guidance, or a comforting presence—to be unmistakably clear. In this case, the sign you received seems to be a gentle but firm nudge from your Aunt Nancy, encouraging you to move forward with something you may be hesitating about. It's as if she's reaching out from beyond, offering her support in even the smallest moments, like joining you for breakfast.

Aunt Nancy's presence in this way is a reminder that her love and influence continue beyond this life. Her signs are not just fleeting occurrences but part of an ongoing connection, reassuring you that she is still with you. Expect more of these blessings, messages, and reminders from her. They may come subtly, but each one is a powerful confirmation that she is nearby, watching over you, and guiding you through life's challenges.

The people who touch our lives in meaningful ways are not always connected to us by blood. Some of the strongest bonds are formed with those we choose—friends who become family, or "Framily." These chosen loved ones remain with us, even after they pass, continuing to serve as guides and protectors. They, too, can send signs, often in the form of the name game, where a name repeatedly appears to get our attention.

Sometimes, like in this story, the name is unique, like Grancy. Other times, a more familiar name will appear over and over again, making sure we take notice. When this happens, it's worth pausing to reflect on the message being sent. The connection we share with those we love may be missed until their presence finds ways to make itself known just when we need it most.

Gifts from My Son
Dara Falco

My son Jordan took his life two years ago on April 29, 2020. His birthday was May 8 (he would have turned seventeen). This time of year will always be hard. Since his birthday is close to Mother's Day, I am always in a particular state of dread. However, Jordan has always sent me signs.

I was away at a business conference. While there, I was chatting and having dinner with a young woman named Jordi. She told me during our meal that she was named after her grandfather, Jordan. While flying home from the conference there was a beautiful break in the clouds, with the sun (son) streaming in as we passed through a double rainbow. Thank you, Jordan!

Judith's Insight:
What a story filled with Heavenly signs and messages. Your incredible son went above and beyond to make sure you knew he was with you. The name game is one of the clearest and most heartfelt ways he could reach out, ensuring that you recognized exactly who was sending you those comforting hugs and reassuring moments. Meeting someone with his name was not a coincidence; it was his way of making sure you felt his presence.

Find comfort in the things Jordan left behind, whether it's something you wear, a piece of furniture, or an object that was once special to him. These belongings serve as personal touch-points, allowing you to feel connected whenever you need to reach out or simply talk to him. Just as Clarence in *It's a Wonderful Life* appeared to guide and uplift, Jordan's signs are meant to lead you to moments of peace and understanding, often in ways that catch you by surprise.

Rainbows, with their brilliant colors and fleeting beauty, carry messages from beyond. The sky that day spoke volumes, a vivid and unmistakable way for Jordan to say, "I'm here with you, and you did an amazing job." Even though he is in his Heavenly space, he is making sure you know that your connection remains unbreakable. These signs are his way of reminding you that, while he may no longer be physically present, he is never truly gone.

Rainbows are universal signs, yet they carry different meanings for different people. Their colors shift, just like the emotions and experiences they reflect. Maybe you're feeling blue and need reassurance. Maybe you're crossing into a new chapter of life and need guidance. Maybe the yellow in the rainbow represents the sunlight breaking through after a difficult time. How can something so universal also be so personal? It's the same way stars fill the sky—countless and ever-present, yet each with its own unique brilliance.

When you see a star, it may offer comfort on different days and in different ways, not always for the same reason. Like the stars that shine just to get your attention, take note of the colors that draw you in when you look at a rainbow. Guardian Angels have a way of keeping you guessing. It's not about whether they show up, it's about recognizing that they always do.

Ave Maria

Maryjo Delehanty

This is a story that I will always remember. My grandmother, Nonnie, lived to be 105 years old. She had extreme faith in God and the Blessed Mother. This faith was the foundation that got her through many difficulties and hardships throughout her life. One day I went to visit her while she was living with my mother. Nonnie always had revealing dreams throughout her life. Sometimes we wanted to hear the dreams and sometimes we didn't. However, most of the time her dreams were good.

I went into her room and sat down on her bed. She told me that the Ave Maria had come to see her. She said she was beautiful, all dressed in pink with brown hair! At that time, I was pregnant with my sixth child. My oldest was a boy followed by four girls. I never found out the sex of any of my children before childbirth. I felt it was God's plan so always left it in God's hands. She told me the Blessed Mother had come to her all dressed in pink. When I heard the word "pink" my heart skipped a beat. I asked, "Nonnie, am I having another girl?" She just looked at me, smiled, and said, "A beautiful girl named Maria."

Judith's Insight:

This story beautifully intertwines the realms of Heavenly and Earthly Angels. Your Nonnie, a guiding spirit, was instrumental in bestowing upon you a precious gift—the life of your daughter. In choosing her name, she left behind a living legacy, a treasure for you to cherish always. Guardian Angel stories weave their own paths to our hearts, allowing us to relive magical words, unforgettable moments, and messages of profound hope. The arrival of your daughter was no mere coincidence; she is a beacon of light, standing out in the world with a grace that reflects the love and guidance she has received.

Earthly Angels often appear in our lives, offering subtle guidance and support. While some may recognize these signs and messages immediately, others may only come to appreciate them after these Angels have transitioned into their roles as Guardian Angels. Both living and Earthly Angels, much like Guardian Angels, are there to lend a hand through our struggles, impart life lessons, and help us navigate fear, grief, milestones, and moments of joy and memory-making. Their presence, whether seen or unseen, continues to enrich our lives in meaningful ways, knowingly or unknowingly.

Brandy My Fine Wine
Lizbeth Kall

I lost my beloved golden retriever, Brandy, at the age of fifteen this past March. While at Lake George last weekend, I got into the elevator and when the door closed there was a picture of a dog on the door that looked exactly like Brandy. It's as if that exact picture was meant for me to see. Even her eyes looking at me made it clear she was in the elevator with me. Although my heart is shattered in a million pieces, it reminds me of the days she would follow me into the kitchen or back yard or lay with me in my bed or on the couch.

Judith's Insight:
Now you know for sure that she will always be by your side. Brandy was a source of comfort and protection, showing you that she remains by your side, especially when you travel away from home. Her presence during your vacation was a gift, a reminder that her love and guidance continue to surround you. Brandy was more than just a dog; she was family. The pain of losing her and feeling your heart shatter reflects the depth of grief. It knows

no limits and affects us profoundly, no matter who or what has left an empty space in our hearts.

Pay close attention to the other messages you've received, particularly those connected to the word "Lake" and the name "George." Water, represented by the lake, may continue to carry her messages to you. The name George may not always be literal; it could represent a male figure in your life who serves as an Earthly Angel. If you haven't met this person yet, keep an open heart. If you were on vacation with someone, this could be Brandy's way of showing her approval, letting you know that this person holds a special place in the journey of support and love she continues to send your way.

Losing a pet, whether a dog, cat, or any cherished companion, can leave an imprint that is always with you. You may find yourself feeling their presence at unexpected moments, sensing them close as if they never left. If you always sat on the couch with your dog, you might feel their warmth beside you in the middle of the night while watching a movie. You may hear the familiar squeak of a toy, knowing full well it was tucked away in a memory box. Whether it's paws or claws, love doesn't fade. Pets always find a way to remind us that they are still with us, holding our heart, just as they always have.

My Nana

JoAnne Turner Connolly

When I was a young girl, my Nana was my absolute favorite person in the world. Everyone around us thought I was her favorite, and if you promise to keep a secret, I'll admit it—I was. Nana had an incredible way of making me feel truly special.

I visited her often, and many wondered why I preferred her company over others. She didn't have the latest games, toys, or gadgets. Being one of many grandchildren, some younger than me, what drew me to her? The answer was simple: Nana was "My Nana," a unique and irreplaceable character. From the moment I entered this world, I felt that we were kindred spirits.

Though she didn't have a multitude of toys, Nana had a big jar of pennies. I would spend hours on the floor, arranging them into patterns and creating little pictures. Losing Nana was one of the hardest experiences of my life, it felt like losing the one who had chosen me. As time went by, I noticed that a penny seemed to appear on every special occasion and daily moment. It was as if Nana was always with me.

Years later, while working at our family deli, I faced a frightening situation when I was held up at gunpoint. The thief demanded all the money, yet the pennies remained untouched in the register. Looking back, I realize that Nana was there with me, through every struggle, every mundane day, and every extraordinary event.

I believe throughout my life my Nana brought me good fortune and made sure I felt her presence through each penny from Heaven. To this day, she is my Guardian Angel, always sending me little reminders of her love.

Judith's Insight:

If you find a penny, pick it up; you never know who is looking out for you. Life is a tapestry laced with memories and connections that leave lasting imprints on our hearts. Your Nana is undoubtedly your Guardian Angel, and she chose pennies as her way of making sure she always captured your attention. She knew these small, simple coins would stand out, allowing you to instantly recognize them as her special sign.

In her own magical way, Nana turned a single cent into a powerful symbol of her love and presence. When she reaches out to her beloved grandchild, a penny is the perfect choice. If you reflect on the significant moments in your life, you may notice that pennies — or the number one — have appeared at just the right times. This is her way of saying she is there with you, celebrating your successes and offering comfort during difficult times.

Imagine starting a special jar to collect these pennies. Each coin is more than just money; it's a hug from your Nana, a kiss from Heaven, and a tangible reminder of her unwavering love and protection. Every penny you find is a small but meaningful message, reassuring you that she is near. Keep those pennies close, they are the whispers of her spirit, reminding you that you will always be her number one.

Childhood memories and games can sometimes hold clues to the greater journey of life. Guardian Angels don't just show up in moments of struggle; they are also there for the joy, the excitement, and the moments that shape who we become. You may find them on the soccer field, guiding you to make that winning goal, giving you confidence to ask someone to dance, or nudging you toward a new adventure. Sometimes, they even come along for the ride. Angels aren't just present in our darkest times; they are there to cheer us on, check in, encourage us, and celebrate with us on the dance floor when life gives us something to smile about.

Faith or Fear

Judith Turner

I am in New York City, and today, someone I love is having surgery — my darling husband. Prayers are flying! The morning started a little rough with the worst Uber driver ever! I kept saying prayer after prayer. All morning, my thoughts were consumed by my mom in Heaven. I asked her to please help me, saying a silent prayer for a sign to get me through this difficult day.

To lift my spirits, I posted on Facebook, seeking more prayers and support from my friends. Then, I decided it was time for my preferred morning drink, a Diet Pepsi. I went to three different food trucks, but none had diet soda. As I waited at yet another truck, the woman in front of me was ordering her breakfast. When it was my turn, I asked if they had Diet Pepsi. The girl behind the counter said there was one, but it was all the way at the bottom of the ice. The woman who had just ordered her breakfast offered to dig it out while she waited for her food.

I was overwhelmed by her kind gesture. As she rummaged through the bucket of ice, our conversation went like this:

"Wow! That is so nice of you!" I said.

"I got you!" she replied.

I went back to the food truck window and told them I would like to buy her breakfast. The woman immediately said, "No! I am buying you this diet soda. I need to do this for you."

"I need to do this for you!" I insisted.

Then she said, "I'm paying it forward."

"But you made my day!" I said.

"We will meet again," she said.

Emotionally, we both hugged. I asked her for her name.

"My name is Judi," she said.

"Oh my God! My name is Judi!" I exclaimed. Then I told her that the most important thing was that my mom's name was also Judi, and I had just been wishing for a sign from her.

We were both in tears. It was my sign from Heaven. My very long day just got shorter.

I forgot one important piece of the story. She asked me for my middle name and said she would faint if my middle name started with the letter "F." I told her my middle name starts with an "E." So, I asked her for her middle name.

"My middle name is Faith," she said.

That is all I needed to hear, the word "faith."

Judith's Insight:

Heavenly Angels often bring us Earthly Angels, using people, places, things, and sometimes even electricity to capture our attention. For me, the presence of an Earthly Angel became unmistakable when I heard the name Judi and the word Faith. This was a perfect example of the name game, where names show up out of nowhere, echoing those loved ones, best friends, or people with whom we've shared moments of life. Names can present themselves in the most unexpected places and ways, guiding us and ensuring we recognize the Guardian Angel lending us a helping hand.

In that moment, the alignment of beautiful kindness was bestowed upon me, cutting through my preoccupation with fear. It is truly magical when our eyes and hearts open to these signs, as mine did upon hearing my mom's name. The flood of tears and the sense of hope that followed were undeniable. This was not merely a coincidence, but a profound connection orchestrated by my mom from beyond.

The universe has a way of guiding us and providing comfort, often in the most surprising ways. You don't have to believe in God to have faith, but having faith can dispel fear, even when common sense tells you otherwise. Faith allows us to trust in the unseen, to believe in the support and love that surrounds us, even when we can't always see it.

This encounter was a powerful reminder that our loved ones are always with us, watching over us, and finding creative ways to communicate their presence. My mom, through the Earthly Angel named Judi, made sure that all would be okay. She sent me a message of faith, reinforcing that even amidst fear and uncertainty, she was standing right next to me, always within reach.

Here's Looking at You Kid

Mary

When I was about fourteen years old, my mom had a baby boy. I was thrilled to have a new brother. Despite my excitement, he cried a lot, and I was always the one who would get up to comfort him. It seemed as though he never stopped crying, but no matter the time, I would get up, walk over to him, sing to him, and do whatever I could to soothe him. From the very start, we had a special bond.

As the years went by, I continued to find ways to take care of him. I got married, moved away, and had my own children, but our special connection remained unbreakable. I nurtured him, spoiled him, chatted with him, and, most of all, loved him deeply. Our relationship was unique and cherished.

On one of my visits to see my family, my brother pulled me aside and said, "I made this for you!" It was a painting. To be honest, it wasn't quite to my taste, but my heart was touched that he had created it just for me. He kept insisting, "This is for you! I made this for you! I want you to have a piece of me. I am an artist." The painting depicted a skeleton in nature, which I understood was his creative expression.

Last year, at the age of thirty-five, my brother passed away. The pain of losing him was immense, he was so young. It was heart-wrenching and profoundly sad. Recently, while moving things around in my closet, something fell off the shelf. It was the painting my brother had given me! I sat down and cried, feeling the weight of my grief. As I looked at the painting, the beauty of it began to come to life in a way I hadn't seen before.

In that moment, I felt a deep connection with my brother and the love we shared. It was as if he were reaching out to me, offering a sign that he was still with me. The painting, once overlooked, had become a poignant reminder of our bond and his enduring presence in my life.

Judith's Insight:

This touching story vividly captures the love and bond between you and your brother. The painting he created was his way of leaving a piece of his legacy with you, ensuring that you would have a tangible reminder of his presence. It was his advance gesture of comfort, a sign he intended for you to turn to whenever you needed him. You were like a second mother to him, offering care and affection throughout his life.

I hope that painting now finds a place on your wall, where you can glance at it and draw strength from the love he infused into every brushstroke. The fact that the painting fell from the closet is a poignant reminder that, although he is no longer physically present, he is still very much with you.

This is a gift that keeps on giving. Sometimes we receive gifts or relics that may not seem to our taste at the moment. However, these items often take on a new significance after the giver has passed away. What once seemed like a simple or unremarkable token can become a cherished memento or heirloom, full of deep meaning and connection. Remember, gifts—even those from the living—can grow on us with time, life experiences, and even through the process of grieving.

Your brother's art, initially overlooked, has become a profound symbol of his enduring presence and love. Expect these signs and symbols to appear when you least expect them, reminding you that he is still watching over you. Just remember, he's still looking out for you—especially when he knows you are looking out for him.

REFLECTION 4

Serenity

It feels like a wish granted from the Heavens above, filled with patience, blossoming in a garden of love, and as free as a butterfly drifting by. Don't question why, just have serenity.

—Judith Turner

It's a Wonderful Life

Judith Turner

I remember sitting in my living room, staring blankly at the television that was on but barely registering. My dad had passed away earlier that month, and the weight of his loss left us all feeling shattered. With three young children—ages eight, seven, and eleven months—I felt completely overwhelmed. The thought of pulling together Christmas felt impossible. I hadn't bought a single gift, and even the idea of shopping seemed insurmountable. My mom, heartbroken and grieving, was constantly on my mind. My parents had been together since they were twelve, married at eighteen, and had devoted their lives to doing what was best for us.

Lost in my thoughts, I kept wondering how I could make Christmas special for my family when I could barely keep myself together. Suddenly, my eight-year-old son came down the stairs, walked right up to me, and said, "Mommy, did you know it's a wonderful life?" He was always a quiet child, and even now, twenty-five years later, he is known as a man of few words, yet he's now a lawyer and a comic. I often said he only spoke when he had something truly meaningful to say. I turned to him, taken aback, and replied, "Yes! As a matter of fact, I do!" In that moment, something washed over me. It was as if my dad was sending me a message, urging me to shake off the sorrow and create a joyful Christmas for my family.

It felt like my Guardian Angel father needed to hear the bells ring so he could get his wings. The irony of my son's words wasn't lost on me because, growing up, my family had a Christmas tradition of watching *It's a Wonderful Life* every year. My sister and dad would quote lines from the movie year-round, as if they had written the script themselves. As we got older, my dad would call us whenever the movie aired on television, making sure we were watching. Since his passing, every time the movie comes on, it feels like a clear sign, a reminder to celebrate Christmas and to remember that, truly, it is a wonderful life.

Judith's Insight:

It's no wonder *It's a Wonderful Life* holds such a special place in my heart. Growing up, it was more than just a holiday tradition; it became part of our family's fabric. Watching it each year was like welcoming a beloved friend into our home, one that brought comfort, laughter, and warmth. The movie's messages weren't just entertainment, they became a source of guidance and inspiration.

What made that moment with my son even more extraordinary was that he had never seen the movie before. If it had been anyone else who had said those words, I might not have recognized their significance. But coming from him, someone who rarely spoke without purpose, I knew it was more than a coincidence. I am certain that my father was speaking through my son, reminding me to hold on to hope and the true spirit of Christmas.

My siblings and I often reminisce about the countless times we watched the movie together, reciting our favorite lines and replaying cherished scenes in our minds. Those movie nights are more than just memories—they are woven into the very essence of who we are.

Looking back now, as I write this book about Guardian Angels, I realize how deeply connected I have always been to the themes of hope, guidance, and unseen support that *It's a Wonderful Life* represents. It's as if my lifelong bond with the movie and the memory of my father have all led me to this moment. The connection is undeniable, a beautiful reminder that everything in life is interwoven in ways we might not fully understand.

Pay attention to the moments that shaped you in your early years, the stories you tell over and over again. Who knew we were marking a trail along our journey, creating memories that would later reveal their significance? Who knew which moments would stay with us, waiting for the right time to remind us of something greater? There is a saying that every time a bell rings an Angel gets its wings. And sometimes, after a Guardian Angel or a guide has helped you in a way that feels nothing short of miraculous, don't you ever wonder if, in that moment, they finally earned their wings? The good deeds or help they provided just earned them their wings.

Unique Dreams
Lenniece D'Anna

I don't know if this happens to anyone else, but lately, when I dream of my mom or dad, they never speak. They are just there—moving through the dream—while I'm the one doing all the talking. The scenery always feels familiar, yet it's blurred and shadowy, almost black. When I wake up, I feel as if they have visited me—especially when I see a cardinal or two outside my window or perched on the phone wire. I'm always left trying to decipher the meaning of these dreams.

Judith's Insight:
Your dreams of your parents coming to you in silence are just as much a visit as if they had spoken aloud. It's actually quite common for loved ones to appear without words. Their presence alone says everything; it speaks volumes.

Next time you have one of those dreams, try writing it down in detail. It may not make sense at that moment, but when you revisit it later—days, weeks, even years down the line—you might see things differently. Clarity often comes with time and distance.

Dreams like these can be both frustrating and comforting. Frustrating because they don't always make sense, and comforting because, for a little while, you feel like you've seen them, felt them, almost like you were hugged by them. Even if there's no physical touch, it's as if their energy wraps around you for a moment.

But then, you wake up. And the weight of their absence settles in again. For a moment, or maybe hours, the grief resurfaces. That ache of knowing they are gone.

Still, there's something sacred in knowing that when you close your eyes at night, there's a chance you'll see them again. Maybe next time, you'll even hear a word or two.

Sometimes, when people whisper — or say nothing at all — we listen more closely. In silence, we feel more deeply. And in those quiet spaces, we often hear everything they're not saying.

The message is this: feel. Just truly feel. Tune in to your own emotions and to what others around you — especially the silent ones — might be feeling too. Pay attention. Feelings matter.

Best Bargain Ever
Judith Turner

Every day, I look for signs from my Guardian Angels to help me navigate life's challenges. It's how I find comfort and guidance, especially during difficult times. Many years after our mother passed away, my sister, who was very close to her, was diagnosed with cancer. Since then, I've searched for signs from Mom, hoping to receive messages that might bring my sister comfort. I make it my mission to bring a smile to her face every day, whether by surprising her with small gifts or simply acting silly to make her laugh. I truly believe laughter is the best medicine, and I'm using it to help her heal.

Recently, my sister mentioned finding a beautiful coat in a consignment shop. Being frugal, she hesitated to buy it since the shop wouldn't negotiate the price. She had inherited her love of bargain hunting from Mom, who was an expert long before it became trendy. I kept the coat in mind, considering reaching out to the shop to buy it for her. However, I had something else planned first. She was attending a wedding the next day, and I knew she had appointments at two different places — one for her hair and makeup, the other for her nails. Wanting to surprise her, I paid for all her services in advance, just to make her day a little brighter.

While driving to finalize her appointments, she called and asked me to pick up something from a store and drop it off at her house. As we spoke, I realized I was right in front of the store she mentioned. I hadn't expected to see her that day since she was busy with wedding preparations, but I took this as a sign from Mom that I was on the right path. I suggested we meet for coffee, even though neither of us drinks it, and she agreed.

When we met, I handed her the item she needed. Immediately, I noticed she was wearing "the ring" — a piece of jewelry I had bought for Mom, which Mom had later given to my sister. Seeing it felt like a message from Mom, as if she were sitting beside me. It was a special moment. We briefly talked about the coat and how perfect it would have been for the wedding.

After she left for her hair appointment, I sat in my car and spoke aloud to Mom: "Okay, Mom, prove to me you're here. The consignment shop wouldn't lower the price. Let's go do this!" As I drove to the store, I kept asking Mom to help me get a better deal. I needed to get a bargain — because if you knew Mom, you'd know she never paid full price for anything, not even a scratched and dented coffin.

My sister and I were regulars at the shop, so the place was familiar. When I walked in, I asked the saleslady about the coat my sister had admired the day before. She showed it to me, and I asked if they could offer a discount. She said no but suggested I speak with the coat's owner, who happened to be in the store.

I approached the owner and explained that my sister loved the coat but was hesitant to spend the money on herself. I also mentioned that she had cancer. The owner shared the coat's history, telling me about its details. Then, when I asked if she could lower the price, she agreed—to the tune of ninety dollars. That was all I needed to hear. I started to tear up. In that moment, I knew Mom was with me, helping me get a deal.

But the story didn't end there. As the owner continued talking about the coat, the saleslady and I became teary-eyed. She asked if I was alright. I explained that I was fine but that my sister had cancer and wouldn't spend money on herself, so I was trying to get her a good price on the coat—though I planned to buy it for her regardless. I stood at the counter, ready to pay, when the owner suddenly said, "I've changed my mind!"

I was momentarily stunned until she continued, "I can't charge you. This is a gift! Someone out there is telling me to do this. I cannot take your money. Please, go give her the coat. I need to do this!"

Everyone in the store was crying. I took the coat, found a gift bag and ribbon in my car, and placed the package on my sister's front seat while she was at the salon. Later, when she called me, overwhelmed by the coat and the other surprises, I told her it was from Mom. We cried together, both feeling that Mom—our Guardian Angel—had shown up to give her the hug she needed, along with the coat.

Judith's Insight:

Guardian Angels have a remarkable way of sending messages that feel deeply personal and perfectly timed. Sometimes, these messages arrive in the form of a bird or butterfly. Other times, they unfold as an intricate story, weaving together events in ways we could never predict. These moments serve as profound reminders of the presence of our Guardian Angels, offering comfort and guidance when we need it most.

In this touching story, the series of small signs and the unexpected generosity at the consignment shop illustrate how our Angels make their presence known. The deep connection I share with my sister and our late mother is undeniable, and this experience reaffirmed the ever-present work of Angels in our lives. My need for reassurance that Mom was still with us was answered in a beautiful and undeniable way.

This story also highlights the role of other Angels—like the coat's owner and even her late mother—who became part of this extraordinary moment. The tears shed that day weren't just tears of sadness but of joy and love.

As you read this, you might think back to your own unexpected journey—one that, in hindsight, was leading you toward a moment of love, clarity, or healing. Sometimes, the signs are years in the making, revealing themselves at just the right time. The evolution of a guide story can be in the making for many years, long before you may realize this was all a part of a plan, a reveal, a comfort, and a very unique and emotional Guardian Angel story.

Clearly Kevin's Messages
Judith Turner

My editor and I had set a goal to complete a draft of my book by Thanksgiving and send it to my friend Kevin. A highly respected film and television producer in Hollywood, Kevin was leading the charge to share my manuscript with his colleagues and industry contacts. He had already received encouraging feedback from two of the biggest agents in Hollywood on the initial chapters. His support was incredibly motivating, and having such a brilliant creative force in my corner inspired me to push forward. It was empowering to know that someone I deeply respected saw and appreciated my vision as an author.

Tragically, Kevin passed away suddenly. In the midst of my shock, sadness, and disbelief, I resolved to stay on course with the book, hoping that someone else in the industry would recognize Kevin's vision for the project. Although I missed the Thanksgiving deadline, my determination to complete the book remained strong.

As I worked toward my new deadline, I needed help with my media kit and book cover graphics. I reached out to my friend Arlene, whose daughter Kaitlin is a graphic designer. Arlene gave me Kaitlin's phone number, but when I called, I was surprised to hear an answering machine message that said, "Hello, this is Kevin. Please leave your message at the beep." Startled, I hung up and tried again, only to hear the same message. Something about it unsettled me. I contacted Arlene to confirm the number, and she quickly apologized, realizing she had given me the wrong one. She then provided Kaitlin's correct contact information.

As soon as I ended the call with Arlene, my daughter walked in, and I told her about the strange voicemail. Curious, I decided to call the number one more time. This time, a man answered.

"Hello, is this Kevin?" I asked.

"No, this is not Kevin," he replied.

I explained that I was trying to reach someone named Kaitlin and apologized for the mix-up. The man chuckled and said, "Actually, you called me twice. Okay, this is Kaitlin."

I laughed. "I know you're not Kaitlin!"

He then said, "Oh, okay, then I'm Kevin."

Something about the moment gave me chills. I told him that I was working on a book and found it incredibly strange that, while trying to get help with it, I had somehow ended up reaching someone named Kevin. I shared the story of my friend Kevin, who had been championing the project before his unexpected passing, and mentioned the book's tentative title, *You Are Never Alone, Hugs from Heaven.*

His response took me aback. "So, I am Kevin, and I am sending you Kevin's hugs from Heaven." For a moment, I was speechless.

He asked me to keep his number and call him when the book becomes a success. He also requested that I mention him as Kevin from Wayne, New Jersey. "I promise I'll buy the book," he said. Then, before we ended the call, he added, "I will leave you with this: Kevin is sending you hugs from Heaven."

Judith's Insight:

Have you ever thought something was just a coincidence, only to later realize it was something more? To some, this might seem like a random mix-up. To others, it could be a sign to keep going. I truly believe Kevin is finding ways to reach out—not just to me, but to others who loved him. His family and friends have shared similar experiences: Who found a coin today? Who heard that song? Who had an unexpected visitor? Who felt his presence? Who came across old photos at just the right time? These moments suggest that Kevin is still making himself known in ways both big and small.

The phone call was especially meaningful because I was seeking help with something Kevin would have been instrumental in handling. When I dialed the wrong number and heard an answering machine for "Kevin," it felt like more than a mistake. It was as if Kevin had found a way to remind me that he was still guiding this journey.

The fact that I ended up speaking with someone named Kevin feels like a scene from one of Kevin's own films, an unexpected twist that leaves you wondering how it all came together. But that's how life works sometimes. When we think we're lost or off track, we might actually be exactly where we're meant to be.

Maybe this was just a wrong number. Or maybe, it was Kevin's way of making sure I knew he was still here, still watching over me, and still supporting this book—just as he always had.

Have you ever taken a wrong turn, shown up somewhere on the wrong day, or come across a name in an unexpected place? Did you stop to wonder if there was a reason? The universe speaks in mysterious ways. The signs are all around us — we just have to be willing to see them, hear them, and embrace them in the way the story is being told to us.

Naomi's Hug

Danielle Pecile

I lost my daughter this year. I was driving with my partner on vacation. I took his hand in mine and while holding it said, "I miss Naomi. I wish she was here." Immediately as we turned the corner on the road, the sky was full of pink. I took it as a sign that she was with us.

Judith's Insight:

This was no ordinary moment — it was a profound connection. One of the most remarkable experiences with Guardian Angels is not just sensing their presence but *knowing* exactly who the message is from.

The pink sky that evening wasn't just a beautiful sight; it resonated deep within you, as if every part of your being recognized it as *her.* Your little princess painted the sky in soft hues of love, ensuring that her presence was unmistakable. And when you spoke of missing her, the sky responded instantly — a breathtaking, undeniable sign. *"I'm here. I hear you."* She illuminated the sky to wrap you both in a comforting embrace, allowing you to feel her presence in a way beyond words.

And then, there was *the moment* — when you instinctively reached for your partner's hand. That simple gesture was more than a reflex; it was a thread binding the three of you together in that brief but powerful instant. Naomi is still with you, walking beside you, gently guiding you toward love and completeness. She's resourceful—always finding ways to communicate.

So, when you find yourself wondering about or longing for her touch, her voice, her laughter—look up. She's there, painting messages of love across the sky in the colors of dawn and dusk.

The Heavens are *always* speaking to us. Even if you simply sit on the ground and gaze upward, you will *feel* something stir within you. It may not always be a direct message from a Guardian Angel, but the sky holds a language of its own. Whether it's a feeling, a vision, or an unexpected sign, the celestial canvas has a way of reaching us—if only we take the time to listen, watch, and feel.

For some, the sky is a place of meditation. For others, it is life's grand canvas, where images, colors, and whispers of the wind merge to create a personal message. We take what we see, blend it with the sounds around us, and in doing so, we craft our own unique mental motion picture, a story written just for us. And sometimes, in the most extraordinary moments, the sky becomes a love letter from above.

Angel Numbers
Deborah M. Light

I have always had Angels around my home, mostly ones I made in ceramics class. I have always believed in my Guardian Angels. Since the passing of my partner, I have been learning about Angel numbers. They have been profoundly correct!

Since the end of November, I have been waking up at 2:43 a.m. That's the time he passed. I was very angry at his treatment and the cause of his death. Yesterday, I looked up Angel 243 and discovered it's the Angel of forgiveness. It wants me to let go of the anger.

When I see numbers repeating, I look up the meaning and have found they hold true each time. These numbers can be on a clock, television, license plate, article, mailbox, almost anywhere. I hope this can be of help to people who are struggling. It has definitely helped me.

Judith's Insight:

Numbers have a way of appearing in the most unexpected places—on the clock, the radio, a receipt, or even while waiting at the Motor Vehicle Department for your number to be called. But these moments are rarely just coincidences. More often than not, they are *messages*, a direct line from your Guardian Angels. These numbers are subtle winks from above, gentle nudges of reassurance, and, most importantly, the warmest of hugs when you need them most.

Everyone seems to have a number that holds deep significance in their life—a number that carries meaning, a story, a connection to something or someone greater. Over time, we begin to notice that certain numbers repeat themselves in ways too meaningful to ignore. These numbers are often a bridge between this world and the next, a way for those we have lost to reach out and remind us that they are still near.

In your story, you've been given the incredible gift of recognizing the numbers your Guardian Angel sends—proof that their presence is always with you. I have no doubt this realization has brought you immense comfort, time and time again.

It's fascinating how many of us feel inexplicably drawn to numbers. If you were to write them down each time they appeared—alongside what was happening at that moment—you'd find that they tell a story all their own. Patterns would emerge, guiding you in ways you may have never imagined.

Pay attention to your own reaction when you see these numbers—notice the immediate sense of peace or familiarity they bring. It's like *medicine* for the soul, a quiet reassurance that you are never alone. And while their sudden appearance might take you by surprise, deep down, you aren't truly shocked. Because a part of you *expects* them. A part of you *knows* they will show up.

If you are someone who continuously looks for your Angel numbers, it means you have accepted this form of divine communication. Your soul has chosen to recognize and embrace the sacred bond between you and your Guardian Angel—a connection with no explanation. There is magic in Angel numbers.

Saved by My Guardian Angel
Joe

It had rained for days. When it finally stopped, I took a ride to my girlfriend's house in the next town. I was seventeen years old at the time and hadn't been driving very long. There was a river and a single-lane bridge I had to go over to get there. On my side of the river, the street was elevated about five feet above the water, but on her side, it was only about a foot above the water. This part of the bridge used to flood all the time. I drove onto the bridge and stopped at the edge before I went down to the lower road level. It was dark, but I could see the street was flooded on the other side. They always closed the road when that happened. When I saw it wasn't closed, I figured the water was not too deep, so I drove down off the bridge.

I only drove ten feet, and my headlights were already completely underwater. I could see the light beaming in the water. I was scared to back up, thinking water would end up in the exhaust. I wasn't thinking clearly as the exhaust was already underwater. I proceeded to drive through it. A few seconds later the water was over the hood of the car and three-quarters of the way above the bottom of the window. I started taking on water through the doors. Suddenly, all the warning lights lit up on the dashboard, which told me the engine had stalled out. I was so deep in the water I couldn't even hear the car. I started to downshift and throttle the gas pedal. I was panicking. Now the car started to move sideways into the river because the current was pulling me in. I didn't know what to do. I couldn't even exit the car because I would never get the door open as it was almost completely submerged.

Suddenly, my Guardian Angel arrived. I know this because the car started to get pulled out of the river and back onto the road! I kept steering the car and I finally came up onto the road incline and was completely out of the water. I pulled over, got out, and looked back. There was no explanation for what had just happened. For the engine to run, you need spark, fuel, and air. I had no spark, the engine stalled! I had no air because the engine was completely underwater! I bailed the water out of the car and drove away to dry off the brakes. That was fifty-two years ago. I still can't explain it other than someone or something pulled me out of that river to safety.

Judith's Insight:

You are meant to be—right here, right now. Your Guardian Angel ensured it. When there was no room for you at the inn— Heaven's gate—it was decided that your journey on earth was not yet complete. This is a true miracle, and sharing your story helps illuminate the purpose behind your fifty-two years of life since that moment. You were saved, protected, and guided by your Guardian Angel. And just like yours, there are countless stories of miraculous survival that must be told.

Miracles happen every day, often in ways beyond explanation. Many who have faced life-threatening events can only attribute their survival to something greater, a divine intervention, an unseen protector. Reflecting on our lives, most of us can recall a moment when we found ourselves saying, "Thank God! I know

He sent my Guardian Angel to help me," or "There's no other explanation—it was a true miracle that I'm still here today."

Veterans who have survived war (or boot camp), firefighters and first responders who put their lives on the line, police officers who answer the call every day—they all know this truth. Whether you call them Guardian Angels, God, Hashem, or by any other name, in the moment of greatest need, they are there. Even when you didn't realize you were calling for help, your Guardian Angel heard you. And that is the greatest miracle of all.

Blue Roses

Lindsey Tesher

I was visiting my brother in San Francisco when, out of nowhere, I was stopped in my tracks by a bouquet of beautiful blue roses in a shop window. Something about them caught my eye. I snapped a photo, continued with my day, and later made that picture the background on my phone.

Fast forward a year. I was sitting with a friend, getting ready to take my first solo trip to Europe. Out of the blue, she asked me, "What's the significance of blue roses?" Specifically, blue. I smiled and said, "Well, funny enough, the background on my phone is a picture of blue roses I saw in San Francisco."

Her face lit up. "Wait," she said, "I have a single blue rose in my car. I need to give it to you. It's a sign from your grandma. When you go to Europe, you'll see blue roses—and you'll know it's her. It might be a good sign, or a warning." I laughed, not knowing how true her words would soon feel.

A week later, I was in London, getting ready to head to Prague with a friend. We walked into the train station, and I glanced to my right—there, in full view, was a large bouquet of blue roses.

My stomach dropped. Something felt off. As it turned out, we were at the wrong station and missed our flight. But somehow, I knew we weren't meant to be on that plane. I automatically thought of my grandma and said, "Coincidence, not so much!"

Now, eight years later, blue roses seem to follow me. Friends send me pictures of them, and I receive a bouquet every year for my birthday. That single blue rose from my friend? It turned out to be the beginning of a connection that feels otherworldly. I'll always be grateful for her and for the beautiful way she became a messenger on this earth along with now knowing every time I see a blue rose, my grandma is telling me something. Forever thankful.

Judith's Insight:

It had to be blue! It had to stand out from the crowd. That's how signs work—they catch your attention, speak to your soul, and make you feel something.

Most people pass by flowers without a second thought. But it's the ones that grab your eye and steal your heart—the ones that stop you mid-step—that hold meaning.

Roses already tug at the heartstrings. They're full of love, charm, and energy. But a blue rose? That's a one-in-a-million bloom. It's not commonly seen, so it will make you take notice. A blue rose is a rare, ethereal messenger, and when it appears, you know it's for you. A blue rose says, "I'm here. I'm talking to you." It's no coincidence—it's communication from the Heavens.

You don't have to believe in guides to recognize a sign. Just pay attention to what's happening around you when one appears. The blue rose isn't a symbol of sadness—it's the opposite. It's illumination. A guiding light. A gentle nudge that says, "Take a closer look."

Those soft blue petals are like a grandmother's whisper, reminiscent of a handwritten recipe passed down in a dish you stumble upon in a quiet restaurant, the one that tastes just like hers. It's her way of saying, "I'm with you."

Blue roses might just be her love in bloom, wrapped in grace, sent with perfect timing. Always standing out in the crowd, even when she's whispering.

And you? Be proud of yourself. You're listening. Roses aren't always red, and violets aren't always blue. No matter what the flower is, remember someone is speaking to you.

The Words I needed to Hear One More Time
Peggy D.

My grandmother had a standard saying every time I traveled anywhere. It didn't matter the time of year, she would always say, "Remember, bridges freeze first." It was our private message. Many years after she passed away, I was driving to Vermont in the predawn hours of Thanksgiving morning. It was a trip I had made hundreds of times, and, on this day, there was a light drizzle the whole trip. As I approached Rutland, Vermont, there was an elevated roadway with a sharp bend just before it. As I was coming around the bend, my foot was literally pulled off the gas pedal, and "bridges freeze first" echoed in my head. I hit the elevated roadway at a slow glide and slid safely across between many other cars that were up against the railings.

My Nana was definitely my Guardian Angel that morning.

Judith's Insight:
"Bridges freeze first." Those were your grandmother's words, simple yet profound. And whether in life or beyond, she continues to guide you as your Guardian Angel.

It's incredible how often we find ourselves revisiting the words of those we've lost, sometimes without even realizing it.

While not every piece of advice will save a life, *this one did*. Her wisdom, spoken long before you needed it, resurfaced at just the right moment—a testament to how deeply our loved ones remain connected to us, even after they're gone.

The words of those we cherish are stored in a sacred space between the heart and mind. Some fade into the background, while others stand the test of time, waiting for the exact moment they are meant to return. The ones that come back to us—sometimes whispered in our thoughts, sometimes loud and clear—are the ones that carry purpose. That's how we know our Guardian Angels are still watching, still guiding, still protecting.

Words left behind by those we love are like treasures tucked in the pocket of life. They resurface when we need them most, carrying with them comfort, wisdom, and sometimes even a miracle. Their lessons don't just shape our past; they shape our future, ensuring that a part of them continues to walk beside us, lighting the way. We still recognize their voices as we hear those words all over again, and we know clearly those are the words that matter.

Karma

Mary DeHope

This happened about eighteen years ago. I was going out on walks two times per day to lose weight and listen to my thoughts. On my morning stroll, I found a $20 bill on the road. It was the most money I had ever found. I decided to put it on the porch of the home I was passing in case they or their company dropped it. Later that night, I was out on my second walk and my preteen daughter had reluctantly agreed to come with me. We set out on the long, hard stroll around our local lake.

Less than halfway around, she started complaining that she was thirsty. We were deep in conversation. I told her about how

I found the money that morning and how right it felt to leave it to someone who may have or may not have lost it. I told her karma was an amazing thing and that when you do something selflessly it can set off a chain of good things. After she moaned about being thirsty for the third time, I said we could ring a bell and ask someone for a glass of water (she said no way, too embarrassing). After walking a half mile more we saw a man washing his car. I suggested we ask if she could drink from the hose, but she rolled her eyes and again said no way.

At that point, it would take just as long to turn around as to continue the loop back home. I felt sorry for her as I had worked up my stamina over the past weeks, but she had not. Slowly walking up the steep inclines, she was feeling exhausted and thirsty. I was feeling guilty as we rounded a bend to see a parked utility truck. The man immediately said, "I have cold water in my cooler, would you like one?" I believe he was our Guardian Angel that day. We still talk about that walk!

Judith's Insight:

Sometimes, the rewards of good karma arrive in the most unexpected and delightful ways. In this heartwarming story, you shared a moment of kindness with your daughter, showing her firsthand how generosity creates ripples of positivity. The man with the cold water, appearing at just the right time, was no coincidence—it was a sign from your Guardian Angel, a gentle reminder that support and care often come when we least expect them.

This isn't about grand, life-altering miracles, but rather the quiet, everyday moments that make life richer. In this instance, water symbolizes more than refreshment—it represents a deeper longing for connection, renewal, and fulfillment. Whether it's from a hose, a bath, or a simple bottle, these moments of nourishment serve as reminders that your Guardian Angels are always near, offering their love and support.

Water is more than just a source of refreshment; it is the essence of new beginnings. It brings forth life—babies, animals, and even the renewal of the soul. It signifies transformation, whether through family, personal growth, education, or stepping into a whole new community. Water washes away the past, allowing for fresh starts and unexpected journeys.

One way or another, *water nurtures, restores, and enhances life.* Just like the presence of Guardian Angels, it is always flowing, always guiding, and always ready to bring you exactly what you need.

Wake Up!

Anastasia Clarke-Tinik

Back in the late '70s, I was a toddler running around my house in a dangerous wheeled walker. At the time, my mom was trying to sleep off a migraine. Suddenly, she heard a commanding voice calling her name:, "Ellen, go now!" She quickly jumped out of bed questioning where she should go. She felt a force leading her through our upstairs hallway and down the stairs into the kitchen where she discovered my grandpa washing dishes. She asked him, "Where's the baby?" My mom then felt compelled to turn toward our basement door, which was cracked open. There she discovered me on my tippy toes about to plunge down our basement stairs, walker and all. No doubt she would have flung herself down after me. My life was absolutely saved by an Angel that day. My grandpa's response to my mom was funny:, "Please don't tell your mother!" My grandma would have killed him!

Judith's Insight:

Angels certainly know how to make their presence known—even if it means waking you from a deep sleep. When they need to send a message, they do so with unmistakable clarity and purpose. On that particular day, a Guardian from the other side was watching over you, ensuring your safety. While they can't always prevent every challenge life presents, when they *can* step in, they do so with extraordinary care.

It's incredible how they reach us through dreams, serving as silent protectors in the stillness of the night. It might feel like magic, and in a way, it is — a divine orchestration by your Guardian Angels, using dreams as a pathway to guide you through life's journey. When distractions arise, paying attention to these subtle messages allows your Angels to assist you more effectively. Trust in their guidance; it is a testament to their unwavering love and protection.

Everyone, at some point, has experienced — or witnessed — what I call a heart-shaking moment. The kind that leaves your jaw on the floor and sends shivers down your spine. Sometimes, it's the split second of a sudden noise, an unplanned stop, a glance at just the right moment, or even the ringing of a phone that alters the course of events. Moments like these make you wonder how destiny would have played out *if* God, a Guardian Angel, or a miracle *hadn't* intervened.

These are the moments that leave you speechless. And yet, they are also the stories you never stop telling.

The Penny
Judith Turner

Today I had to have the first of quite a few surgeries. Although I was so lucky to have people praying for me with true love and passion, I was looking for a special sign. For me, it's a "know it when you see it" moment, when something just stands out and speaks volumes.

The day did not go easily at first. While I waited on the gurney, I just lay there and meditated with my deceased mom coming in for a visit. I spoke to her and said I needed her guidance and help with this surgery, and with that my deceased dad came through too. Then the nurse came into the room and told me they were having a delay and asked if I needed to use the ladies' room before we left for the operating room. I said sure and walked into the small bathroom and looked out the window overlooking the city. On the windowsill was a penny. It was my sign! It immediately brought me great relief. I picked it up and walked out to nurse Gary. I told him I needed to keep this penny with me throughout the surgery. I was wearing only a hospital gown and there were very few places to hide it. He looked around and told me he'd take care of it and told me he knew where to put it. Then he taped the penny onto my hospital gown.

He said there you are, now you have your lucky penny!

My surgery took much longer and was far more complicated than expected. I also had a terrible reaction to the anesthesia. When they finally wheeled me back to my hospital room, I was more alert and asked my operating room nurse, Grace, "Where's my penny? It's taped to my gown." At first, we couldn't find it, but, thankfully, we eventually did. Grace was blown away and swore it wasn't there during the surgery.

After I told her the story, she smiled and said, "Oh, it's a lucky penny." I responded, "No, that's my penny from Heaven!"

Judith's Insight:

This is a true "penny from Heaven" story—a vivid reminder that sometimes the universe sends us signs in unexpected ways. I've often wondered if there were other subtle hints along my journey that I might have missed. Yet, there are moments when our Guardian Angels feel compelled to deliver a clear, breathtaking message, ensuring that we don't overlook their presence.

In everyday life, we might notice gentle reminders—a bird's song, a butterfly fluttering by, a sudden rainbow, recurring numbers, or even a dragonfly dancing in the sunlight. These signals often serve as soft whispers from the divine, quietly saying, "Hello, it's me." However, when circumstances demand reassurance, these familiar signs might not be enough. In such times, a more dramatic sign—like the unexpected appearance of a humble penny—emerges as a powerful symbol of guidance.

Today, that very penny was my gift. It wasn't a product of mere delays or complications, but a deliberate message meant to comfort me and remind me that I am never truly alone. That tiny token brought with it a profound sense of peace and the reassurance that a loving, unseen hand is always ready to hold mine.

The beauty of Guardian Angel messages lies in their lasting impact. They are not confined to a single moment; their influence can extend into the hours, days, or even weeks that follow, offering hope and strength long after the initial encounter. Recognizing these signs also calls for self-awareness that we all have our vulnerabilities. For instance, I'm keenly aware of my own health challenges. For me, "white coat syndrome" is real, and a sudden spike in blood pressure can be a stark reminder of deeper issues that lie beneath the surface.

There are times when it seems as though God answers our prayers in ways we never consciously sought. When He is busy, He often speaks through His helpers—those we come to recognize as our Guardian Angels. Their messages, woven into the fabric of our everyday lives, remind us that we are supported and guided, even in our moments of weakness.

In embracing these experiences, we learn to trust the subtle interplay between the divine and our daily existence. The penny from Heaven was more than a fleeting coincidence; it was a testament to the enduring presence of love and guidance, encouraging me to reinforce life's miraculous signs.

Kevin Was Never Alone!

Jan Turen

I recently went to visit my daughter-in-law Evelina, her family, and of course, my two grandsons. I say "family" because Evelina's mother, Barbara, lives with them—and not only is she an amazing cook, but she's also one of the kindest people I've ever known. My son Kevin and Barbara had an extraordinary bond. I'd describe her as a second mom and a best friend rolled into one.

Barbara owns a floral business and goes once a month to the wholesale flower market in downtown Los Angeles. Over the years, she became very close with her orchid supplier—they even call each other soul sisters.

A couple of months after Kevin passed away, Barbara returned to the market. The moment her friend saw her, she knew something was terribly wrong. Barbara broke down and told her what had happened.

It was a Sunday morning. Kevin had been driving home from a tennis tournament with his ten-year-old son, Jack. Suddenly, Kevin passed out behind the wheel. Jack threw water on him, and when he didn't respond, Jack jumped onto his lap, steered the car across three lanes of highway traffic, and safely pulled over. Then he called 911 and gave them their exact location.

Through tears, Barbara told her friend that Jack must have had a Guardian Angel that day. By chance—or perhaps by fate—they had taken the Tesla, which was in auto-drive mode and had already begun to slow down because of an earlier accident. That gave Jack the opportunity to steer the car off the road. Both women were crying uncontrollably. Then, suddenly, Barbara's friend went quiet.

She asked, "When did this happen?" Barbara told her the date. Her friend went pale.

"That traffic, it was from an accident that morning," she said.

"My truck driver was killed. He was delivering a full load of orchids to me. The crash scattered them across the highway—it took hours to clear."

The two events—Kevin's passing and the truck full of orchids—had occurred at nearly the same time, on the same road.

A few days later, Barbara offered to drive me to the airport for my flight back to New Jersey. On the ride, she told me this story. I've been shaking my head in disbelief ever since. Every time I think of it, tears come to my eyes. It touches so many chords deep inside me. I had to tell this story. It's one in a million—just like Kevin.

Judith Insight:

Jack was the Earthly Angel in this story, which features Earthly Angels, Guardian Angels, and Crossing Over Angels all intertwined. Jack certainly had an army of Angels protecting him during this life-threatening experience. The word "speechless" comes right to mind as I read that part of the narrative with chills running up my spine. This reaction, where your body feels something so profound that it strikes an emotional chord in both your heart and brain at the same time, is a common reaction to near-death stories. It plays out in our minds like a scene from a movie that is so frightening that you have to close your eyes. In moments like these, the unexplainable can only be attributed to knowing there was a Guardian Angel present.

We find kindred spirits as we navigate through our daily lives. We might refer to them as acquaintances, or even friends. Sometimes, it's as if you are instantly bonded, while other times it develops slowly, and one day we realize how closely we have connected. As we grow closer, we reveal things we wouldn't normally share with our best friends. Within these connections, we find a common thread of life. We exchange stories, pictures, and maybe grab a cup of coffee to divulge the aches in our bodies along with the pains of life.

The reason for this connection often remains uncertain, yet we often feel and grow a unique love for these individuals. Then one day, like in Barbara's case, the reason becomes crystal clear. They were brought together by multiple Guardian Angels, with a hidden agenda to share the bond of loss, understand each other's tears, and shed tears together. They shared the pain from their losses, each heartbreak intertwining with the other.

As this story unveiled itself, it delves very deeply, casting a wide and extensive net over two souls who shared their journey back to their true home in the Heavens. Just as Barbara and her friend shared the road of conversation about their mutual loss, the two young men leaving to return to the other side also shared the same road. We've all attended funerals and have seen many flowers scattered around the room. Each of those petals was destined to create the Heavenly path for their way home.

This reveals that Kevin was never alone on his passage into the Heavens. He did not leave alone. One could find solace in knowing the truck full of white orchids was sprawled along the road. The beautiful Heavenly path that the young men took to Heaven was adorned with white orchids, symbolizing purity (representing a journey without pain), innocence (indicating a departure without struggle or fight), and passion that they carried with them. Honor and peace were on the stairway to Heaven along with many tears that were flowing from the crowds that mourned these souls like royalty.

REFLECTION 5

Love

*Every day, Angels join the Heavens —
but not every day is it someone you know.*

*This morning, as I sat down to write about how much I
miss my mom, I was reminded that there's always a reason for the messages we receive. If you're lucky enough
to see a sign, feel the love, or hear the message, take a
moment to say thank you.*

*Gratitude keeps them close, standing by your side, always
watching over you—that's love.*

—Judith Turner

White Feather from Heaven

Elena Williams

My brother-in-law passed away last week. It was a very emotional week for everyone. Yesterday the sign that I received entering the funeral home was a white feather that landed on me. The Angels were around for sure.

Judith's Insight:

The most beautiful thing about feathers is that they are deeply personal, they land exactly where they are meant to. When you receive one, it's like being handed a small piece of Heaven, a gentle reminder that you are loved and watched over. Some believe feathers come from older Angels who have long since earned their wings. But today, this feather was meant *just for you.*

I believe it's from your mom. Maybe she had a strong connection with your brother-in-law, or perhaps she simply wants you to hug your sister a little tighter today. Feathers drift down as symbols of warmth and protection, sometimes offering comfort, other times redirecting your focus when you need it most. No matter the reason, the message in this story is clear: *You are deeply protected.*

Feathers have a way of appearing *out of nowhere* — and that, in itself, is often the greatest sign. They remind us that unexpected blessings can arrive when we least expect them. Have you ever noticed how rare it is to see a feather and not smile? We all need that small, gentle lift, a "feather in our cap" to lighten the weight of everyday life.

In the language of Guardian Angels, feathers are reminders to release stress, to breathe, to feel lighter. They help shift our thoughts, nudging us toward peace and joy. And sometimes, they are simply a way of saying, *I remember you.*

There is something so pure and loving about feathers, yet

they can appear in a million different ways—on your lap, on your clothing, resting at your feet, or floating down from nowhere at just the right moment. However they arrive, they always carry a message, and that message is one of love and light.

March 23

Janice Nolting

The last few months, I have had a tough time medically. In the past, every time I had surgery, my sister-in-law Cheryl came and stayed with me before I went to the hospital. Sadly, Cheryl passed away. When I found out that I needed more surgery, I was very nervous. I was thinking about how much I missed her and how worried I would be without her. So, I started talking to her and praying for her to watch over me. And I asked her to send me a sign. When the surgical coordinator called me and gave me my surgery date, it was March 23, Cheryl's birthday.

Judith's Insight:

This morning, I woke up with a sudden and undeniable urge to write this book. It's been years since I've written one, and while the idea has crossed my mind before, I never quite pulled it all together. I needed a sign from above to move forward.

So, I put out a simple Facebook post, asking friends to share their own Guardian Angel stories. *Yours* was one of the first to appear. As I read your words, I saw the very sign I had been searching for. My Earthly Angel—my grandson, Campbell—and your sister-in-law, Cheryl, share the same birthday: March 23. That day holds immense significance for me and seeing that connection felt like a message straight from Heaven. I'm taking this as the sign I needed to move forward with my *Guardian Angels* book.

Now, about *you*. You were in such deep emotional pain, and this Angel — Cheryl — chose to give *herself* a birthday gift by showing up for you. She made her presence known on *that* day so you would *never* have to doubt it was her.

Guardian Angels often pick meaningful dates — ones from their life or yours — because it makes their message unmistakable. It's their way of making sure the pieces of the puzzle come together more easily. So often, we second-guess ourselves, letting logic or doubt cloud what our hearts *know* to be true. This story is clear as day, with not a cloud in the sky.

Cardinals and Pennies
Carole D.

I have lived in my home for over twenty years. We have always had birds in the yard, but never cardinals. After we lost our parents, we started seeing a few, we are now up to three couples that live in the backyard. They are always there. Whenever I'm at the kitchen sink one of them is always staring at me through the window.

My mom passed away from COPD. Right after she passed away, I smelled sulfur from a lit match in the house. No one was lighting matches. A couple of weeks ago my sister moved into my home. Ever since, I have found lots of pennies and dimes in the most random places. After vacuuming, I came back into the room I had just cleaned, and there was a penny in the middle of the floor. I know we're always surrounded by Angels, but some of the signs just touch me more.

Judith's Insight:
What a beautiful story! Cardinals are powerful messengers, symbolizing life and the importance of *living*. When they appear, it's

often from someone strong, someone with a lot to say. They tend to show up frequently because you have unanswered questions, and, deep down, you look to them for guidance. When they visit, they are bringing you the answers you seek.

Cardinals may also come in pairs, representing bonds that transcend life—married couples, sisters, mothers and children, cousins, or even best friends. Their presence is a reminder that love endures, no matter the distance between worlds.

When the sign involves a match or smoke—symbols of fire, urgency, and action—these signs often want to *ignite* something within you. If you smoke, they may even be nudging you to quit.

Pennies, on the other hand, carry messages of trust and peace. The phrase *"In God We Trust"* and words like *"Liberty"* remind us to have faith and embrace freedom from worry. A penny is also stamped with *"one"* and *"cent,"* symbolizing unity and the small but meaningful ways our loved ones reach out. Pay attention to whether the penny is heads or tails up, as it may hold personal meaning for you. My favorite sign is a *penny from Heaven*; when you're searching for reassurance, and, suddenly, *one* appears. That's a hug from above, a gentle reminder that today matters. Looking at the date or the moment you found it can trigger an even deeper insight.

Guardian Angels sometimes need a little help, from their friends, from *your* friends, or even from family members. Receiving multiple signs can mean one Guardian Angel is reaching out in different ways, or that several are watching over you. Not every Guardian Angel will send the same symbols. In fact, their messages can change constantly, evolving with your journey.

When something draws your attention, what feels like a message usually *is* a message. You'll know it in your heart and soul. Maybe you will get a tingle or two up your spine.

$2 Bills from Heaven

Maria Greco Shanley

My mother recently passed away. We needed to find her Social Security number, so I looked through her wallet. I thought it was odd that I found a few $2 bills. My mom previously told my sister-in-law that my dad gave them to her, and she always carried them for luck. I didn't know this. When my young grandson, her great-grandson, was told of her passing, he asked his parents if he could give something in her honor. He presented a $2 bill. When I was told of this, obviously it was no coincidence to me. I was blown away.

Six days after her passing, I was out with family members enjoying a snack break. My mom's daughter-in-law casually told us she was given a $2 bill in her change. Again, I said this is no coincidence. My mom was sending these $2 bills to us all. She's always with us.

Judith's Insight:

This message is clear: Your loved one has landed safely in the hands of Angels. This is why so many of you received a $2 bill, a subtle sign lingering in your hands, a gift that carries a unique meaning. I always say that our Guardian Angels have distinct ways of communicating with us, often arriving in forms that are unmistakable and personal. The $2 bill or the amount itself might have seemed ordinary to you once, but now, it holds a special significance, a cherished notification from your mom—and perhaps even from your dad. There's no coincidence in this message, especially given how it occurred more than once. Your Guardian Angel was making sure the message reached you, a comforting shout from Heaven saying, "Hello, I'm here, sending love, and sending you hugs from the other side." The story doesn't stop there. The number two carries its own powerful symbolism. This number represents partnerships, spouses, bonds, and friendships—connections with others that help us navigate life's journey. Whether it shows up alone or in the company of other numbers, two serves as a reminder that you are not alone. Even when you may feel like you're walking through life in solitude, the number reminds you that you are supported and accompanied by a deeper presence—whether visible or invisible. The number two embraces the essence of connections: the twin flame, the soulmate, the best friend. It's a divine greeting, saying, "I'm here with you, standing alongside you, even if you can't see me." It's a call to trust and take chances—"Take a leap of faith with me." It embodies the magic that ensures you never have to feel alone; it carries the reassuring heartbeat of companionship and the promise that you are cherished, always.

All about Mom

Judith Turner

Today, my client Bryan walked into my office with an excited remark: "Wow, I was lucky to get an appointment with you today." At that moment, I barely registered his enthusiasm—I was preoccupied, collaborating with my assistant on a press kit for my new book. We were racing against a Thanksgiving deadline to send it off to my friend Kevin Turen, whose sudden passing just a few days ago still left me in shock and disbelief.

The only reason Bryan's appointment was available was because I had been scheduled to meet Jan, Kevin's mother—a meeting that was obviously canceled at the last minute. With that slot open, Bryan was added to my schedule. We retreated into a private room for our session, where Bryan peppered me with questions about the book before we continued with our work.

After our meeting, I excused myself to use the restroom. When I returned, I found Bryan still standing in the room — a rare occurrence, since clients typically leave as soon as their session ends. He approached me, phone in hand, and repeated, "Look at this," showing me a picture of Marlene Dietrich. He then pointed out that, by all odds, he wasn't even supposed to be in my office today; his appointment was nothing more than a fortunate fluke.

At that moment, I was too overwhelmed with grief over Kevin's untimely death to fully grasp what Bryan was trying to communicate. I couldn't understand why he was fixated on an image of Marlene Dietrich. Then, in a gentle yet mysterious way, Bryan explained that he had been looking at pictures of Marlene Dietrich that very morning and suddenly found himself in my office. My confusion deepened until Bryan stepped away and gestured toward the wall. "Do you see this?" he asked, pointing to a framed original poster of Marlene Dietrich from the 1920s hanging in my office.

In an instant, tears welled up in my eyes. "Oh my God, Kevin gave me that poster — it was from him!" I recalled the conversation with Jan when she was downsizing her home. I had mentioned my admiration for the poster, and although Jan initially hesitated, she eventually called me later to say, "Kevin said give it to Judith." In that moment, the poster transformed from a mere piece of art into a poignant symbol of the interconnectedness of our lives.

Judith's Insight:

This is a reminder of lost loved ones, unexpected miracles, and the mysterious ways in which fate works to bring healing and meaning when we need it most.

There are two intertwined stories here, each with its own message of divine timing and support. The first story weaves through the experience of my client, Bryan. A last-minute opening allowed him to arrive in my office on that specific day, and he truly felt it was kismet. Bryan had been searching for pictures of Marlene Dietrich, a woman he viewed as embodying qualities his own mother had—strength, uniqueness, compassion, and generosity. Little did he know that the very image he had been pondering would unexpectedly appear before him in my office, where a framed original poster of Marlene Dietrich from the 1920s hung on the wall. In that moment, Bryan felt blessed with a sign from Heaven, a message from his mother, affirming that he was, indeed, moving in the right direction in his life.

The second story unfolded within my own heart, where I received a connection to my dear friend Kevin, who had recently passed away. Kevin, who had been a film and television producer, had left behind passions, memories, and messages for those he loved. The name of the Marlene Dietrich film on the poster was *The Blue Angel*, and this taped connection landed precisely where it needed—to deliver a message from Kevin to his mother, Jan. That message was one of hope: "You are not alone." It was as if Kevin had orchestrated this moment, ensuring Jan felt the support of his presence, just as Bryan felt the energy of his mother guiding him forward. What began as a powerful, artistic gift— the Marlene Dietrich poster—transformed into a broader, spiritual shared experience that transcended its material form. Those who witnessed it understood its deeper meaning: Sometimes, it's not just one soul but two, or more, coming together through an unexpected sign or gesture, helping each individual receive the clarity, comfort, or message they need at that exact moment.

Messages from the other side do not always come in traditional messages; sometimes, Angels are joined by the help of friends, whose efforts create mass resonance. When this happens, multiple lives are touched simultaneously by a message that crosses realms of existence and offers healing to hearts wide apart. This simple yet significant object—the Marlene Dietrich poster—took on a whole new life as it carried profound meaning to two people navigating their separate journeys. It reminded us that we are never truly alone, that our Angels and departed loved ones have clever and unexpected ways of reaching out to us. Pause for a moment to look around at the objects you see in your everyday life. Tomorrow, the very thing you glance at could take on an exceptional new meaning—one that brings insight, comfort, and clarity that you never expected. Look around, there's a message waiting patiently for you.

The Church Lady

Lisa Warner Jansen

My mom passed away at the age of ninety-six in 2020. Her birthday was July 26, and she will forever be affectionately known as "the Church Llady," as she was the secretary for several churches in our neighborhood. Last evening, I attended an outdoor concert featuring an Eric Clapton tribute band. It was a perfect evening, and the sunset was absolutely mesmerizing with an array of colors. During one of the songs, I could have sworn I heard church bells. I looked over at my friends and asked, "Do you hear bells chiming?" They all said yes. It happened twice during the concert. I think it was my mom letting me know she was with me on her birthday! There couldn't have been a clearer sign from the Church Llady.

The beautiful thing about bells is that they can appear in so many places—echoing from churches, chiming on street corners during Christmas, or even ringing in your own ear. Every time a bell rings, an Angel gets its wings—which means they've found a way to teach you.

Think about what you're currently facing or looking forward to. The bells were your mom's way of getting your attention. The closer you are to someone, the stronger the connection you'll feel even after they're gone. When you feel their presence, it means they're right there beside you. Bells are also a signal—a sign of a lesson learned, or one being taught. So the next time you hear a bell, pause and consider: Am I in the middle of learning something? Or am I being prepared to teach it? And if you're struggling with that process, don't be discouraged. The answers will come. The bells will ring. And perhaps the most important lesson of all? You are worthy.

Timing and Tattoos
Mildred B.

I often wake up at 12:21—a time that holds deep meaning for me. It's the date of my uncle's passing, and it's inked into one of my tattoos, which I wear proudly in his honor.

Judith's Insight:

It's all about guidance. That's why you find yourself noticing the clock—at 12:21 or at other moments when the numbers seem to leap out at you. But it's not just clocks: it's hotel room numbers, paperwork, raffle tickets, scoreboards—little breadcrumbs scattered along your path.

These "Angel numbers" you've chosen to connect with become a kind of sacred scavenger hunt. You're playing it with the universe, or with your Guardian Angels, checking in to make sure you're still heading in the right direction.

You may find yourself making a significant purchase, and only when your Guardian Angel number appears will you feel satisfied. When the timing is right and the sign becomes visible, that's when you'll realize it's no coincidence. That's the sign.

If you pay attention, these numbers become part of a bigger game—one of faith, reassurance, and connection. They're the universe's way of saying: "I'm here with you. You're not alone. I know you're scared and in pain—but keep moving forward. I'm walking with you."

Consider yourself lucky. That number, 12:21, is a heavenly marker, your Guardian Angel number. Maybe it's tied to a birthday, a passing, a childhood address, or a significant turning point in your life. You'll discover that one number, or a set of them, will walk with you forever; a quiet companion, a guide. That number becomes part of your story. And as life's next domino falls, it helps lead you down your own yellow brick road or cobblestone path, step by step.

The tattoo? That was you choosing him to be your guide, your Angel—engraving his date into your body as a symbol of honor, remembrance, and connection.

Of course, you don't need a tattoo to commemorate someone. There are countless ways to carry someone with you: a piece of jewelry, an urn from cremation, a scholarship fund, a legacy plaque, a cherished keepsake, a handwritten note, or even the headstone at their grave. Some people even step up and volunteer in honor of people who have passed.

Whatever you choose, they know. They see it. And they walk with you, always. Because no matter how you decide to remember them, you are wearing your heart on your sleeve, letting your Guardian Angel know that you picked them too.

Fireflies

Michelle Goffredo

My man and I were watching television. We looked out of the window and this firefly (aka my mother) was watching us. She was there until we went to bed. I have never before seen fireflies in May.

Judith's Insight:

Your mom was letting you know she was there with you—*and* showing you the light. She wanted you both to feel her presence, reassuring you that she is still guiding you, even in moments of darkness. And you *knew* it was her, because only your mom would choose to appear as a firefly in May. She was shining a light on life's simplest pleasures: relief, comfort, and the joy of just being together in the warmth of home.

Fireflies, flames, flashing lights, or even fireworks have a way of capturing our attention, sometimes evoking both awe and unease. They are meant to stir something deep inside us, bringing hidden struggles to the surface. Sometimes, they serve as a needed distraction, offering a brief but meaningful escape from stress. Other times, they illuminate a secret you haven't spoken aloud yet, giving you a moment of clarity or relief.

But beyond that, they are symbols of joy, hope, and renewal. A firefly's glow might simply be an accent on an already exciting day, a gentle reminder to embrace the magic around you. Whether the moment is good, bad, or uncertain, these flickers of light appear to remind you that even in the darkest times, there is always a spark of something beautiful.

Dragonflies from Heaven

Christina Sleckman

Several years ago, I lost a dear friend named Diane. The day she passed away there was a dragonfly on my shepherd's hook holding flowers in my garden. The dragonfly just stayed there for quite a while, even while I took pictures. Soon after, I started seeing the number forty-four over and over again. I associated this number with Diane.

When I attended her memorial service, her urn had dragonflies on it. A couple of years after her passing, two other good friends and I went to my clubhouse pool. It was the anniversary of her passing. While we were in the water, a dragonfly hovered over us for several minutes, just going round and round. I told them that it was Diane!

I still see number forty-four often, mostly on license plates. I know and acknowledge that these signs are from my friend telling me she's okay and still with me.

Judith's Insight:

I truly love the numbers in this story. Pay attention when you see signs that seem to speak to you, sometimes, they just *stand out*. At first, you might wonder if you're imagining it, trying to make it happen. But then you realize—you *can't* make it happen. It happens all on its own.

Numbers can feel like a silent but consistent hug, a reassuring presence reminding you that you're not alone. Dragonflies, on the other hand, will keep you guessing. They carry a mystical energy, a strong presence, and a way of making sure they get your attention. If you find yourself searching for answers or feeling uncertain about something, dragonflies may be a sign that clarity is on its way.

Some people find flying creatures unsettling, while others are drawn to them. That's no coincidence. When you feel a connection to a certain creature, it may be because they carry a message meant just for you. If a dragonfly is your Guardian Angel, you'll see a continuous pattern of them showing up.

Dragonflies have a way of being both protectors and messengers. While numbers inspire and spark stories, *dragonflies are the story.* In this story, your Guardian Angel will certainly find a way to fill your garden.

Near Death at the Dentist
Jackie Castaldo

When I was about sixteen years old, I had a terrible toothache, so I went to the dentist around the corner from my house to have it checked. After examining the tooth, the dentist decided it needed to be extracted. I sat in the chair as he prepared the anesthesia, unaware that I was about to have a life-altering experience.

As the gas took effect, I suddenly found myself somewhere else: a beautiful park, bathed in light. I was dressed in pure white, peacefully picking flowers, feeling a deep sense of calm. Then, I heard a soft, soothing voice. "Jackie, you have to go." I ignored it, continuing to pick flowers, lost in the moment. Again, the voice whispered, this time more insistent. "Jackie, you have to go now." Confused, I asked, "But why?" "Because it's not your time." At that very moment, in the background, faint but growing louder, I heard a nurse's panicked voice: "I'm losing her! I don't have a pulse!"

An eternity seemed to pass. Then, suddenly: "Wait, she has a pulse!" I didn't see a white light. There was no tunnel. But as I came back, I fixated on the dentist's cabinet, the gleaming tools on the table. My body felt completely numb, not just from the gas, but from something far deeper. Without much explanation, they let me go home, as if nothing had happened. But something had happened.

Even now, decades later, I know in my heart that I was saved by my Guardian Angel. The experience left me with a profound, lingering fear—not just of dentists, but of doctors, anesthesia, and the idea of surgery itself. Now, in my seventies, I have never had surgery and have gone to great lengths to avoid doctors altogether.

Judith's Insight

This chilling yet deeply revealing Guardian Angel encounter is something many experience but hesitate to share, fearing they won't be believed. But your story is undeniable proof of divine intervention. At that moment, your Guardian Angel stepped in, pulling you back from the edge, ensuring that your life's journey didn't end that day.

What makes this experience so profound isn't just the memory, it's the feeling that stays with you. The mix of fear and relief, the blend of trauma and comfort. It's easy to dismiss such moments as dreams, but when the unexplainable can only be explained by the presence of a Guardian Angel, we must pay attention.

The gentle, persistent voice calling you back was no ordinary dream, it was a guiding force, ensuring you returned to the life you were meant to live. And as the years have passed, the fact that you've reached your seventies without ever needing another surgery is no coincidence.

Your Guardian Angels are still at work, still protecting you, still guiding your path. And as your story reminds us, sometimes the most extraordinary miracles happen in the most unexpected places, even in the dentist's chair.

Our dreams often carry meaning, and this one served a clear purpose—it was the moment that decided you weren't meant to leave this world that day. There was still so much more for you to do, so much more life for you to live.

For anyone who has ever experienced something like this, let it serve as a reminder: *You are here for a reason.* Your journey has greater purpose than you may realize. Even when you question it, even when you don't see the full picture, know that there is more ahead for you, more to give, more to experience, and more to become.

Touched by an Angel
H. B. F.

I was driving back home from graduate school after a late-night apartment fire in the building I was living in. It was about 3:00 a.m. as I was traveling southbound on the Palisades Parkway. I dozed off for what must have been a few seconds, and felt a hand on the side of my face push my head straight that woke me up a split second before I would have crashed my Honda Civic. Since that fateful night, I have never felt anything like that in my life.

Judith's Insight:
Your story unfolds like a scene from a thriller film. In that terrifying moment, you escaped a raging fire in your apartment building—a brush with what could have been a devastating injury or even death. At the time, you may not have fully grasped the magnitude of your escape, but it was clear that fate had intervened.

It felt as though a Guardian Angel was right there with you, guiding your every step. The surge of adrenaline propelled you into action, fueling your rapid dash to the car that carried you away from imminent danger. Later that night, as you made your way home, you couldn't shake the sensation of an unseen presence riding alongside you—a silent protector whose energy sent chills down your spine.

In the midst of the commotion—the probably blaring radio and the overwhelming fatigue—you dozed off for a brief moment. That slumber, however, could have been your last if not for a gentle, fatherly touch on your face. This subtle caress, imbued with strength and determination, stirred you awake. Though your eyes struggled to remain open, that delicate spark of energy left an indelible mark on your soul, altering the very course of your destiny.

Throughout that long, fateful night, it was as if your Guardian Angels had gathered around you, steadfast and vigilant. These experiences, as inexplicable as they are transformative, become etched into your heart and mind forever. In the quiet moments of reflection, we all recall those uncanny instances—those "Aha!" moments—when an unseen force reached out, changed our perspective, and even saved our lives.

Such encounters remind us that there are mysteries beyond our understanding, gentle guides that hold our hand in our darkest hours. Whether you believe in Guardian Angels or simply in the serendipity of fate, these moments inspire awe, leaving us with questions and gratitude for the inexplicable forces that sometimes alter our lives in ways we never imagined.

Mourning Doves
Sami

I had surgery approximately two and a half years ago. I came home from the hospital and things took a turn for the worse. I became septic. During this time, two mourning doves would sit outside my window every day. While I was going through one of my nine surgeries, my brother passed away. Every time I came home from the hospital the doves would sit outside my window. My last surgery was in October 2020, and I never saw them again until yesterday. I think they know when you are going through a rough time, and I do believe it is my mom and my brother looking out for me. It's these little signs that help you get through the day.

Judith's Insight:

Your mother and brother discovered a perch that brought you healing, a truly remarkable sign. Remember that you were not alone then, you are not alone now, and you will never be alone on your journey ahead. All the surgeries and challenges you endured filled you with a fear you had never known. In your desperate search for answers and comfort, you needed a tremendous amount of help.

During that trying time, two doves appeared to offer the support you so desperately required. Their presence was a message, a gentle reminder that you were being cared for. When they eventually departed, it signified that you had reached a point of clarity where the constant need for daily signs was no longer necessary. And even now, they may send subtle reminders from time to time.

Now, as fear resurfaces in your heart and mind, these doves return to remind you once more: You are loved, supported, and continuously aided by your Guardian Angels. Mourning doves, in particular, are symbols of new beginnings and endless possibilities. Their appearance invites you to pause and reflect on the questions and dilemmas you face each day. They may have arrived during your darkest hours to extend a helping hand, but they also appear when you consider taking a risk, stepping into a new phase, or simply when you are in a state of celebration. They stand with you as you dance, play pickleball, and in every moment that brings struggle and joy.

Loving People That Love You!

Judith Turner

When I was a kid, both of my grandfathers were *my people*. They lived just around the corner from us, so I saw them regularly, and I loved them both deeply. But I had an especially extraordinary connection with my dad's father; he was one of the people I loved most growing up.

My mom always said he was one of the nicest people she had ever met. He was full of life, easy to be around, and just radiated warmth. She often called him *a very nice man*, but to me, he was even more than that. He reminded me of my own personal Santa Claus—always jolly, always making me feel special. Looking back, I think he was my first Guardian Angel.

I was always thrilled to see my grandfather because he *paid attention* to me. And every time I saw him, he would give me a quarter and say, "It's going to be a great day!" It didn't matter if I was at his house or if we just happened to run into each other— he would always hand me a quarter. It was our special bond.

But the quarters weren't what made me love him so much. It was how he made me *feel*—completely loved and cherished. The quarters were just his little way of showing it. When he passed away when I was eleven, I found comfort in every quarter that came my way. Whenever someone handed me one, I would quietly tell myself, "This is from Grandpa. He's reminding me, it's going to be a great day."

Sometimes, I would sit and stare at a pile of quarters, concentrating on them just to *feel* him again. It always worked. After he died, I wrote a poem about him, and my parents hung it on the wall. I need to find it. I would love to see what my eleven-year-old self wrote about the man who meant so much to me.

As I grew older, I worked in a deli and later owned restaurants, so quarters constantly passed through my hands. And still, to this day, there are so many moments when I think of him and smile, whispering to myself, *It's going to be a great day!* Somehow, no matter what, a quarter always seems to show up when I need it most.

I owe all my *awesome* days to my grandpa, because even now, he still finds a way to remind me that every day can have a quarter in it.

Judith's Insight:

Sometimes the simplest recurring gifts become signs from our loved ones. While our Guardians are alive, we often don't realize that the little things they do—their traditions, their words, their laughter—are quietly preparing us to recognize them when they are gone. It might be the holiday they never missed, the kind words they always shared, a joke that still makes you smile, or a cherished memory you've replayed a hundred times. And when you feel their presence, trust it, it's real. In time, with faith, the picture becomes clearer and clearer.

What is the meaning of a quarter, you may ask? It was once a small token of love, and now, it has become a sign of something magical. If you pay attention, you'll realize that countless quarters pass through your hands every day. But every so often, one will stand out—perhaps appearing just when you need a little reassurance, like an umbrella in the middle of life's storm.

A quarter can hold many meanings, but in this story, it's as simple as memories. Every day may not bring a dollar, but my grandpa taught me to remember a quarter could be just enough.

Friends Matter

Judith Turner

When I was fourteen, I moved to a new town, started at a new school, and stepped into an entirely different world. The very first person I met there was a girl named Eileen, and from that moment, we forged a bond akin to sisterhood. I affectionately called her mother Ma, and she called my mother Mama.

Since that day, we have shared years filled with laughter, joy, tears, prayers, hugs, and deep conversations about solving the world's problems. Together, we've created countless memories — from trips and spa days to parties and celebrations. Our connection is so profound that my son and her nephew are best friends; he has been the closest person in her life, especially since she was never blessed with children of her own.

When we were eighteen, Eileen's mother had us cleaning the local Catholic Church on Sundays. Although I wasn't raised Catholic, this experience eventually led me to join the Rites of Christian Initiation of Adults program. Over the years, our lives have intertwined even more — we married boys who lived next door, our birthdays fall just two days apart, and she has worked for both my parents and me. When she landed a great job, she even helped my sister and many of our friends secure employment. While our journey is full of memorable stories, this narrative is about our shared spiritual path.

Eileen has faced incredibly hard times. Her health has declined, and she now battles memory issues while living in a nursing home. I, too, have endured a difficult year marked by complex medical challenges. Throughout our phone conversations during this trying period, Eileen often spoke of a tree outside her bedroom window, where she watched birds come and go all day. Although she always insisted I shouldn't visit because it was over a two-hour drive, deep down I knew she longed to see me. Even then, she would pray for me, gently urging, "Take care of you!" Her kind soul shone through every word.

About a month ago, she pleaded, "You need to come and visit me! I need to see you. I really need to see you." Her urgent request took me by surprise; its directness almost frightened me. Yet, I promised I would visit her during the week of July 4.

The week before my visit, while browsing in a store, I purchased a print of two birds perched on a branch. It was a simple piece, yet something about it resonated deeply. When I hung it in my living room, my sister asked what I intended to do with it. I wasn't sure—maybe I would gift it or perhaps keep it—but I knew it spoke to me in a profound way.

Later that week, as I gathered things to bring to Eileen, it suddenly struck me: I needed to give her that print. It symbolized us—two birds that, though in different places, always flock together. My sister agreed, suggesting I first check Eileen's room to see if there was a spot for it.

Walking into the nursing home, I glanced to my right and saw a print on the wall nearly identical to the one I had purchased—except it depicted only one bird. I got chills. In that moment, I felt an overwhelming sense of relief and knew there was a deeper purpose to my visit. It was as if our Guardian Angels were speaking to us, confirming that I was meant to have that print. I believe our Ma and Mama Guardian Angels were working tirelessly to bring us together, to help bring Eileen peace amidst her pain. I resolved to hold on to the two-bird print until the perfect moment arrived to gift it to her.

When I finally entered her room, she greeted me with a scream and tears—an expression of emotion that only the closest of friends can share. It became clear that not only did she need to see me, but I also needed to be there for her. Our journey as life-long cherished friends continues, and I am profoundly grateful that our Guardian Angels ensured this special day was filled with beautiful, meaningful signs.

Judith's Insight:

Sometimes, as we journey along life's winding path, we search for answers to questions we never even knew we had. Whether in our darkest moments or during the happiest celebrations—weddings, birthdays, or other milestones—we all crave a comforting embrace, a hug from Heaven. Our Guardian Angels are always present, gently guiding us and reminding us that we are never alone.

Every sign we encounter carries profound meaning. In this story, the birds symbolize the deep bonds we form with others, the family we choose along the way. The connection I share with one special person doesn't replace or diminish the other relationships in my life; instead, it enriches my journey. Life is a tapestry woven with countless relationships: some fleeting like a sprint, and others enduring like a marathon. Each friendship adds color and depth, enabling you to share your experiences while still enjoying the freedom to live your separate lives.

The meeting with my best friend was no mere coincidence; it was a divine reminder to trust in the lifelong bond we share. No matter how many new connections you forge, nothing can interrupt the unique journey that you and your kindred spirit travel together. Even when distance separates you physically, the bond of the heart endures. The birds, as messengers from above, delivered a celestial hug—a sign that this enduring connection is lovingly watched over by our Guardian Angels.

Ultimately, souls come together for a reason, and every relationship matters. The bond we share was built long before life's complications, including health challenges, and will continue to flourish well into the future. The mysterious forces that connect us are more fascinating than we can ever fully understand. Every relationship you nurture contributes to the vibrant rainbow of your life. Along this path, you benefit not only from the support of your Guardian Angels but also from the comforting presence of your Earthly Angels, the friends and loved ones who hold your hand through every joy and every sorrow.

REFLECTION 6

Answers

*An Angel's message is always there —
you just have to notice it!*

*Look for the signs your Angel is sending you:
rainbows, butterflies, pennies, whispers in the wind,
flickering lights, repeated numbers on a clock, or
even unexpected animals like birds, cows, or pigs.
Messages can also appear in songs, the familiar scent of
perfume, old photographs, or lost items suddenly found.
Some signs take our breath away, shifting our perspective
in an instant. After feeling a Heavenly hug, you may
begin to see the world a little differently. And in that hug,
that's where you'll find your answers.*

—Judith Turner

Seeing Clearly

Judith Turner

I find myself facing a series of daunting surgeries. Recently, my doctors discovered a pituitary brain tumor, which means I must have cataract surgery on both eyes—not only to improve my vision but also to allow them to monitor my optic nerve. The thought of undergoing cataract surgery on both eyes fills me with anxiety, a fear rooted in a childhood memory. When I was nine, a doctor warned me that I would eventually go blind, a statement that has haunted me ever since. Because of that, I've always trusted only the best Torick contact lenses from the very start of needing glasses.

After my first cataract surgery on the left eye, I took time to heal. The doctor later informed me that I could wear a contact lens in that eye and that my vision had improved enough to drive again—a small beacon of hope amidst the challenges I faced. Then, on Father's Day morning, my world turned upside down: I lost my only good contact lens—the left one. Friends and family sprang into action, frantically searching for it while I spent the day in tears and desperation.

Amidst this chaos, my one-year-old granddaughter approached me and pointed at my phone in my purse. I couldn't shake the feeling that she was trying to tell me something important. In that moment of vulnerability, I turned to prayer, begging God and calling on every Guardian Angel I could think of for help.

I reached out to one of the places where I had purchased my Torick lenses in the past, but they were closed due to COVID restrictions. Another eye center I contacted was also closed. Finally, the next day, Monday, I called Visionworks, a trusted supplier from my past. I explained my situation, and they informed me that my name wasn't listed in their digital files—they would have to dig through old boxes to find my chart. Anxiety mounting, I watched the clock as I waited for their call.

After eight and a half excruciating hours, I finally received a call. The gentleman on the other end said, "You're not going to believe this, we found your paper file. And what's in it is really going to shock you, as it shocked all of us. We found a contact case attached to your file. The right eye box was empty, but in the left eye box, there was a contact lens." He paused, then asked, "Isn't that the one you need?" Overwhelmed, I could only cry, "Yes! Yes!" Neither of us could quite believe that the left lens was still there after all this time. He cautioned, however, "Don't get too excited just yet, you need to come in so we can check the fit, because these lenses are made for an individual eye and this lens is five years old."

That very night, my brother sent me a picture of a butterfly. Every day of her life, my mom wore a butterfly pin or patterned garment—a subtle reminder of her presence. The image of the butterfly stirred cherished memories and filled me with warmth.

The next day, I went to the Visionworks office to try on the left contact lens. Miraculously, it was a perfect fit! The doctor exclaimed, "Do you know what a miracle this is?" and I could only reply, "Absolutely!" In that moment, I offered silent thanks—thank you to God; thank you to my Guardian Angels; and thank you to my butterfly Mom—for guiding me through this challenging journey and reminding me that even in our darkest times, hope and miracles can find us.

Judith's Insight:
Sometimes, the answers we seek are hard to see, hidden behind the veil of everyday life. It often takes the support of both our Earthly Angels and those watching over us from above to guide us toward clarity and self-discovery. Journeys like this one can feel like a lifetime of challenges, yet reaching out to God and my

Guardian Angels—calling in reinforcements when I needed them most—was exactly what the doctor ordered. There were no coincidences here; this was a reassurance, a divine message meant to restore my faith.

The protection I needed began the moment that contact lens was placed in my file, quietly waiting for the day I would need it. This experience has surely renewed my belief in the power of prayer. It marks only the beginning of many Guardian Angel encounters that will offer me a continuous embrace of hope, healing, and support from beyond.

Even when I didn't realize it at the time, my prayers were being answered. It only took a little time for the signs to become unmistakably clear. That butterfly—sent by my mom—was a gentle reminder that help was on its way. Embracing the timing of these events is a crucial part of the Guardian Angel story, showing us that everything unfolds exactly as it should.

We all face our own versions of hell, fear, and drama—not just for our own sake, but for the sake of those we love. Little miracles appear every day, often in the smallest of ways. It might be a traffic light that forces you to stop and inadvertently prevents an accident or taking a day off that coincides with a tragedy you narrowly avoid. Many remember the inexplicable moments surrounding events like 9/11. Other subtle signs—finding batteries just before a storm, a cherished photo falling out of a closet, or stumbling upon the perfect outfit—are all gentle nudges from the Heavens, guiding us and reminding us that we are never truly alone.

Each of these moments is a small, yet powerful, helping hand, lovingly extended by those in the Heavens to support us through life's twists and turns.

We Never Walk Alone

Lisa Bonhotal

As I began walking and making healthy changes in my life, I started to notice signs. First, it was the birds, ducks, and geese greeting me along the way. I began taking pictures and sharing them. Then I started photographing the sky, and it felt as though the Heavens were speaking to me every time I walked. Even walking in the rain seemed to send a message.

The more I walked, the more intense the signs became, and the more I felt attuned to them.

I'm one of the lucky ones who sees religious symbols in unexpected places. I've seen angels appear in the swirl of my drink. Jesus once appeared on my mirror. I also saw the Blessed Mother's image on my shower door.

Wherever I went—whatever I was doing—there were signs. Initials. Dates. Messages in passing license plates. It became a daily occurrence. Time after time, I found myself saying, "You can't make this stuff up."

Judith's Insight:

Encouragement, that's what these guardians are putting on your path. The signs, the winks, the nods, they may be multiple Angels, working together to keep you on track, and to continue motivating you.

You must be calling in spiritual reinforcements often, because these signs are everywhere, touching every corner of your life.

And the rain? That's no accident. That's cleansing. Even when you don't ask for it, it's there to wash away what weighs you down, to renew you when you feel overwhelmed by the clutter of everyday life.

Your Guardian Angels are doing their job. In your story, they're helping to recreate, to reinvent, to purge pain. And the most powerful part? Your walks have become more than just steps, they've become a path to healing. You feel less alone, less fearful, and less lost.

This is a journey of self-discovery, a path that's setting you free. The constant flow of signs is no coincidence. They're leading you to doubt less, to believe more, and to grow in positivity.

Even the smallest details—a shape in your beer foam, a swirl in your martini, the whipped cream in your hot cocoa—can carry messages. The answers aren't just blowing in the wind, they're everywhere, and they're showing up just for you. These Angels are about self-esteem and self-worth. Remember, you are valuable.

Every Time a Bell Rings
Mary

I lost my brother just before Christmas. He was one of my most favorite people. There was a big difference in our ages, but not in our hearts. I was heartbroken when he died and for many reasons I couldn't be there for the end of his life.

A friend of mine told me that bells would be a sign to look for from him. As she told me that, my mom sent me a picture of her shopping and buying bells. This brought tears to my eyes and I hoped that there would be more bells in the future of which I would take notice.

It's easy around the Christmas season to seek out bells, but what I think we all look for are the signs that stand out when they aren't expected. I have never mentioned the bells to anyone in my daily life or to my family, some of whom live very far away.

Recently, I came home from work and there was a box addressed to me on my counter. I opened the box and there was a bell with a blessing for my brother accompanied by a "sorry for your loss" note. Of all gifts, he sent a bell! It was incredible because I knew the sender had no idea the impact of receiving a sentimental bell would have on me. I rang that bell to make sure my brother, my Angel, got his wings!

Judith's Insight:

This story is like a gift that keeps on giving. Bells carry deep sentimentality, symbolizing peace, harmony, and connection. Think about the feeling you get when church bells ring—their sound brings a sense of calm and tranquility. As a sign from your Guardian Angel, bells remind you of peace, unity, love, and especially family.

There's a saying: *Every time a bell rings, an Angel gets its wings.* These wings signify that your brother has arrived in Heaven, but more importantly, that he is still by your side. Wherever you go, he will be there, his wings guiding you toward the places you're meant to be.

If you come across a bell that isn't ringing, it may be your Guardian Angel encouraging you to ring it—perhaps a gentle nudge to take charge of something you've been neglecting. On the other hand, if you hear a bell ringing, it doesn't just mean an Angel has earned its wings. Sometimes, it's a signal that *you* are being called to take a leap forward, to embrace change, and to allow yourself to soar.

That subtle spiritual tug on your collar—the quiet push you may not even realize is happening—is always meant to propel you toward something better. Bells are never a sign of stillness; they are a message of movement, of rising, of growth.

So, the next time you hear a bell ring, listen closely. Someone may be trying to get your attention.

Those that have lost siblings, whether close or not, will always feel like a piece of them is missing when the sibling has passed. As bells ring, always allow it to bring in the joyful memories of the siblings you've lost. Know that a bell ringing when you've lost a sibling is a sign of sharing as you share more than DNA. You are blood sisters or blood brothers.

The Winner Is

Marie S.

My husband retired, so for the time being, we needed to live off our savings. I needed to keep my spending in check, and it didn't help that inflation and gas prices are so high right now. Our budget is going to be very tight.

I am chairman for a cancer organization and happen to be running our fundraiser in the upcoming weeks. We usually auction off many raffle baskets for the fundraiser, but donations were coming in very slowly and we didn't have enough prizes.

My daughter was going to Las Vegas, so I decided to give her some money to play a slot machine for me. Before she left, I found dimes everywhere I went. My mother-in-law loved to play ten-cent slot machines. I took this as a sign from my mother-in-law. When my daughter asked me what machine I wanted her to play with the money, I told her to play the $10 machine. I soon found out my machine hit the jackpot, and I won $650! Hours later after finding out about my Las Vegas windfall, I happened to reach out to a friend and found out I won $100 in a raffle. Amazing! Now I can now buy more baskets and contribute these winnings to my cancer organization.

Judith's Insight:

This is such an incredible story, especially with the winning guidance you received from your mother-in-law! You weren't just lucky to win; you were divinely supported. The help you received wasn't just a gift for you, but a blessing for your cancer organization and all those it serves. You are an Angel yourself for the work you do, and it's no wonder you can feel the presence of your Guardian Angels. Your mother-in-law is still looking out for you, helping to answer not only your needs but also the needs of others.

This was nothing short of divine intervention. The timing was a jackpot in itself, aligning perfectly so you could meet the needs of others. Sometimes answers arrive in ways that feel almost orchestrated—like when someone tells you about a top doctor in their field, and just days later, a friend calls asking if you know a specialist in that exact area. Then, that very doctor ends up saving your friend's life. Or perhaps you make a wrong turn and stumble upon a road you never knew existed, only to find yourself living on that very street years later.

It makes you wonder just how many Angels are working behind the scenes in moments like these. The path to becoming a "winner" isn't always obvious. Often, we are winning in ways we don't even realize, playing a game we never knew we entered, guided by forces beyond what we can see.

Wondering!
Donna Lanza

I had the strangest sleep last night. I lost a dear colleague yesterday, and he appeared in my dreams, right in the middle of a work-related scenario. I suddenly woke up because I felt someone gently rubbing my arm, as if trying to wake me. I was sure it was my daughter, but there was no one there. After that, I couldn't fall back asleep.

Judith's Insight:
So often, we're left wondering what just happened. What did it mean? Should I tell anyone about what I just experienced and

what I just felt? This clearly seems to be a reaction to something unexplainable. Yes, maybe you were just restless and unable to sleep, but consider what you felt: You sensed someone touching you, yet no one was there. Are you crazy? I don't think so.

Many people experience brief, mysterious moments like this—split-second visits, sensations, or visions that can't be explained. One second they're there, and the next, they're gone.

I believe your colleague came to comfort you. In your grief, especially after a sudden loss, you likely called out to him in your heart, wondering how he was doing, where he was. When things like this happen, the most important question becomes: What do I believe it is? More often than not, your instincts will know.

No, it can't be proven. But does that really matter? What matters is what your soul knows and what your intuition feels—that quiet, steady voice that connects us to something greater.

Your soul holds answers to many of life's unanswered questions. It speaks the language of the universe, the divine, the eternal. So, at the end of the day, I leave you with this: It's okay to believe what brings you comfort, whether it's proven or not.

Believe in the touch. Believe in the visit. Believe in the love that reaches across time and space to bring you peace. You have been touched. If you find yourself wondering, maybe now you won't have to wonder anymore.

My Best Friend
Ally Deptuch

I was so lucky to meet a girl named Holly when I was in pre-kindergarten. To me, she felt like she'd been in my life forever, or at least as long as you can call someone your best friend. Holly was the funniest person I ever knew. I remember playing softball with her—while I would sprint to first base with all my energy, Holly would casually stroll or maybe even skip with her own unique swagger. We also had a friend named Jaiden. We weren't just the Three Musketeers; we were more like the Trio of Life. Our years together were filled with laughter and making countless videos. Those videos created a bond that made us laugh at ourselves for hours.

We did everything from playing "church" to dancing to our favorite songs, always with a sense of having it all figured out. We must have made thousands of videos, and anyone who came along was pulled into our wild dancing and singing adventures. Our friendship was so close that we lived in each other's lives and homes. Holly even called my Aunt Jeri "Aunt Jeri," and we made her a special video for her fiftieth birthday. We danced so hard in those videos that sometimes we'd fall flat on our faces, only to burst into laughter.

Even as high school ended and we went our separate ways to different schools, I always thought that since Holly was my person, there would be a day when our paths would cross again in the same way they used to. But life had other plans: college, COVID-19, and everything in between, although we did catch up for lunch or dinner from time to time. Then, it seemed like out of nowhere, I got a text from Holly asking if we could have lunch the next day. I told her sure but that I was off on Tuesday so if we got together then, we'd have more time. Holly agreed, and we made plans to meet.

But then, on the Sunday before our lunch, my mom broke the news to me that Holly had been found dead. I was devastated. I felt like a piece of my heart had been ripped away. I spent the next few days watching our old videos and going through a mountain of photos on my computer. From when we were eight, I'd been documenting our friendship with silly pictures and videos.

The wake was incredibly tough, but seeing Holly surrounded by thousands of pink flowers was a small comfort. I knew she had received all the love and attention she deserved. I knew the giant pink heart among the flowers brought a smile to her face. I was restless and wanted to put something special in her casket. My mom asked Char, Holly's mom, who kindly said, "Of course, anything Ally wants." Even though I knew Holly's mom was incredibly kind allowing me to do so, I was petrified to ask in my overwhelming grief. I left my girl Holly a bottle of Gucci perfume, because I knew she would love it and I hoped that it meant she would be "Gucci," aka, all good, in Heaven. It meant so much to me that her mom allowed me to give her one last gift. It was my way of saying goodbye, the one I never got to have, and she could take a piece of me with her.

A few weeks later, as I stood by Holly's grave, I was talking to her, trying to feel her presence and asking her for a sign: "Come on, Holls, send me a sign right now! I know you hear me." Just then, Holly's mom appeared out of nowhere. It felt so surreal, like a scene in a movie where wishes are granted instantaneously, almost like magic. The timing was unbelievably perfect, as if Holly had arranged for her to be there exactly when I needed it most. It was an emotional moment, leaving me knowing that Holly was reaching out to me through her mom. I felt her love.

Judith's Insight:

We often form deep, soul-nurturing connections with people from a young age — friends who feel like soul sisters, blood brothers, or family by choice. The sheer amount of time spent together in childhood, from endless playdates to shared adventures, forges bonds that are incredibly strong and enduring. Losing a best friend, no matter how old we are, can be profoundly heart-wrenching. The impact of losing a friend who has been with us through countless moments and memories can be even more intense than losing family members. As adults, it's harder to create such deep connections because we don't spend the same hours and days together. Your bond with Holly was extraordinary, a beautiful blend of youthful joy and unwavering support.

Holly was more than a friend; she was like an Earthly Angel in your life, always there with a laugh, a smile, or a comforting word. How do I know she's still watching over you? The timing of her mom's appearance right after you asked for a sign was no ordinary coincidence. It was as if Holly orchestrated this moment to give you the hug you desperately needed, providing comfort in your deepest time of grief. Her mom's unexpected visit was Holly's way of reminding you that her spirit is still very much present, offering you solace through her loved ones.

As time goes by, you might notice that Holly continues to send you signs—little moments that feel like answers to your heartfelt prayers or echoes of a song from your joyful days of dancing and video-making. When you're feeling blue, remember Holly and "think pink." Her vibrant spirit is always around you, a splash of color and love that brightens even the darkest moments. Holly's presence remains a warm, reassuring reminder of the special bond you shared and the joy she still brings into your life. When you're walking, sitting, or dancing on the dance floor and you get a whiff of fragrance, you'll always know that Holly is dancing with you.

A young friendship bond never truly ends. When a young person passes, they take pieces of many hearts with them. But if you think about it, they also leave behind countless pieces of themselves—filling the empty spaces in your heart, as if they were always meant to be your guiding Angel.

From the moment you met, this Angel was already watching over you. Your laughter, memories, and the love you shared are signs for you to keep living, to carry your spirit forward. Have no fear, you are never alone. The treasure of your best friend, now an Angel, will always be with you, guiding you just as she always has. This Angel will always make sure you're Gucci.

The Black Crow's Message: A Symbol of Change, Guidance, and Protection

Rachel Zitomer

I saw two crows at the park today, and one got rather close to us. Is this a bad sign? I am kind of scared about it now.

Judith's Insight:

There is no need to be afraid. Guardian Angels have their own ways of getting your attention, sometimes switching things up so their message comes through loud and clear. Not all signs arrive in the form of flowers, butterflies, or pennies. Sometimes, they take a different shape—one that demands your awareness.

Black crows have long been regarded as symbols of transformation, signaling moments of change, growth, and deep self-discovery. If you've been noticing them more often, it could be because you are standing at a crossroads in life, searching for clarity, or undergoing a personal shift. They are not there by coincidence; they are guiding you.

I like to think of black crows as wise, old guardians—perhaps even the spirit of a grandparent watching over you. There is something knowing about their presence, something that suggests they carry messages from beyond, offering protection and insight. Though they are often misunderstood, these birds are not omens of misfortune but rather messengers, nudging you toward awareness and change.

The sight of a black crow may startle you, and that reaction is often intentional. Unlike a bluebird or cardinal, which may bring a gentle reassurance, a crow's presence commands attention. And sometimes, attention is exactly what you need. Imagine a moment when you were urged to take action—perhaps rushing a loved one to the hospital, making a sudden decision that changed everything, or stepping back just in time to avoid danger. That moment of fear or unease may have been the very thing that saved you. Fear isn't always a warning; sometimes, it's a wake-up call, a force that shakes you from complacency and demands that you listen.

Guardian Angels work in mysterious ways, sending the signs you need, not always the ones you expect. Sometimes, they reroute you, gently—or forcefully—pushing you onto a different path, one that holds the answers you've been searching for. The black crow didn't intend to frighten you; it came to prepare you, to stir something within you, to make you pay attention.

And in the end, that moment of recognition, that shift in awareness, led you exactly where you needed to be. Right place, right time.

Standing Close By
Lisa Warner Jansen

Over the last several weeks, I've had very vivid dreams of people that I've been close with who have passed. They are alive and well in my dreams, smiling and laughing just as if they were on Earth! Are they trying to tell me something?

Judith's Insight:

Signs from Heaven often come to us just as they are—through dreams, whispers of intuition, or unexplainable moments that touch our hearts. Dreams, in particular, provide an open gateway for these messages, allowing them to gently infiltrate our minds and souls while we sleep. If you are worried about someone in your life, these dream visits may be a way for your Guardian

Angels or departed loved ones to help you cope, offering reassurance, guidance, or even confirmation of your fears.

No matter the reason, Guardian Angels come with one purpose—to remind you that you are never alone. Whether they appear to celebrate with you, support you through a transformation, or guide you through uncertainty, they are holding your hand every step of the way.

Many of us wait with bated breath, longing to see our loved ones in dreams, or even begging for a sign—any sign—that their presence is still near. Even if a dream seems fragmented or unclear upon waking, the presence of our loved ones is never without meaning. They are always finding ways to comfort us, easing the grief and pain of their passing. Some find peace in believing their loved ones have become Guardian Angels, watching over them in ways both subtle and profound.

How do we invite these visits? There is no magic formula, no guaranteed way to summon them into our dreams. But in my experience, simply asking can make all the difference. Before you sleep, speak to them—tell them you are open to their presence. Some people find that placing lavender in their pillow or keeping a glass of water by their bedside promotes a restful sleep, making it easier to recall their dreams with clarity. The more relaxed your mind, the more vivid the memories of their presence can be.

In the stillness of the night, when the world is quiet, our loved ones find their way to us, not through logic or reason, but through the unseen connection that many of us choose to live with.

Once a Hero Always a Hero
Rose Ciolfi

I had the weirdest moment ever in my life. I was cleaning out my garage, and I found my dad's fireman's windbreaker. When I picked up the jacket to hang it up, my father appeared right in front of me with a big smile on his face. He seems a little shorter than I remembered, and his coloring was good with rosy cheeks. In the next second, he was gone. I started to cry, and my day was ruined as I was emotional all day.

Whenever I enter my garage now and pass his jacket, I don't know what to do with it. I can't donate it because his name and department are all over it. I'm keeping it, and I guess I'll just keep walking by and saying hi to it and him. Nothing like this has ever happened to me before. I receive plenty of signs and am very receptive to them. However, I'm clueless about this sign. The experience kind of freaked me out.

Judith's Insight:

This is a battle of hope, and whether you realize it or not, you must be asking your dad for guidance. You are far more intuitive than you give yourself credit for—a sensitive soul who sees, feels, and understands beyond the surface.

When you picked up that jacket, you unknowingly called out to him. Our guardians have a way of making their presence known, especially when they have a message to share—a guiding light for something ahead, a silent reassurance for a challenge you are about to face. They step forward when we need them most, even when we don't consciously seek their support.

That jacket wasn't just fabric in your hands; it was a symbol of his love, his protection, his unwavering presence. He was reminding you that he is with you, wrapping you in warmth, strength, and hope. Sometimes, even in our happiest moments, we find ourselves gripped by unexpected fear, anxiety, or emotion. He was there to wipe away those feelings, to ease your worries, to hold you the way he always did. That embrace—that hug from beyond—was real.

You may not fully understand why you need his guidance right now, but in time, you will. Life unfolds in ways we cannot always predict, and as circumstances change, so too will your understanding of the messages he's sending. But know this: Whatever lies ahead, he is there. He walks with you, offering strength when you falter, courage when you doubt, and wisdom when you seek answers.

Your dad is not just a guardian, he is a warrior, standing beside you with an unbreakable coat of armor. His love, his presence, his essence—it is woven into the fabric of your existence, loud and clear, for all to feel and know. A hero in life, and a hero still. Always.

But signs don't just come in the form of jackets. Sometimes, you're in a store, cleaning out a closet, wandering through an antique shop, or simply going about your day when you see something that brings a flood of memories. In an instant, someone who touched your heart but is no longer here pops into your mind. These moments are not coincidences; they are triggers to the soul.

When this happens, pause. Ask yourself *What is happening in my life right now that is bringing this person to mind?* Sometimes, the answer is simple, an echo of a thought, a gentle reminder, a connection to something you've been contemplating. Other times, it is deeper—an answer to a question you didn't even realize you were asking. And yes, for those who feel lost or lonely, especially when attending a wedding, a party, or an event where you wish a loved one could be present, these signs become even more powerful. That item, that memory, that moment, it *is* the gift. It is the presence you long for, the hug you miss, the love that never left. So, embrace it. Enjoy it. And know, without a doubt, that it is certainly no coincidence.

Four-Leaf Clover
Betty D.

It has been a rough few days. I just walked out the front door and a green four-leaf clover landed at my feet!

Judith's Insight:

I truly love the simplest of stories — because sometimes, the smallest signs carry the greatest meaning. A four-leaf clover appearing in your path isn't just luck — it's a message. A sign that the tides are shifting in your favor, that "lucky" moments are about to unfold. The fact that it was right in front of you could mean that the answers you've been searching for are closer than you think. Or perhaps, you are about to step into a brand-new beginning. The Angels among you are being quite clear — you, my dear, are one lucky lady.

If you're a betting woman, maybe this is your sign to bet on the number four horse. But beyond luck, pathway messages like this bring comfort, guiding you forward through both the hardest and most beautiful moments in life. Press this clover between the pages of a book and cherish it as a sign from Heaven — a quiet whisper from above, reminding you just how treasured you truly are.

Beyond its personal meaning, a four-leaf clover is a symbol of *hope, new beginnings,* and *changing tides.* But perhaps, the most magical part is what lies unseen, the hidden wish waiting to come true. Not necessarily a brand-new desire, but one you've already made. A soul wish — one buried deep inside, never spoken aloud.

Some may call it a miracle wish, the kind that carries the weight of the heart, much like an ultimate birthday wish or a secret wish upon a star that, against all odds, actually comes true.

Above all, this is a heads-up, a reminder that while fate is at work, patience and persistence will play their part, too. Timing is everything. And with a little more faith—and perhaps a little more elbow grease—the perfect moment will soon land right at your feet.

Orb

Rachel Zitomer

We were on vacation, and I took a picture of my daughter, and a green orb showed up next to my daughter's foot! It was amazing.

Judith's Insight:

Orbs are widely considered to be a true manifestation of an Angel's presence. These ethereal spheres of light often bring comfort and reassurance, serving as a bridge between the spiritual and physical realms. Frequently, you might feel that an orb represents someone who exhibited angelic qualities during their earthly life, a person who radiated kindness, compassion, and warmth.

The appearance of an orb carries profound significance. It embodies attributes such as softness, kindness, and hopefulness, much like a gentle ray of sunshine breaking through the clouds. When you come across an orb in a photograph, it invites you to delve deeper into the image and uncover the hidden narrative it holds. Each orb tells its own unique story, sometimes evoking cherished memories of loved ones who have passed on, and other times, guiding you with encouragement and wise counsel as you navigate a new path in life.

Orbs can be seen as celestial messengers, offering a sense of peace and a reminder that you are not alone. They often appear during moments of introspection or significant life events, gently nudging you toward a sense of clarity and purpose. The presence of an orb can be incredibly comforting, suggesting that a benevolent force is watching over you, providing support and love from beyond.

In the depths of our hearts, we often intuitively recognize who is sending us these luminous hugs. Whether it is a departed loved one, a Guardian Angel, or a spirit guide, the orb's presence reassures us that we are cared for and protected. Embracing the beauty and mystery of orbs can enrich our lives, filling us with a sense of wonder and connection to the divine.

Where's My Hug from Heaven?
Teresa Blewangel

It's been forty-two years since my dad tragically passed away in a motorcycle accident. I never dreamt about him. What does that mean?

Judith's Insight:
Not everyone remembers their dreams or receives visits from loved ones while they sleep. That's why Guardian Angels send signs, hugs, winks, nods, and slices of Heaven when you are awake. Each person's experience is unique—no two signs are ever the same.

If you believe you've never received a sign from your dad, consider this: Some people simply don't notice signs, while others dismiss them as mere coincidences. But those who are truly open know that there is no such thing as coincidence.

If you feel in your heart that someone you love is sending you a sign, they usually are. Your intuition will guide you, taking you exactly where you need to be when you see it. Hugs from Heaven don't hide; they stand out like food at a banquet when you're starving, or like a sore thumb that needs some loving attention.

In the meantime, try to relax. Drink a warm cup of milk, tuck his picture under your pillow, and before you rest, spray your pillowcase with lavender. He is certainly around you; just keep your heart open, and you will feel the love, the presence, and the unbreakable bond that never fades.

The yearning for loved ones is a natural part of grief. We never truly "get over" a significant loss. Instead, we learn to carry it differently, moving forward in our own way and in our own time, whether or not we ever say those words aloud. Somehow, we begin to release grief when we recognize that our loved ones are still with us, presenting themselves in subtle but profound ways.

Maybe you're not someone who receives messages through dreams. Your signs might come in other forms—a hawk perched outside your window, a unique rock that catches your eye in a neighbor's garden, an American flag waving in the center of town, or a blue rose handed to you by your daughter at graduation.

Signs can come through sound, too—a waiter at a restaurant speaking a foreign language just like your grandfather did, a line from a comedian that echoes an inside joke, or even the innocent words of a child who unknowingly says exactly what you needed to hear.

And then there's the name game. Just as Angel numbers repeat in meaningful ways, so do Angel names. You might see the same name over and over again, in a song, in the newspaper, or in a stranger you meet. When a name keeps appearing, it's not random. It's a whisper from beyond, a gentle tap on the shoulder reminding you that love never leaves.

So, when these moments happen, pay attention. When something makes you pause, let that be your sign. Because it is.

REFLECTION 7

Healing

What may not bring you joy today could absolutely thrill you tomorrow. The challenges we face add depth and meaning to our lives.

Focus on what truly matters and let go of what doesn't. Savor the good moments, and when times are tough, trust that someday—somehow—it will all make sense, even if it doesn't today.

Take a deep breath, embrace the journey, and let the healing begin.

—Judith Turner

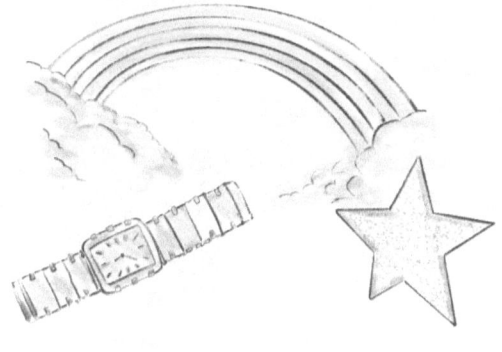

Double Take

Lizbeth Kall

I know there are scams on Facebook, but today I got a friend request from a dear friend who died last January. It was so weird to see this on my phone. We also share the same birthday but ten years apart. Is this a sign? My mom also passed away last January; did they find each other?

Judith's Insight:

You've got to love the new ways Guardian Angels find to communicate with us! Social media has become a modern, hipper way for them to remind us they are near. In the past, they relied on flickering lights, unexpected electronics turning on, or even mysterious phone calls—rings with no one on the other end, often on a meaningful day like a birthday. Sometimes, a song with deep significance would start playing out of nowhere, as if orchestrated just for you.

Today, their methods have evolved, but their messages remain just as powerful. Your friend was certainly sending you a sign; matching birthdays is no small coincidence. It's a reminder, a signal, a touch from beyond. As you step into this new year, pay attention to the changes and opportunities ahead. That matching birthday? That's a hug if I ever saw one. Your friend is reaching out, offering a helping hand when you need it most.

Have you ever felt a tap on your shoulder, turned around, and found no one there? Someone was there. You may not see them, but you can feel them.

I love those moments when I catch a glimpse of someone out of the corner of my eye—only to look again and realize no one is there. That's a double-take message. A momentary presence meant to make you pause, to let you know you are not alone.

And then there are the digital signs. A word, a phrase, or

a post appears right in front of you, seemingly out of nowhere, speaking directly to something on your mind. It makes you do a double take, questioning whether it's real. But here's the truth — if you think it's a sign, it is a sign.

Your thoughts, your feelings, your experiences, they are what matter most in your story. Trust them. Because someone is always finding a way to reach you.

Dream of Hope
Vicki D'Auria

I'm hoping for an interpretation of a dream I had last night. It was an upsetting dream about my son who passed last year. Since his passing, I've only had about three dreams about him even though I openly invite and ask for dreams of him often.

In my dream, I had an appointment to go to the funeral home for myself. While waiting for the appointment, someone sent me a video of my son Brian's funeral. In the video, I saw him breathing with his chest rising while lying in the casket. His eyes were also open but not staring at me. Next, I saw cotton come from his mouth like it was stuffed, and as soon as the cotton fell out of his mouth, he began to breathe. Almost as if he took a breath of comfort. Next, I was running for the funeral home to try to cancel my appointment, but I was standing in a very long line, and it was very crowded as I tried to get to my son's funeral where I belonged. There were also numerous red poinsettias floating in the water. I was concerned that I wasn't dressed appropriately for a funeral, but I was so desperate to get to his service that I didn't care.

In real life, I didn't miss any part of his funeral and was blessed to be at his side holding his hand when he passed. It was a very weird and disturbing dream, and I'm hoping you can shed some light on what it means.

Judith's Insight:

This is both a dream interpretation and a profound sign of love from above. As for the dream itself, it reflects the weight of your grief—the deep, unrelenting burden of losing your son. The anxiety and pain you felt in the dream mirror the emotions you carry every day. This loss has been an overwhelming heartbreak, a sorrow that has shaken your soul. It is natural to experience conflicting dreams—your mind and heart are still processing an unimaginable reality. You endured a profound calamity, and with it comes an immeasurable depth of grief.

The sign from Heaven is clear: Your son knows you always showed up for him. He finds his way to you not only in dreams but in the moments when you are awake—when your eyes are open, when your heart is searching, when you need reassurance the most. His presence is a reminder of your unwavering love, of all that you did for him, of the things you could control rather than the ones you could not.

Even more, he wants you to recognize truth from illusion—to understand what is real and what is not. This is a deep, hand-holding kind of message. With every breath you take, he wants you to know he's got you. You are not alone. You do not walk alone. You do not breathe alone. He sees all that you did for him in life and knows he was never alone—just as you are never alone now.

Losing a child is one of life's most devastating experiences. The grief is paralyzing, and even the most faithful hearts struggle to find meaning in such an unbearable loss. The question "Why?" is one that lingers, often unanswered, with no explanation that feels justifiable to those left behind. Every grieving soul wonders: Why didn't my loved one get to live out their life?

But perhaps young souls ascend with a higher purpose. Perhaps they take on the weight of Heavenly miracles, becoming the strongest of Guardian Angels—doing the mighty, unseen work of saving and guiding lives from above. They spend their time earning their wings, not in a distant way, but in a hands-on way, protecting and lifting those they left behind.

Losing a young soul is a grief unlike any other. But know this: They make their presence known. They are the chameleons of Guardian Angels, spreading their wings wide and strong. Their signs come in unexpected, unexplainable ways, answering prayers we didn't even know we were sending. So, when the signs appear—big or small—trust them. Expect the unexpected. Believe in the impossible. Because they are the miracle answer.

The Painting That Speaks
R. M. B.

I painted a picture when my grandson passed away on July 11, 2013. The painting was of a flower I picked up at his burial. It was never my intention to paint his face in the painting, but as the days go by, more and more I see the reflection of him through the flower. I thank him every day for finding his way, not only into the painting, but into my life. I thank him all the time for picking me to be his Nana.

Judith's Insight:

That is one incredible painting. Sometimes, life moves in reverse—circling back to remind us of what truly matters. That flower didn't just follow you home from the funeral; it found its way into your heart, just like your grandson did. The flower you painted became a symbol, a tribute to his life, a remembrance of his journey. But your grandson had his own plan. He found a way to place himself in the painting, making sure you knew he would always live on.

With every brushstroke, he gently guided your hand, ensuring his presence was embedded in the colors and shapes before you. He painted himself into that work of art, not just on the canvas, but into your heart—where he will always be, holding your hand from beyond.

Paintings, sketches, sculptures—any form of artistic creation—is open to interpretation. Even the work of a contractor, a builder, or a craftsman can hold unspoken meaning. Just as art is subjective, so too are the messages we receive from our guides. We may not always understand them at first, but when the time is right, the meaning becomes clear.

Have you ever looked at a picture, a painting, or even a piece of wood that has been in your home for years, only to suddenly notice something new, something you never saw before? You may wonder, "Why now? How did I not see this before?" That's how our guides work. They bring things to our awareness through the pathways of our hearts. When someone suddenly stands out in your thoughts, there is always a reason—a message, a hint, a hug, or maybe just a simple hello.

Go ahead, I dare you—look at a picture, a painting, or even an ordinary object you pass by every day. Really look at it. I bet you'll see something you never noticed before. And when you do, take a moment to wonder: "Who is speaking to me?" Because someone is. And they want you to know they are right there with you. I bet when you do, you will realize that there's something there that you never saw before. Then you may start to think about who is telling you something.

A Birthday Wish

Lizbeth Kall

My birthday was June 16, and I visited Colonial Williamsburg, Virginia. The last time I was there was twenty years ago with my parents and my children. When I happened to sit down for a break, two cardinals landed very close to where I sat. I felt at peace and knew my mom and dad had come to wish me a happy birthday.

Judith's Insight:

This is a perfect example of hugs and hope sent straight from Heaven. If we take a moment to look around, we see millions of birds, especially in the warm month of June. But the fact that two birds landed right by your side on your birthday was no ordinary moment. That was a sign, a message that spoke directly to your heart. And that's what caught your attention.

It wasn't just the sight of the birds—it was the energy, the presence, the unmistakable feeling of your parents' souls surrounding you. If it had been any other day, you might not have noticed. But these two souls came with purpose, bringing you love, warmth, and reassurance on your special day. This experience was more than just a sign, it was a gift of comfort, a gentle nudge forward as you embrace new beginnings. Birthdays, after all, are like our own personal New Year's Eve celebrations. They don't just mark time; they invite us to turn the page, to start fresh, to step into a new chapter of life.

But these birds? They weren't just helping you turn the page. They were there to remind you that you're not just stepping into a new chapter, you're creating an entirely new book. A book filled with new life, new relationships, new family, and new hope. This was their way of celebrating you and all that is still to come. So, from above and beyond, Happy Birthday from Mom and Dad.

Birthdays are more significant than we often realize. As the author of *The Hidden World of Birthdays*, I can tell you with certainty—these days hold a power beyond just cake and candles. Think about it: We light candles, close our eyes, and make a wish. Candles, one of the most timeless and sacred symbols, have long been used to reach out to the Heavens. They are meant not only to illuminate the darkness but also to bring light to our emotions, our prayers, our thoughts, and our deepest hopes and dreams.

But who are we really making that wish to? Who is listening? Who is helping us make those dreams come true? Birthdays are an extraordinary time for our Heavenly guides to show up, to listen, and to catch those unspoken wishes in the air. Whether we say them aloud or whisper them in the quiet of our hearts, our wishes are heard.

A birthday is more than just a celebration, it's a moment to reach out, to set intentions, to step into the new year of your life. It's a sacred day to send your dreams into the universe, or, more often than not, directly to your Guardian Angel.

Of course, birthdays aren't the only special day for this. There's also October 2—Guardian Angel Day, a day that has been recognized since the 1500s and officially celebrated since 1608. But beyond that, don't forget to wish, pray, and hope every day in between.

So, as you celebrate this year, know that you are surrounded by love, guided by light, and held in the embrace of those who walk with you from beyond. Happy Birthday to you.

Cardinals Bring Hope and Peace
Catherine DeCoite

When my sister was very sick in the hospital, I saw a beautiful red cardinal on my deck. It gave me so much hope and made me happy that Angels were watching over her.

Judith's Insight:
Cardinals are extraordinary messengers of peace, hope, and love. Their presence is often a gentle yet powerful sign that someone from beyond is watching over you, reassuring you that they are by your side every moment. They offer a sense of strength, prayer, and healing energy, guiding you through life's challenges.

In your case, the cardinal carries a deeply personal message—one from your mom, bringing you the hug you need, exactly when you need it. Keep looking for these signs. Cardinals are often the earthly reflections of Guardian Angels, appearing to remind you that you are never alone.

When you encounter a cardinal, don't just notice it, observe it closely. There is often a deeper message hidden in the moment. Look into its eyes; sometimes, you may feel a direct connection to the soul it represents. Pay attention to where it appears, how it moves, and what surrounds it. These details hold significance. If the cardinal is perched on a branch, take note of the tree or location. Different trees and settings can symbolize different messages, perhaps a reminder of a place or a connection to a past memory. If the cardinal appears near your home, it is a strong sign of protection and comfort, reminding you that love continues to surround you. If the cardinal lands somewhere unexpected, it may be urging you to pause, reflect, or take notice of something important in your life. If a cardinal flies by at just the right moment, it's a sign of movement—encouraging you to move forward with something you've been contemplating. It's a nudge to take action, trust yourself, and embrace the next step. If a cardinal hovers or lingers, it could be a moment of deep spiritual connection—an opportunity to listen closely to your heart and find peace in the presence of your loved one. Seeing a cardinal in a picture—whether a painting, a magazine, or even on social media—could be a reminder to slow down and be present. It asks you to pause and reflect on something happening in your life at that moment. If you repeatedly come across images of cardinals in different places, it may be a message of reassurance, confirming that your Guardian Angels are near and guiding you.

When you see a cardinal, trust that it is not a coincidence. The circumstances in which they appear can provide profound insights and direction. Their presence is a gift, an opportunity to feel connected to your inner wisdom and to the spirits of those who love you.

The next time a cardinal crosses your path, take a deep breath, listen to your heart, and embrace the message it brings. Your loved ones are near, watching over you, and sending you love in the most beautiful way.

Can I Have Your Attention, Please
Karen Laggner

My parents never smoked, but since I moved into my new place a little over three years ago, I occasionally smell cigarette smoke. I just assumed the people who lived here before me were smokers and they were coming to visit!

Judith's Insight:
It seems you may have more than one Guardian Angel reaching out to you—perhaps one who smoked, or maybe someone who did when they were younger. Guardian Angels don't always come from those you've known; they can be souls who passed long before you were born yet still watch over you.

The scent of smoke could be their way of getting your attention, a wink, a nod, a whisper from beyond. Always take note of what is happening in your life when you detect this scent. Often, there is a clear message tied to your current situation, guiding you toward clarity, comfort, or reassurance. Regardless of who is sending the sign, one thing is certain: It is meant to help you cope and bring you hope.

Scents are some of the most powerful triggers for memory and emotion. They grab your attention, stir your soul, and evoke feelings that words often cannot. There's an old saying: "Where there is smoke, there is fire." But in this case, where there is the scent of smoke, someone is reaching out to you.

Even if your Guardian Angel wasn't a smoker, the scent has successfully captured your focus, hasn't it? Smell is one of the five senses that deeply connects us to memory, emotion, and the unseen world. Some say fear has a scent, just as burning does. Others recognize specific fragrances tied to people, places, or moments from their past, memories embedded deep within the soul.

Think about it: The scent of your grandmother's house suddenly envelops you. The familiar fragrance of a church, a school, or an old book can transport you back to a bygone era. A whiff of perfume or cologne can instantly evoke feelings for someone you miss.

These are not just memories; they are triggers placed in our soul, signs that reveal the presence of those we love and the guidance of those who watch over us. Next time a scent stops you in your tracks—especially if it appears suddenly or without explanation—pause and reflect. What are you thinking about? What are you feeling? What is happening in your life at that moment? Keep noticing. Keep telling your stories. Keep paying attention. The more you do, the more you'll realize these moments are not random—they are invitations to listen, to remember, and to understand what your Guardian Angels are trying to show you. So, breathe it in. Embrace the adventure. The more you open yourself to these signs, the more life and meaning they will bring to you.

Hidden Agenda

Rhonda Charles

Tomorrow is a big day for my family. Today when I was leaving the house, I saw something I had never seen before anywhere near my house. I saw a cardinal. I have never seen a cardinal in this area.

Judith's Insight:

That's so incredibly amazing! It seems like tomorrow is already filled with prayers from the Heavens for you. I'm sure you are calling on your Guardian Angel to ensure the day is blessed. But this isn't just any cardinal—he is a master, commanding attention in a way that cannot be ignored.

You can see the Tree of Life standing tall beside him, a powerful symbol of strength, growth, and connection. This is a sign full of life, bursting with energy, making sure you take notice. What a wonderful gift this is as you wait for another.

This cardinal is more than just a simple sign—it is a pearl of wisdom, like discovering a hidden treasure or finding a pearl in an oyster while fishing. What makes this cardinal different from any other Guardian Angel sign? It had been hidden, something you had never noticed before, until now.

This moment is like a big reveal, showing you what you need to focus on as you take your next few steps forward or make life-changing decisions. This is a cardinal of distinction, one with full determination to be there at the exact moment you walked out the door, ensuring it caught your eye just when you needed guidance.

This cardinal appeared with purpose—to make you stop, take a breath, and ask yourself: "What does this cardinal mean at this exact moment? Is someone trying to tell me something?" And the answer? Yes, absolutely.

You are being guided. You are being watched over. Someone out there definitely has your back. It doesn't mean the road ahead will be without challenges. There may still be bumps along the way, but what it does mean is you will get there. And you are not walking alone.

So, take this as a sign. Take this as encouragement. You've got this! At any moment we can find ourselves taking steps and suddenly noticing something we never did before. That's called a hidden agenda from our Guardian Angel. It may not be a cardinal, but it will certainly be something you take notice of.

Red Rose of Hope
Ginalaura Virgintino Harris

Feathers, birds, songs, coins, butterflies, the smell of roses, or seeing roses when not expecting to, all have a special and unique meaning to me. When my husband was sick last year, my yellow rose bush bloomed with a red rose.

Judith's Insight:
Every once in a while, life gifts us with moments that feel like an "Aha!" revelation—sudden, striking, and full of meaning. These moments may seem puzzling at first, but with time, their deeper significance unfolds. In this case, the appearance of a red rose on a yellow rose bush was one of those extraordinary moments.

This striking sight was no accident. It was designed to capture your attention, a message of hope, a whisper from the other side, a heartfelt connection from soul to soul.

Whether by instinct or intuition, we often recognize who our Guardian Angels are. They are the souls with whom we share an unbreakable bond, a love that transcends space and time. Though your husband has passed, his love remains everpresent. He may not always appear as a red rose blooming on a yellow bush, but that rose is now a symbol of his eternal love for you.

Roses, universally recognized as expressions of love, carry deep emotional weight. Red roses symbolize passion, devotion, and an undying connection, while yellow roses, reminiscent of the sun, radiate warmth, strength, and friendship—bonds that continue to thrive even in physical absence.

Your Guardian Angel husband will always find ways to touch your heart, guiding you to notice the extraordinary hidden within the ordinary. You will feel his presence through unexpected signs, reminding you that love, once deeply shared, never truly leaves.

For those of us with stories to tell—whether knowingly or unknowingly—there are moments in life that feel like finding diamonds in the rough. You may believe something is unfolding for one reason, only to realize later that it was leading you somewhere entirely unexpected.

Perhaps you reluctantly attend a party, only to meet someone who offers you the perfect job, or even becomes the love of your life. Maybe your car breaks down, and the tow truck driver turns out to be a long-lost friend of your late father. Or you step through what you think is the entrance to an ice cream shop, only to discover it's actually a hidden speakeasy.

These moments are not random. They are doors opening, paths redirecting, signs appearing, all leading you to the message you are meant to receive. And on the most remarkable of days, someone may present themselves to you as a rare, but wonderful rose—a reminder that love, guidance, and destiny work in ways beyond our understanding.

So, when the unexpected happens, pause. Pay attention. It just might be a sign leading you to something even greater than you imagined. It's always a great day when someone presents themselves as a rare but wonderful rose.

Dad Watching Over You

Kristin Figueroa

I've been seeing my father's badge number everywhere. I want to believe it's him telling me something. I wish I knew what! It's a fairly random number, and this last week it was everywhere. I had surgery last week and I prayed that he would keep me safe. Perhaps he's just here for a bit longer watching over me.

Judith's Insight:

Badge numbers hold a special significance, especially when they belong to someone we love and honor. These numbers are more than just digits, they are etched into our hearts, symbols of duty, service, and unwavering protection.

It's incredible how, when you ask for a sign, one appears clear as day. His badge number, in any order, will always be a message that he has your back. Badge numbers carry strength, just as the people who wore them did. If you take a moment to reflect, or simply look around, you may realize that signs were all around you that day and will continue to appear. You may have even passed a police car, fire truck, or ambulance, giving you an extra wink and nod, a subtle reassurance that he is still with you.

These signs are Hugs from Heaven, small but powerful gestures sent to ease your loneliness, bring you comfort, and help you heal, especially as you navigate health challenges or uncertain times.

A badge is more than a piece of metal — it represents a life of service, honor, and respect. Imagine your Guardian Angel as a protector standing by your side, much like the head of security for the President of the United States or the firefighter who waits patiently for the next call to save a life. This earthly savior commanded honor when he walked into a room, and now, from the other side, he continues to watch over you.

He is the one sending warning signals, the one who made sure you had a tire iron in your car before you got a flat tire. He is the one who sends smoke signals, nudging you to turn around at just the right moment, helping you avoid disaster.

This fun-loving, wise, and protective presence was always a master of riddles and rhymes, the one who could make you laugh, teach you life's lessons, and still be the strong force that others looked up to. He is the same person who taught you right from wrong, and maybe even had a beer in hand while giving you his best advice. He's the one who showed you what it meant to belly laugh, to appreciate the little things, and to never take life too seriously.

Maybe this was someone you drank milk and ate cookies with as a child—or maybe it was someone who stepped in as a father figure, even if he wasn't your biological dad. Either way, you will know him because he was the man who wanted the very best for you.

Whether you believe this Guardian Angel is your father, mother, godfather, best friend, or mentor, it doesn't matter. What matters is how they make you feel. You will know them by the unconditional love that continues to flow from them, even from the other side.

When you see those signs, when you catch a glimpse of that badge number, or when you suddenly feel a presence beside you—trust it. Because he is still here, guiding you, protecting you, and loving you every step of the way.

The Dive

Teresa Blewangel

In June 2017, while in Sal Salvador, Bahamas, I had just completed my open water scuba diving course. As we were returning to land, I was so excited I had accomplished one of my bucket list items. Just then, I looked up and I saw a heart-shaped break in the clouds, clear as day, and took a picture. This was a sign from my dad, who had passed away in 1980 in a motorcycle accident. I know he was sending me this sign that he was so proud and was present in spirit.

One afternoon, I was sitting in my yard in Upstate New York with a group of people reminiscing about the good times, specifically when my father was alive. Suddenly, a butterfly landed on the top of my foot and stayed for half a minute! This was a sign my father was present in spirit.

Judith's Insight:

This is a perfect example of what it means to live life to the fullest. When you reach out to your Guardian Angel—in this case, your dad—he doesn't just send a single sign. He makes sure the message is loud and clear.

In both cases, there were likely more signs than you even realized, perhaps even clouds forming a heart in the sky, whispering "I love you." The seat you were sitting in at the time may have held numbers and letters that added another layer to the story. Every detail matters when messages from beyond are being sent.

The scuba diving represents the search—the continuous journey of discovery, of diving deep into the unknown. The water represents peace, assuring you that your dad is helping you find serenity in your heart.

Him sending you a sign at the very moment you were passing your scuba diving test was no accident. It was his way of applauding your many accomplishments, honoring your perseverance, and celebrating your courage. It was his proud smile from beyond, cheering you on as you embrace life.

Your dad was a daredevil, a fearless spirit who rode motorcycles and took on life with passion and adventure. And in the same way that he once felt the rush of the wind through his soul, you now feel the invigorating power of water surrounding you as you dive into your own experiences. This was more than just a sport—it was a shared spirit between father and child, a mutual embrace of life's wild and wonderful energy.

Then came another sign, the butterfly. At the exact moment you and your loved ones were acknowledging memories of him, a butterfly appeared, sending you a cosmic high five. And when it landed on your foot, it wasn't just a beautiful coincidence. It was a message of movement, a push forward, a reminder to keep exploring, keep experiencing, and keep living.

This dad is not just a protector from beyond, he is a teacher, a guide, a force of encouragement. His message to you is simple: Keep making memories. Keep sharing your stories. Keep embracing life the way he did. His adventure didn't end—it continues through you. So, dive deep, ride fast, feel the wind, feel the water, and feel the love. He is right there with you, every stroke and dive of the way.

"Girls Just Want to Have Fun"
Gianna Lanza

I am a sophomore in college and last year I lost my grandma, "Mimi," who was my best friend in the whole world. She lived with my parents before I was born. I was with her every day of my life until August 2020, when my family decided the best decision for her safety was to put her in an assisted-living facility. My earliest memories consist of us constantly singing, "Girls Just Want to Have Fun," by Cyndi Lauper. We would sing in the car, in the house, just anywhere we were. Recently, I was out with my friends on the weekend. As we were going into the bathroom that song came on. When I opened the bathroom door, there were two heads-up coins on the floor. I just knew as soon as I heard the song and saw the coins that Mimi was there with me.

Judith's Insight:

This message truly warms the heart when you read it! The arrival of that song is no mere coincidence, it's your Mimi reaching out, letting you know she's still there, listening, and ready for a chat, just like old times. But she's not just stopping by for a quick hello. She has more to say—more than just a few words, more than just two cents' worth. In fact, she might be giving you eleven cents' worth, a number that holds a special, Heavenly significance, reinforcing that this message is, without a doubt, Heaven-sent.

Your Mimi is making sure you know she's with you, even on your nights out with the girls—whether it's in the "morning light" or the "middle of the night." Her presence will be felt, a comforting embrace that reminds you she's by your side in all those cherished moments.

Songs tell stories. They capture emotions, bring comfort, and help us recognize the signs around us. Certain lyrics arrive at the exact moment we need to hear them, making our hearts react, remember, and heal.

Think about artists like Taylor Swift, whose music resonates deeply because she puts words to feelings that so many have experienced—pain, love, joy, longing. The same happens with our Guardian Angels. They are our personal storytellers, our celestial songwriters, validating our emotions and reminding us that we are never alone.

Just as music artists become Earthly Angels, Guardian Angels often use their lyrics and melodies to deliver messages, ease grief, restore hope, and set us free. So, whenever a song hits differently, when lyrics feel like they're meant just for you, listen closely. It may be a whisper from above, a message wrapped in melody, a hug in harmony. And let's hope the music never stops.

Because through music, our Guardian Angels always find the right words to reach us and penetrate our souls.

"The Electric Slide"
Cathy Adams

I received the call that my mom had passed away, so I packed the car and began my drive home to New Jersey from Maryland. I was driving up the New Jersey Turnpike and the radio was playing, but I wasn't really paying attention; my thoughts were focused on my mom. Suddenly, an unusual song came on the radio: "The Electric Slide." Everyone who knew my mom understood how much she loved that song. If we were at a party or a wedding reception, she always made the DJ play that song because she loved to do that dance. This is not a song you normally hear on the radio, so I knew she sent it to me. I cannot fully explain the feeling that washed over me, but I felt my mom's presence in the car with me.

Judith's Insight:
"Unusual" is the perfect way to describe a Guardian Angel message. Our Guardian Angels love to stand out, ensuring we take notice when they reach out. And this time, they choose to slide into your life with the lively tune of "It's electric!" What a vibrant, joyful, and unmistakable sign!

This message was meant to bring you relief and reassurance, a rhythmic reminder that she is with you on your journey. This song, along with many others, will become one of the ways she sends you hugs, courage, faith, and foresight. While you may not hear a song every time you need guidance, stay attuned to the events in your life. If you listen closely, you'll realize that your mom is speaking to you — clearly, profoundly, and always in perfect timing. She will continue to use the unusual to grab your attention, offering messages of support, love, and encouragement in the most unexpected ways.

At times, the words of a song become more than just lyrics; they become a legacy. Like an unforgettable plot twist in a movie, these messages come in ways we never could have predicted. In this story, the writer didn't know that she herself would become a Guardian Angel before the publishing of this book. This is her gift—a lasting message to her family and friends, intertwined with music, reminding them that she will be here, living on and on.

In this story, Cathy refers to heading home to New Jersey. The funny thing is, Cathy signed an agreement giving her permission to include this story in the book on August 9, 2024. That very same day, only hours later, Cathy was called home and was promoted from being an Earthly Angel to a Guardian Angel, allowing her to leave her words behind, a lasting impression for all to read and sending the message loud and clear, "Make sure my story is in the book!"

So, keep living. Keep listening. And above all, keep dancing.

A Drawer That Opens My Heart

JoAnne Turner Connolly

I have been a nurse for almost forty years. Recently, I took a different job in a doctor's office. It was a great move because in this office I'm so comfortable and like the people so much that it actually feels like it's my home.

The office is fairly typical as we have individual rooms in which we put the patients. Whenever I am working in one particular room, this one drawer just opens. At first, I thought something was wrong with the drawer. After this phenomenon happened repeatedly, I named it "the ghost." Whenever it happened, I would always say, "The ghost is back!" Eventually I realized the opening drawer could only mean one thing: it was a sign from my dad. He was my biggest fan of me becoming a nurse. When he was older and sick, I was his special medical person who took care of him. It only seemed right that I would feel him sending me his support and hug when I am at work. Now, I look forward to that drawer opening. It means he's showing up to help me get through life.

Judith's Insight:

Of course, it's your dad. Deep down, we usually know who is helping us or sending the hug we need. If you took note of the times the drawer opened and compared them to what was happening in your life, you'd likely know exactly why he showed up that day. He's making sure you remember how proud he is of you. He's also reminding you that he is there for you, just as you were there for him. Never underestimate the power of your bond. Your dad wants to be noticed, and he is.

The opening drawer is a perfect example of how our loved ones find ways to reach us. Others may have similar experiences—doors opening, unexplained noises, even thunder and lightning at just the right moment. Our Guardian Angels sometimes go to great lengths to make sure we pay attention, even if it means making a little noise. They often repeat actions or patterns, seemingly random at first, but ultimately meant to signal us to keep our eyes open and be aware of what's happening around us.

These signs don't always come during difficult times. Even in moments of joy, we can use a reminder that we're supported. And when life's challenges arise, our loved ones send extra hugs to help us through. They are there to make us feel cherished and protected—even though they may scare the heck out of us at times by opening and shutting doors, making noises in the middle of the night, and finding ways to keep us off our guard. They really know how to make a big bang.

REFLECTION 8

Gratitude

Remember, you're not the only one who misses them—they're finding ways to show you they miss you too!

Those who recognize the presence of their Guardian Angels are truly fortunate. Once you open your heart to their guidance, hugs, winks, nods, and quiet support, you'll realize just how blessed you are. And for that, you will be grateful.

—Judith Turner

A Picture-Perfect Day

Ginalaura Virgintino Harris

My husband passed away in June, and these past few months have been hard. Every day I look for little signs to help get me through. This weekend was especially hard as we first met and spoke on February 12. Today a friend posted a photo from her wedding, and when I looked closer, my husband was in the background. That was my sign for today.

Judith's Insight:

This was a sign from your husband to help you through the day. Yes, he may have had a little help from your friend, but he wanted to remind you how important your wedding was and how deeply he loved you. Your Guardian Angel is kind and humble, still ensuring that your special days feel meaningful. Guardian Angels often work through others, weaving together different people and stories to deliver their messages. That number 212, February 12, may hold even more significance than you realize. His love continues, and your Guardian Angel will make sure that holidays and special occasions never go unnoticed. You are truly fortunate. The love you shared endures beyond time.

Anniversaries, birthdays, Christmas, and Thanksgiving are moments when we instinctively search for signs, even if we're not consciously aware of it. Some of us look for them every day. When two people are soulmates, twin flames, or bound by marriage or commitment, the stories that emerge are remarkable. It's not that these are the only times signs appear, but these dates carry deeper meaning, making us more attuned to their presence. It's incredible how often loved ones pass away on significant dates—holidays, birthdays, anniversaries—as if marking their presence in a way we cannot ignore. Even those who don't actively believe in Guardian Angels often find themselves recounting experiences that happened on these special days without realizing their significance.

You don't have to believe in Guardian Angels to notice these moments, but they do make you wonder. Have you ever zoomed in on a picture—maybe one on Facebook—only to spot someone in the background who is familiar? Maybe it was someone you didn't expect to see, yet there they were, perfectly placed. The things that appear in your path are never random. They may not make sense today, but one day, they might. Sometimes, it's not the picture itself that's extraordinary, it's what's in the background that holds the true meaning.

Beautiful Scene
Betty D.

I was sitting in my car in my driveway and out of nowhere, something hit my back passenger side window. I turned around to look and there was a beautiful red cardinal sitting on the window ledge tapping on my window! I instantly knew it was a sign from Heaven. I said, "Hi Mom. Hi Babs." The bird then proceeded to fly around and around my car several times. Then it flew away and sat in the woods watching me. I was overwhelmed by this sign from Heaven from my mom and sister.

Judith's Insight:
You were sitting there, and they thought, "Let's have some fun." This encounter was a little something to brighten your day. A beautiful Guardian Angel always finds a way to send a message from above. While not every sign is the same, in this case, they wanted to lift your spirits, remind you that you are supported, and bring a little joy to the moment. Their intention was to put a bounce in your step, add life to the party, and make sure you all shared a few minutes of happiness together. You may have

thought you were alone — but on this day, you definitely weren't.

Why is it that some days, birds perch nearby, and you barely notice? Yet on other days, they capture your attention, and you feel drawn to them, as if they are familiar souls. Why is it that sometimes two birds appear, and you instinctively name them, as if they were old family members or friends, maybe even grand-parents or godparents? Is it something in the air, something in their eyes? Maybe it's both. Sometimes, it's just the perfect align-ment of time and circumstances.

In this story, it happened to be cardinals, but it could just as easily have been two bluebirds chatting on a street corner or a single bird landing beside you on a park bench. More than the birds themselves, it's about the bond you shared with those who have passed — the ones who were always by your side, your clos-est companions, your ride-or-die people. Just reading this might remind you of moments when you've felt a presence nearby, a fleeting visit from a loved one.

These moments, no matter how small, feel like something out of a storybook. They leave you longing for more, more signs, more connections, more proof that love never truly leaves us. The feel-ing of a Guardian Angel's presence is like sitting by a warm fire, wrapped in a blanket of love knowing they are near. It's simply about sharing a slice of life together, even from different worlds.

Sea Angels
Christina Sleckman

I love the sea and sea creatures. I also believe strongly in signs from Heaven. My mom's Heavenly sign to me is 444, which I see very often. It means that you are surrounded by Angels. During two instances, my Angels told me they were with me and protecting me.

First, I went to the emergency room after a car accident. They put me in a room, and when I looked up, there was a seahorse on the wall! Second, when I was hit by a car while walking a couple of years ago, the paramedics took me to the emergency room. They took me to a room filled with fish on the walls. Do you think they are signs that my Angels are all around me? Yes, I believe!

Judith's Insight:

Once again, we encounter the significance of number 444. This story, intertwined with the imagery of the sea, explores themes of love, inner peace, and guidance. Your Angels are here to bring you comfort and help you find serenity. Just as the sea offers a vast embrace of tranquility, number 444 serves as a powerful sign of love and reassurance.

Sea creatures and the ocean's natural rhythm symbolize growth, transformation, and the flow of life itself. Fish represent personal progress, while water embodies the ever-changing movement of experiences. When you come across these symbols, whether in the form of fish swimming gracefully or the steady ebb and flow of the tides, they carry meaningful messages meant just for you.

The combination of 444 and these oceanic images suggests that your journey may involve navigating challenges, coping with grief, or embracing change. However, these signs also serve as reminders that you are supported and protected. Your Guardian Angels don't just send messages in times of hardship; they also make their presence known during moments of joy and adventure. Their love surrounds you continuously, offering guidance and strength exactly when you need it most.

Angel numbers have a way of guiding us, taking us on a journey, and dropping hints along the way. If certain numbers seem to follow you, try writing them down—you may begin to see a pattern, a personal road map filled with meaningful stories. Similarly, sea creatures, when combined with the presence of water, remind us to take a deep breath and embrace life with renewed energy. They encourage us to gain perspective, face challenges without fear, and trust that we won't be knocked down by the waves. Even if we don't always feel steady, these signs remind us that we are being guided toward safe harbor, helping us find our balance when it's definitely off.

Help from Above

Anonymous

I was diagnosed with breast cancer back in October 2017. I went through chemotherapy, had a mastectomy, and completed radiation. I recovered and was fine for four years. I was almost out of the woods.

Fast forward to October 2021. I had a horrible right lower quadrant stomachache for a couple of days. I felt an unexplainable urge to go to the emergency room. I was positive I would be diagnosed with appendicitis. I went, and they did a CT scan which showed absolutely nothing wrong with my bowels and belly. What they did find was a lesion on my left hip. That meant that my stage IV breast cancer metastasized to my bones. I was sent home and the stomach pain was completely gone. It never came back. I felt someone/something sent me to emergency room to find the spot on my hip.

After multiple CT scans and a PET scan, the doctors found it was the only spot in my body. I had no other lesions. The cancer was nowhere else. Although I'll probably be on chemotherapy for the rest of my life, I'll hopefully be around for many more years due to finding the spot early. My Guardian Angel is always with me.

Judith's Insight:

Life-saving events are truly a Heavenly rescue. Trusting your instincts is often another way of receiving guidance from your Angels. I'm sure you've noticed other signs along the way that led you to seek help. In the end, those signs prove their purpose and bring clarity to your journey.

There's a saying: "You can lead a horse to water, but you cannot make him drink." In this story, you were led to the hospital so that someone else could provide the answers you needed. These remarkable, life-saving moments have a way of steering you toward the right place or the right people, those who can help keep you safe. If you ever reach out your hand, someone will be there to hold it.

Following the yellow brick road may not always take you straight to the Emerald City, but it will always lead you where you need to go—even if it's not the destination you originally intended. Life can sometimes feel like a version of Mr. Toad's Wild Ride, full of unexpected twists and turns. But the good news is you're not just holding on to the handlebars for dear life. You are supported and guided.

Beautiful presence
Elena Williams

We decided to go to Disney for my birthday in February 2020. We were getting ready to check out of the Port Orleans Resort on my birthday. As my family went back to the room, I was sitting in the front passenger seat of the car. I heard a tapping on the side window and there was a female cardinal on the side mirror. She then flew onto the hood of the car and got all the way up to the windshield. The cardinal was chirping and staring at me. A male cardinal was in the tree we were parked under looking down at me. I truly believe these cardinals were my parents wishing me a happy birthday, which was the exact day of my birthday!

Judith's Insight:

This is like a gentle knock at the door, as if your parents were stopping by for a cup of coffee, just to check in and share a moment with you. Your birthday will always be one of the most significant days of your life, a day filled with love, memories, and the invisible thread that connects you to those who have gone before you. And with every birthday, there should be gifts — not just the ones wrapped in ribbons but also the ones that come in unexpected and meaningful ways. Today, you received two beautiful presents, reminding you that you are never forgotten.

Cardinals tell their own story each time they appear. These cardinals arrived with a message of love, bringing with them the importance of cherishing memories, finding joy in laughter, and remembering to be kind to yourself. They are messengers of the heart, appearing just when you need them most. Listen for them; they will return, and they will certainly have more to say.

As we journey through life, our Angels travel with us, their wings unseen yet always nearby. Sometimes, we don't even realize they are there until we feel that subtle nudge, that whisper of reassurance, or the sudden appearance of a familiar sign. It is in those quiet moments that Heaven reaches out. Or perhaps, it's not us knocking on Heaven's door, but rather Heaven knocking on ours.

Cardinals carry a calming, settling presence. They arrive like a warm embrace, bringing comfort to the heart, especially when we need it most. And if we are far from home, they have a remarkable way of carrying a little piece of home to us.

Good Morning Angel

Joan Essmyer Blendowski

It was a long time ago, probably the early 2000s. I was commuting to my office in New York City. The subway was jam-packed with busy rush hour foot traffic. My subway was a hub so there were a lot of lines converging. I was probably a bit sour and focused on getting to work. I was walking through the station to my next subway transfer when I clearly heard a man's voice say, "Good morning, Joan." I turned to see who could possibly know me here in the subway. At the top of some stairs leading down to a platform was a man I had never seen before. He was older, not incredibly tall, and a bit stocky. He had dark black neatly combed hair. He looked me in the eye and smiled so big. His eyes and face were kind. I had no doubt that it was he who said my name. I do not know if anyone else saw him. He was definitely there. I believe he was my Guardian Angel coming to brighten my day.

Judith's Insight:

It doesn't matter if anyone else saw or heard him. What matters is that *you* did. You heard your name, even if the words never actually left his mouth. Two significant things happened here. First, someone called your name to get your attention, to make you take notice. Second, that man symbolized your Angel.

Hearing your name in an unexpected way is more than just a coincidence, it's a message. It's about speaking up for yourself, recognizing your own presence, or even rediscovering who you are. This moment was a reminder of strength, support, and guidance. On a morning when you needed a friend, a distraction, or just a small reason to smile, someone showed up to say, "Good morning!" And sometimes, that's all it takes to change the course of a day.

There are times when something happens to us, and we only truly recognize its meaning when we hear someone else tell a similar story. If you're reading this and it resonates with you, then it has touched something deep inside—a connection, a memory, a reminder. Much like a chord played on a piano, harp, or guitar, it stirs something within. Maybe for you, it was music that caught your attention. Or maybe it was a smile, a familiar expression that instantly reminded you of someone dear.

Sometimes, in the face of a stranger, we catch a glimpse of someone we've lost. A gesture, a glance, a fleeting moment that feels almost like a whisper from the past. And when that happens, just take it as a little nod from the universe, as if someone is saying, "Here's looking at you, kid."

Rainbow Babies
Joan Essmyer Blendowski

I was pregnant with my older son. I had lost two babies before becoming pregnant with him. I was so stressed at the end of my pregnancy. Also, my grandmother had just passed away. In the middle of the night, I was awakened by the smell of gardenias. The scent was very strong. It was early fall and the windows were open, but no one had gardenias. They were my Gram's favorite flowers. I always felt she was there telling me it was okay. There was a sense of peace after that. My son was born happy and healthy.

Judith's Insight:
There are no coincidences when one soul leaves and another is born. Timing matters in ways we may not always understand. Often, as one soul departs, another arrives—or vice versa—creating a deep and meaningful connection between them. Your

grandmother's passing and the birth of your baby boy are not separate events; they are intertwined. Even if they never met, she is undoubtedly his Guardian Angel. The end of one life often signifies the beginning of another, marking a moment of transition, renewal, and new beginnings.

Gardenias symbolize peace, harmony, and well-being. When you smelled them, it was more than just a fragrance—it was a gift, bringing you the peace of mind you were searching for. When soul's cross paths in this way, there is a natural balance of harmony, hope, and happiness.

Rainbow babies—those born after a loss—carry a special significance. Some believe they are the same soul returning when the timing, body, or circumstances are just right. Sometimes, the universe holds back a soul as an act of protection, ensuring both the mother and child are safe when they finally meet. It takes the energy of many Guardian Angels to orchestrate these moments. If the timing isn't perfect, they wait—watching over from beyond the rainbow bridge—until everything aligns.

My own daughter, at just eighteen months old, once told me, "Mommy, I waited for you. I picked you. I waited until after my brother was born because I wanted you. I needed you to be my mom." That moment reaffirmed what I have always believed: Any baby born to you has chosen you. They needed *you*. They *wanted* you. Because they already *loved* you. This is the destiny of a soul and the enduring love of an Angel. Just remember, they picked you.

Our Teachers of Love and Life
Judith Turner

Death becomes real in a different way when your parents pass. As time has gone by, I've come to see how deeply our family is connected to Guardian Angels. When my grand-father Archie died, the number 217 seemed to take on a life of its own. It was always spoken about, sometimes indirectly, but it always came up. Family members would play it in the lottery, and whenever 217 appeared—on a check, a cash register receipt, or a restaurant bill—it was seen as a good omen, a sign of luck, comfort, or simply a happy moment.

By contrast, the signs from my other grandfather were more tangible—newspapers, the Sears and Roebuck catalog, beer bot-tles, and big scissors, since he was a cutter for the Rogers Pete clothing company. For my Nana Dunn, her signs came in the form of a $2 bill, roast beef, pennies, and marbles. I still remem-ber making her earrings out of fried marbles when I was in kin-dergarten. But the most memorable sign tied to her was a bucket of herring and very thinly sliced ham, a combination that, to this day, makes me smile.

As I reflect on my Guardian Angel stories, I realize that many of these signs were things I learned to recognize through my par-ents. They cherished and celebrated these familiar symbols from loved ones who had passed. If one of these signs appeared, my parents would acknowledge it as a message from beyond. They would recall moments like staying in a hotel room numbered 217 or sharing stories about Nana Dunn's legendary cooking when someone complimented a roast beef dinner. They would remind me to save a $2 bill because Nana always gifted them at Christmas. And every year, my mom would buy creamed herring for New Year's Eve—though no one ever ate it. Looking back, I now understand that these weren't just old traditions. They were signs, reminders that our loved ones never truly leave us.

Judith's Insight

As our loved ones pass, memories become the way we recognize their presence. Each person we've lost represents a piece of the life puzzle we are still putting together. Signs from them help us heal, offering comfort to our souls. Memories are more than just recollections; they create bonds that allow us to feel their presence when they visit.

These moments stick with us, as vivid as if they were happening right now. We hold on to the dishes we ate from as children, or that favorite Santa gift—a Baby Catch-a-Ball doll—because they carry something deeper than nostalgia. Why are so many of us buying record albums again? Because they bring back something familiar. The scents we remember, the keepsakes we hold on to, the numbers that appear over and over again—they are more than memories. They are connections.

The word *familiar* comes from *family*. When we surround ourselves with things that feel familiar, they trigger our senses, allowing us to *feel* something beyond what's tangible. Even objects can act as calls from those we once shared them with. Holding on to these things isn't about refusing to let go of the past—it's about allowing those who have passed to stay present.

444 Signs
Christina Sleckman

When my mom was alive, she would always wake up at 4:44 am and spoke of it often. After she passed away, I started seeing 444 all around. I always took it as a sign from her. The day my dad died I saw it about eight times. That was comforting.

I researched the 444 numbers and found out that it means you are guided by Angels. Seeing 444 is a sign from Heaven to let you know there are Angels around you, watching over you, guiding you, and protecting you.

A few years later I went on vacation to Pennsylvania. I was driving around with my boyfriend looking at the homes. Of course, one house number was 444. While driving, I asked my boyfriend what the mileage was. His answer, 44.4 miles. Then I saw a huge graffiti on a wall that said 444. My boyfriend jokingly said, "Go away Angels, we don't need you," and the GPS fell off the windshield. I cried out, "No, Angels, please come back! I need you!" As I said it, a big tractor-trailer drove by with these words on the side of the cargo area: "God is with you!"

When we got to the house we were renting for the week, there was a little Angel on the table. Another sign. As a memorial to my parents, I got a tattoo. Of course, 444 is incorporated. The tattoo is on my back because I often say they always have my back.

Judith's Insight:

It's a numbers game, but not necessarily a game at all. The number 444 is guided by Angels, and for you, it is truly a miracle number. These numbers are more than just digits; they are messages, speaking to you and offering guidance. Pay attention to what is happening around you when 444 appears, especially if you are carrying a burden or facing a challenge. It's incredible how this number follows you, just as it's remarkable how you've woven it into your story. This is your footprint in the sand, a mark of your journey. Keep looking for those 444s—they will continue to appear, revealing messages of hope and reassurance throughout your life.

Angel numbers have appeared in many ways throughout this book, each story altering the way we see them. These numbers follow you because, in some way, you follow them. You seek them out, you notice them, you interact with them. That number is your guiding message. If you don't think you have an Angel number, start by looking at your birth date. Then, consider the house number from your childhood. Reflect on the numbers tied to milestones in your life, and you may realize that you, too, have an Angel number that has been with you all along.

Tattoos are like artwork for the soul, a sign or symbol chosen to honor a loved one. Not everyone wears a tattoo, but for those who do, it becomes a badge of honor, a permanent tribute to a Guardian Angel they may not have even realized was watching over them. Whether through ink, numbers, or quiet signs in everyday life, these messages remind us of who's missing at our table.

Walking with Faith
Carole Sahagian

As a woman who carries Jesus in her heart everyday, bathes in holy water from Lourdes, and drives around with a cardboard poster of Jesus in her car, I often find myself praying for just about everyone, even people I don't know. When I go for walks, I count how many St. Joseph or Virgin Mary statues I see in gardens. They've become a sign for me, a cue to stop and say a prayer.

Sometimes, before I even drive off in my car, I'll feel a nudge to say a quick prayer for someone. My desk at work has become a kind of shrine—a sacred little space in the middle of a busy office where people stop by to buy insurance or file claims. And no matter what, I'm always praying—not just for myself, but for everyone I know and even those I don't.

And I see the signs that someone's listening. Once, while heading to a cancer treatment appointment, I noticed billboards and license plates that seemed to hold special messages, little clues from the universe. These glimpses of love and grace help me feel close to my parents, and they bring me peace and hope.

Judith's Insight:
This is how you make it through your hardest moments, through valleys where you need more than just a breeze beneath your wings. You need a song in your step and unwavering hope in your heart.

The signs, statues, songs, and whispers, they're all part of it. They lift you when you're falling. They ease your anxiety, calm your fears, and serve as answers to the prayers you send out into the universe.

You don't have to be Catholic, Christian, or religious at all to feel something when you pass a statue of a saint or a cross. No matter what your beliefs, these are signs from Heaven.

Today, you can walk into almost any spa, salon, or home goods store and find symbols like Buddhas, which can trigger feelings of health, hope, and harmony. Or the Star of David, which might spark a sense of strength, nobility, and connection to something divine.

These, too, are like Guardian Angels offering a quiet embrace, like spiritual medicine that soothes your soul.

Sometimes, that's all we need: to feel held. To feel loved. To feel as if someone, somewhere, is wrapping us up in grace.

Neverman's Love Is Never Ending
Susan Monaghan

This morning, my cousin sent me a message on Facebook: "It's your Mom and Grandpa's (Da's) birthday! Didn't he get a fantastic gift when she was born?"

I replied, admitting that I had forgotten it was Da's birthday too. As soon as I closed Messenger, a Facebook memory from five years ago appeared—a photo I had taken of an envelope addressed to my grandfather.

Judith's Insight:
This story brings to life the idea of new beginnings and celebrations. A birthday often symbolizes fresh starts and the joy of shared love, and this serves as a heartfelt reminder of that con-

nection. Your Guardian Angel, who has likely been guiding you for years, has been sending you subtle signs all along. Your mom, your ever-present, hand-holding Angel, wants you to know that both she and your Guardian Angel are actively supporting you in these moments.

Stay open to the signs around you—pictures that catch your eye, flowers blooming in your garden, and celebrations that include cake. Pay attention to the numbers on envelopes, stamps, and addresses; they may hold messages of hope and encouragement.

Every detail in this message adds to its significance. Something as simple as an old letter or envelope might not have seemed important at first, but now it carries new meaning, offering comfort and connection. Keep it close, it holds a lifetime of Heavenly hugs, ready to provide solace whenever you need it.

Even unexpected postal mail can be a sign that someone is reaching out from beyond. Have you ever received someone else's mail by accident? That, too, may have meaning. Look at the name, the address, the numbers—do any of them stand out? These small moments are often the way our guides try to catch our attention. Even the flyers we often discard without a second glance can reveal hidden messages. A single image might shift your entire day. And in today's digital world, love can appear in unexpected ways—perhaps even in a random social media post. Not because it's an advertising ploy, but because someone out there is trying to bring you a little joy.

This One Always Brings You Joy
Kerry

Whenever I am feeling very blue and missing my guy, I pray that he will send me a sign that he is at peace. His signs come as cardinals, or he leaves a dime or penny in the most random of places. I've cleaned an entire room and magically a penny or a dime appeared that wasn't there before. Last Christmas while baking cookies with four of my grandchildren, a cardinal appeared outside my kitchen window. That cardinal stayed for more than two hours on my weeping cherry tree. I have never seen a bird stay anywhere for more than ten seconds. Fortunately, I had three stunned witnesses plus the kids. I believe he was telling me that he's very happy that we continue our Christmas traditions that he loved so much.

Judith's Insight:

That's an incredible story! Your loved one had so much to share that day. Here's what I believe he was trying to tell you: "I'm right there with you, baking those Christmas cookies, and I'll stay by your side until you realize I'm not just any cardinal. I'll make sure you notice me—I'll linger, stand out, and catch your eye. You'll see me, and together we'll celebrate this Christmas and every Christmas, just in a different way. You know how much I cherished these moments."

When your loved one visits as a cardinal, know that he's also surrounded by your other Guardian Angels. The coins you find unexpectedly are little messages from them—magical reminders that they're nearby. Pay attention to what's happening in your life when you discover them, whether you're facing challenges or feeling joy. Their signs won't be limited to one form. If you're by the ocean, they might appear as a seagull, in the sound of crashing waves, or in the rhythm of falling rain. Stay open to their presence. Guardian Angels—especially this one—love keeping you on your toes, finding ways to surprise you and make you smile. And if you ever need a reason to smile, they'll find a way to bring one to you.

Traditions hold deep emotional significance, marking the essence of who we are. They are like engraving our initials into a treasured piece of jewelry or signing a masterpiece—each one a work of art in its own right. The traditions we create shape the road maps of our lives, leaving behind feelings and memories that can be cherished and carried forward for generations. When we share traditions, we share pieces of ourselves with those who walk alongside us. Life, after all, is far more about sharing than simply having.

Godly Message
Lucille Spallone

I have had a lot on my mind these past few days. While in my apartment, I was worried about a few things. When I moved my cedar chest, I found a beautiful prayer card behind it. (It said something similar to this as we couldn't use the original prayer):

"You shouldn't fear.
Don't walk with anxiety.
I am with you.
Those who guide you and believe in you will make you strong.
Someone will always be there to help you.
Give it to the Heavens.
You are never alone."

—Judith Turner

Judith's Insight:
This is a truly divine message, filled with deep significance. It may come from a Guardian Angel, God, Jesus, or whoever was on your heart at the moment you discovered it. Sometimes, when we pray directly to God, we feel an immediate and intimate response. Other times, we encounter signs that unmistak-

ably come from our Guardian Angels, who are deeply attuned to our pain, fears, and uncertainties. In these sacred moments, we receive a message from above, carefully placed to ease our worries and bring us comfort.

Even when we are unaware, our thoughts and silent prayers are heard. God listens to the unspoken longings of our hearts and the deepest yearnings of our souls. When you were searching for an answer, it arrived as a sign—offering reassurance, guidance, and the gentle reminder that you are never alone. Divine support and love surround you, helping to lighten your burdens and guide you through life's challenges.

Our prayers, or simply our conversations with the Heavens, do not always need to be religious. As we journey through life, we sometimes find ourselves on dark and uncertain paths, questioning whether light will ever return. In those moments, whether through words, songs, or even unspoken thoughts, our fears and doubts rise to the surface. But just when we begin to question hope, someone, or something, finds a way to send us the answers that we need.

REFLECTION 9

Hope

Keep in mind that today is only one piece of the big puzzle of life. We sometimes need to let time pass and gather more pieces of the puzzle before today makes sense to us! Try to get through today with some of life's great support. Someone stands with you, laughs with you, and cries for you, giving you hope.

—Judith Turner

Momma's Got Your Back
Linda

My husband and I bought a house in Naples, Florida, in 2021 and it was fully furnished. It was decorated in the exact style of my departed mom, with animal prints, monkeys, and birds. I totally love it! Thank you, Mom!

Judith's Insight:

This is a gift from above, lovingly sent by your mom. At a pivotal moment in your life, as you faced an important decision, she wanted to guide you toward the right path. Her presence was there to bring you inner peace, making your transition smoother and more exciting. These gentle signs are meant to help you feel at home, wrapping you in a sense of comfort and belonging.

As you settle into your new space, know that your mom is right there with you in spirit. Watch for her messages, they may come through in unexpected ways, like the image of an animal, a monkey, or a bird on a magazine cover, a book, or even a passing moment. Her love surrounds you as your new home becomes a place where family can grow, gather, and create new memories.

Her signs are a powerful expression of love and reassurance, reminding you that she is never far away. She is with you every step of the way, offering warmth, guidance, and encouragement as you embrace this new chapter.

Is it truly over? Will this be the right new beginning? These are the questions that echo in our hearts whenever we take a leap—whether moving forward, making a change, or committing to something significant. We second-guess ourselves, feeling both excitement and hesitation. We wonder if we are closing a chapter or if we should even be starting a new one. It's not until we sense that undeniable feeling—that sign, that moment of settling in—that we realize everything is falling into place. And with that, we step forward with confidence, knowing we are onto something better.

Magical Miracles
Jeri Turner Sinnig

One year when my son was little, we were going through a tough time financially. As fate would have it, it was Christmas—a time that should be filled with joy and warmth—but we were still deeply grieving the recent loss of my dad. The pain of his absence was palpable, casting a shadow over what should have been a season of celebration.

My son had his heart set on an Xbox gaming system that year, but I simply didn't have the money to buy it for him. I knew that if I asked, my family would have helped in a heartbeat, but my pride and sadness held me back from reaching out. I was overwhelmed—caught between the grief of losing my dad and the stress of trying to make ends meet.

Amidst all this, we were preparing for a fundraiser for a family friend whose child was battling a serious illness. We had gathered an array of wonderful gifts and prizes for the event, one of the biggest being the very gaming system my son so desperately wanted. Despite my financial situation, I managed to scrape together a few dollars to buy some raffle tickets, including one for the Xbox. I wasn't known for having much luck at these kinds of events, but I figured, "Why not? You can't win if you don't try."

As the night wore on, it was finally time to draw for the big prizes. When they called out the winning number—00120798—I couldn't believe my ears. I had the winning ticket! My son would have his gaming system after all. But as I looked at the numbers on that ticket, something even more astonishing hit me: 12/07/98. It was the exact date of my dad's passing.

In that moment, I knew that my dad — my Guardian Angel — had come through for us. It wasn't just about winning the Xbox; it was a message from him, letting me know that he was still watching over us, guiding us, and making sure we were okay. I still have that winning ticket, attached to a picture of my son, sitting proudly on my desk at work. Every time I see it, it reminds me of how uncanny winning that prize really was. How do they do that?

Judith's Insight:

When we find ourselves in desperate need, we often turn to silent prayers or quiet pleas, hoping the universe will somehow provide what we seek. Whether it's something as simple as a toy for a child or a more profound longing, those whispered wishes can sometimes feel like they go unanswered. But in moments like these, when the impossible becomes possible, it's clear that someone is listening.

Your dad understood the depth of your struggles and the weight of your grief. He found a way not only to help in a practical sense but also to send a powerful message — he was okay, he was still with you, and he would always support you. Christmas, already a season filled with magic and wonder, became the perfect moment for him to reach out. The winning numbers weren't just a coincidence; they were a sign, a reassurance that he was guiding you through even the toughest times.

The Xbox wasn't just a gift for your son; it was a message that your dad was looking out for him too. Even in moments when you feel alone, your dad is there, making sure your son knows he has a Guardian Angel watching over him. Sometimes what seems like a negative situation can reveal itself to be a hidden blessing, a reminder that you and your son are never truly alone.

Pay close attention to these signs, especially around the holidays. The true winning prize wasn't the Xbox; it was the reminder that your dad's love is still very much alive, guiding and protecting you both. This Christmas miracle was your own version of *It's a Wonderful Life*—a story where the bells rang for your Angel, letting you know his mission of love continues.

Manifesting can be magical, something we all do whether we realize it or not. Some people speak about it more openly, finding ways to keep positive energy flowing. The Angels in this story saw the sadness in her eyes, just as your own Angels recognize the sadness in your heart. Their goal was to bring joy, like a classic Santa story on Christmas morning, to replace emptiness with warmth. When we think about what a Christmas miracle truly is, we realize we all experience them in different ways. It may not always come through a winning ticket, but it is always there, revealed in the love that we feel in our own Christmas miracles. Remember to pay attention and look for that miracle every Christmas, and you will find it.

My Heart Will Go On
Judith Turner

Last year, I had a dream about an old friend, Michele Marsh, a longtime CBS news anchor who had passed away five years earlier. Though we hadn't seen each other in years and life had taken us in different directions, I often felt her presence after she was gone. Looking back, I now realize she had been sending me signs for some time.

Just days before my dream, I came across the signature book from her first wedding, the one I had been responsible for getting everyone to sign. I had no idea how I still had it, as I was certain I had given it to Michele all those years ago. Not long before that, I visited the River Palm, a restaurant we both loved. While there, I noticed her picture on the wall, positioned right above the booth where I had been seated. It brought back memories of the first time we went there together, celebrating nothing in particular — just a girls' night out. I also remembered the restaurant's owner, John Campbell, asking me to get that very picture of her, as she was a well-known CBS anchor at the time.

Then came the dream. Michele spoke with heartfelt excitement about finally being with PH, her second husband. She also told me she was with my father and Father Tom, a beloved priest we both adored — both of whom had passed away long before. I woke up around 4:00 a.m. I thought, "Wow, it was such an intriguing and significant moment."

A few days later, the news was dominated by coverage of the OceanGate Titan submersible. The world was captivated by the fate of those trapped inside, and every channel was filled with speculation about their rescue efforts. While watching one of these reports, I heard the name PH, and it immediately caught my attention. There aren't many people with those initials, and Michele had just spoken of PH in my dream.

Shortly after, my friend Sue called to tell me that one of the people on the missing submersible was Michele's husband. I was stunned. Memories flooded back of how Michele had met her husband, PH — Paul-Henri Nargeolet, a deep-sea explorer and Titanic expert known as "Mr. Titanic." She had been fascinated with the idea of communication between the living and the dead and had dreamed of visiting the Titanic wreckage as part of her research for a book she wanted to write, *The Other Side*. Instead, she and PH fell in love and married not long before her untimely passing.

When it was announced that all of the passengers on the submersible had indeed perished in the implosion, it became clear that Michele had been telling me of their fate days before the search and rescue teams confirmed it. As devastating as the

OceanGate disaster was, it brought me peace knowing my dear friend Michele and the love of her life, PH, had been reunited.

Judith's Insight:

Of course, the answer to my dream had to surface through one of the most significant, newsworthy events of the year. When a friend called to tell me that Michele's husband was one of the victims of the submarine tragedy, I realized my dream had been more than just a dream—it was a visitation from a Guardian Angel.

In the dream, Michele mentioned my dad and Father Tom, reassuring me that she was surrounded not only by the people she loved but also by those I loved, like my dad. At first, I wasn't sure if it was a true visitation. I felt Michele's presence, but the significance of PH was unclear. As far as I knew, PH was still alive, so if he and Michele were together, it seemed like it must have been just a dream rather than a message. However, as I started piecing together the details, I began to understand the deeper meaning behind it.

Michele and I had often talked about her desire to write a book on the afterlife. Looking back, it feels as though she was reaching out to confirm her beliefs and to let me know she was at peace. It's remarkable how dreams involving our guardians can seem nonsensical at first, only for their meaning to become clear as life unfolds its answers.

As it turns out, John is the name of Michele's son, which is why seeing her photo at the River Palm triggered memories of the owner, John Campbell, requesting that picture. Adding another layer to this name game, my grandson—born shortly after Michele's passing—is named Campbell. At only four years old, he is a reminder of the continuity of life, a small but powerful symbol of how we are all connected. These seemingly random links reveal how the universe weaves our stories together, keeping us tied to one another in ways we may not always understand.

The signatures in the wedding book and the gathering of people that followed highlighted how PH's story echoed around the world, much like the proverbial "shot heard 'round the world." Though Michele and I never had the chance to say a proper goodbye, I believe she found a way to reach out and say hello. Our journey isn't over—I am certain she will send more messages whenever she feels the need to connect. This latest encounter was her way of letting me know she's at peace, now watching over her beloved son John as his Guardian Angel.

It makes perfect sense that my dream of Michele would become newsworthy—after all, she was doing what she did best, serving as an anchor, delivering a story only she could tell. Her passing, much like her life, was significant, and even in death, she found a way to share a message.

This was not only a newsworthy tragedy but also a profound Guardian Angel story. Even though the message came through a dream, the heart of the story was about finding peace. Messages may come to us while we sleep, but our souls are always awake. Dreams can be powerful triggers, offering glimpses into what is to come. In this case, the dream served as a heads-up, a gentle warning of what was about to unfold. It took a whole community to unravel the meaning, as it sometimes does. But in the end, it was all about the happily ever after.

Window Watching

Catherine DeCoite

My mother shared a Guardian Angel story with me. One early summer morning when I was a toddler, she was asleep, and something woke her up and told her to go check on me. She went into my room, and I was sitting on the windowsill. We lived on the fifth floor of an apartment building in the Bronx.

She said I was staring at a woman from another window trying to tell me to go back inside. She didn't panic and slowly walked over to me and got me off the sill. She always said it was my Guardian Angel watching over me.

Judith's Insight:

This is one of those moments in life where a single second could have changed everything. It's the kind of story that makes you believe in something greater, something beyond explanation.

There are two incredible stories intertwined here. First, your mom—suddenly awakened by an unshakable feeling, as if someone or something was urging her to get up and check on you. And second, the woman across the way, unknowingly playing a pivotal role in saving your life that day. She may never fully grasp the impact of her actions, but she was your Earthly Angel. From that moment on, your mom believed in Angels.

This experience became a lifelong journey, teaching all of you to have faith in signs, to recognize the messages that appear when you need them most, whether in the darkest moments or the happiest times. This story is etched into your heart and mind, a reminder that love, guidance, and protection are always around you. It has taught you how to feel the warmth of unseen hugs.

"Someone saved my life"; simple words, yet they hold such profound meaning. Saying them aloud can send chills up your spine, giving you goosebumps as their weight settles in. The phrase "voice of an Angel" takes on a new meaning when you realize that sometimes, there is no actual sound—yet we hear it all the same.

Right now, somewhere, someone is saying, "Someone is watching out for me." And they're right. The Angels who touch our hearts and shape our lives, they are truly the Eighth Wonder of the World.

"Words" Are All We Need

Elena Williams

Yesterday, I was talking to my husband about how sad I felt about the recent passing of my brother-in-law. I told him I felt horrible about what my sister Diane was going through and how my brother-in-law loved visiting us in Florida. I talked about the great time we all had together when they stayed with us last October. It made me so unhappy to think that those wonderful visits are over. As we were talking, I went to get my phone out of the basket on my scooter, and my brother-in-law's prayer card was on top of my phone. It wasn't there before. I felt that it was a sign from him.

Judith's Insight:

It's truly remarkable when signs appear unexpectedly yet feel deeply significant. In that moment, your thoughts aligned perfectly with your brother-in-law sending you a message. He was clearly acknowledging that when Diane visits, you'll share a wonderful time together, just as you always have. And he'll be there too—perhaps even riding the scooter, if you keep an eye out for him. His message is clear: Continue creating joyful memories, and his presence will be felt in those moments.

This story highlights how communication from those who have passed can come in many forms—through written words, printed messages, or even casual conversations. These signs will always leave an imprint. You might even come across written notes or messages that serve as gentle reminders that your brother-in-law is still with you. He didn't transition alone; he was guided by many Angels who safely led him home. Just as your family members are with him, they are also guiding and supporting you from afar.

Prayers, a mezuzah, or any kind of religious message carries meaning—it is still a message from our guides. Regardless of one's beliefs, the essence remains the same: Our stories connect us. In this case, it was a prayer card, its scriptures resonating with deep meaning. The same could be said for words from the Torah, Buddhist texts, or other sacred writings. Guardian Angels exist across all faiths, their messages transcending time. Words written centuries ago often find their way to us at just the right moment—not by coincidence; remember, divine guidance can be written in stone for you to keep.

Angels need Angels
Janice Nolting

I'm a nurse and today I went to all my pre-admission testing doctor appointments for my upcoming surgery. My last appointment was with my primary care physician whom I've been going to for years. One nurse came into the room and did all my vitals, then my doctor came in and we talked for a little while. When it was time for my cardiogram, another nurse came in and said, "I can't believe you're here! I was just talking about you yesterday. A patient came in who you took care of in the intensive care unit during COVID. He talked about how well you took care of him, and his wife said you were a godsend. She said that you have Angels looking over you all the time because you worked with all those sick people for so long and never got sick yourself." That was my message. Someone was telling me that I have Angels looking out for me. I'm okay now.

Judith's Insight:
Your heart was yearning for a sign, searching for reassurance that your Angels were listening and could help ease the weight of

your decision about surgery. Clearly, they heard you. They used the words of others to deliver their message, making it undeniably clear. More than that, they reflected the impact you've had on those around you, acknowledging you as an Earthly Angel yourself. This was a dual gift from the divine lifting a significant burden from your shoulders while also offering heartfelt recognition and appreciation for the light you bring to others. What a beautiful and reassuring wink from the Angels.

Your surgery was a pivotal part of your journey, providing both clarity and support during a difficult time. Even Earthly Angels, like yourself, need encouragement, comfort, and reminders. Your Angels are walking with you, offering guidance and strength, ensuring that their presence is felt every step of the way.

Affirmations, this is what it's all about. We need them, we seek them, we crave them. When your boss tells you you're doing an amazing job, it fuels your motivation and continued success. When an actor receives applause or an award, it eases their anxiety, allowing them to wait for their next role with confidence. When a student earns high grades and graduates, it inspires them to take the next step, perhaps to pursue a master's degree or attend law school.

And when you're about to enter an operating room, few things are more comforting than hearing someone say, "You have an Angel watching over you." Especially when those words come from the people standing by your side. Affirmations are more than just words; they are encouragement, strength, and the push we need to take our next step with confidence, positivity, and trust. And when you receive that affirmation—you will own it. And you will move forward, stronger than before.

Shining Star

Danielle Pecile

I was up last night reading Guardian Angel stories. I've been trying to think of my own story as I know I've had my moments of connection with a loved one. I was trying to remember the signs my mom has sent me over the years. I went to sleep, and I had a dream of the sky and then saw the outline of a star being drawn. My late mother's name means star. It was also her nickname to some friends.

Judith's Insight:

The funny thing about signs is that sometimes they are more obvious than we expect. A star is a Heavenly light—something we wish upon, navigate by, and feel emotions toward when we see it. Stars carry many meanings, but when "star" is part of someone's name, you can be sure they were a light, a firecracker, or a trailblazer in their own way during this life.

Signs often appear in unconventional ways—through dreams, written words, or even right there in the sky—guiding us through life. Stars shine their brightest in the darkness, but that doesn't mean they disappear in the daylight. Your mom is in your heart, always bringing you a glow in the dark and warmth in the light.

Whether it's the twinkle of a star in the night sky or a quiet sign during the day, her presence is always with you. She will guide you, inspire you, and comfort you through these moments. Now, you might start noticing her passion and the messages she's sending a little more clearly. Keep your heart open, and you'll find her light shining brightly, no matter the time of day.

As you sit beneath the night sky, you may feel a single tear slip down your cheek. You might wonder why that star—usually so distant—suddenly feels clearer, closer, more real. Not always, but on this night, something is different. Along with the shifting darkness, you begin to sense a gentle light. A star that stands out from the rest, shining just for you. The soul you are reaching for is there with you, and, of course, that connection is absolutely real.

Find a Penny, Pick It Up, and All Day Long, You'll Have Good Luck
Jane French

Lately, I've been questioning the financial stability and future profitability of my business, a beautiful shop I've poured my heart into. Before opening my store today, I drove to my landlord's building to pay the rent. As I walked up to the entrance, I glanced down at the marble doorstep and spotted a brand-new, shiny penny. It was heads up, and the sun caught its surface, making the words *In God We Trust* glisten. I knew instantly it was a sign.

My grandmother always told me that finding a penny meant an Angel had dropped it from above as a reminder to keep the faith. Where there is faith, there is hope—and where there is hope, miracles can happen. That day turned out to be the most successful sales day my business had ever seen: $800 in sales.

Judith's Insight:
This message carried multiple layers of meaning, starting with where you found the penny—right as you were paying rent, a moment of financial uncertainty. That penny from Heaven was a direct message telling you, *Do not give up!* Your grandmother's wisdom rang true: *In God We Trust, and we are all helping you.* That was more than just a coin; it was a penny of faith.

Finding a penny and picking it up has long been a symbol

of luck and love, but this one held an even deeper significance. The moment you picked it up, the hope and reassurance it gave you were undeniable. It was as if your grandmother was standing right beside you, gently reminding you that brighter, shinier days were ahead.

That simple penny carried a promise—a token of faith, a sign of the love and support surrounding you, and a small but powerful message. Keep that penny close as a reminder that no matter how uncertain things may seem, the future holds much to look forward to.

The unknown can stir up doubt, even in the strongest of us. We try to stay optimistic, holding our heads high, but reality has a way of testing our resilience. Mistakes happen—sometimes over and over again, with no clear end in sight. That's how life teaches us. There is no formal class on how to avoid missteps; instead, we learn by navigating through them. This journey, however uncertain, must be taken with trust. Trust that there is an almighty captain guiding your ship or rowboat, keeping you afloat until you learn how to swim. Time to set sail.

Footprint of the Heart
Rose Ciolfi

My brother-in-law died unexpectedly on February 14. It was a crazy, emotional week. After his burial, we went back to the church for the repast. I was sitting and eating at a table with my bereaved sister, and there was the smallest little sign of a heart etched on the table so my sister could see it.

Judith's Insight:
Your brother-in-law was expressing his love in the most heartfelt way. The heart is a powerful symbol, made even more meaning-

ful by the fact that he passed on St. Valentine's Day. By sending you a heart, he is showing the unending love he still holds for all of you. This will continue to be his special sign, appearing in unexpected and beautiful places—whether in the clouds, in a newspaper, or even in the frost on a windowpane.

Think of the famous poem "Footprints in the Sand." This story carries a similar message. Whenever you come across a heart, it is his way of letting you know he is with you, watching over you. In time, you and your loved ones will recognize his presence in these moments. Each time you see a heart, know that he is saying, *My heart is carrying yours.* That will be his footprint, his eternal mark of love and support, reminding you that he is always near, walking beside you through life's journey.

Hearts hold meaning on so many levels. They symbolize love, life, breath, health, prosperity, and wisdom. As we move through life, people come and go, blending into the background. But sometimes, without warning, someone or something suddenly stands out. It may be something familiar, something you've seen countless times before, but on this particular day, it feels different. That is when your Angel decides to step in. They place a glow around a person, a moment, or an object, making it impossible for you to overlook. You might wonder why its meaning has changed, why it feels so significant now. It feels real because, in that instant, the heart is involved. And that is the moment you know your Angel has made their presence known.

It Only Takes One
Michele Litzky

I heard a story today that I couldn't wait to share. The friend of my business partner lost her mom last fall. She was missing her terribly and desperately wanted to hear her voice. She couldn't find a saved message on her phone. She needed a new phone and was hesitant because she didn't want to potentially lose anything in the transfer of data. Her husband offered to do the transfer for her promising he would be careful. She went to sleep and when she woke up, all the data had been transferred. She looked at the screen of her new phone and there was one voice message. It was from her mom. She had never heard it before. It was just a normal mom catch- up call. However, she didn't hang up the phone at the end and could be heard just rustling around her house, watching television, and blowing her nose for a few extra minutes. Talk about a sign.

Judith's Insight:

There was only one message. Her mom wanted her to take notice that she was reaching out. If there had been twenty-five messages, your friend might not have listened as closely. But this message was different, it was meant to stand out. Her mom wanted to make sure she was heard, just as she had always done in life. She was the kind of woman who stood out in a crowd, someone who did things her own way. And even in the Heavens, she found a way to make her presence known.

Your friend can expect her mom to continue finding ways to let her voice be heard. Whether through a familiar song playing at just the right moment, a sudden breeze that feels like a whisper, or an unexpected sign that tugs at the heart, she will make sure her love is felt. These moments will be reminders that she is still present, still guiding, and still watching over her daughter.

Capturing a moment is why we take pictures, record videos, or even sketch an image. But who is doing the recalling? The memories, the moments that truly stand out, are the ones that surprise us, making us pause and think, *What are the chances?* You may not have your mom's or dad's voice saved on an old phone, but you likely have photographs tucked away in the attic, waiting to be rediscovered. A gift reappearing out of nowhere can be a priceless reminder of their love, a quiet nod from beyond.

Life is shared between this world and the next, woven together through these small but powerful moments. Every vision, feeling, and sign tells a story. Each piece holds meaning, waiting to be recognized. Sometimes, all it takes is a glimpse, a touch, or a sudden awareness to feel the presence of those we love. And in an instant, it is as if they are swaddling us in the way they did when we were born.

Keep Watering to See What Grows
Diane

My husband just passed away, so I stayed with my daughter for a couple of days. When I came back home, I went to water my plants and found one flower blooming on the Christmas cactus. The plant was from my mother who passed away several years ago. I don't know if it was a sign.

Judith's Insight:

Of course, it's a sign. Not only is your husband at peace, but he is also letting you know that your mom and dad are with him. With the blooming flower, you may soon hear of a new pregnancy or a new relationship entering your world. Heavenly messages often come through earthly things like plants, trees, construction, or even statues. You have a lot of Guardian Angels, and they have a lot to say. Keep nurturing your life the way you would a garden. You never know what else will start growing along with your family.

What's a sign? What's a nod? What's a wink? It's whatever you believe it to be. Think of it as a whisper from a soul reaching out. If it weren't real, you wouldn't have noticed it. The moment you saw it, felt it, dreamed it, or lived it, you already knew it meant something. It's not rocket science. In fact, it's not science at all. It's something beyond explanation, which in turn makes it completely explainable. So, what's your story?

There's No Dragon in This Fly

Maria Greco Shanley

I've always been fascinated with dragonflies. About three months after my son passed away, his headstone had been put into place. I was sitting on the ground in front of his headstone crying. Suddenly, a little dragonfly landed on a flower to my left. I put my hand out and it came to me and stayed on my right hand for six minutes. I got up and walked to my car to get my phone to take a picture. The dragonfly stayed on top of my hand and didn't move. It just felt so right to me as a sign from my boy.

Judith's Insight:
Our loved ones often find meaningful ways to make their presence known. When he walked with you to the car, it was a reminder that even though he is no longer physically here, he will always be with you. Dragonflies symbolize strength, and each time you see one, you will feel that strength. Your son, now stronger than ever, will always find a way to connect with you, even if it is not through a dragonfly. His spirit will continue to reveal itself, always finding a way to hold your hand and offer comfort.

When the dragonfly landed on your hand, it was a sign that he will always be there to hold it. Each time you see a dragonfly, remember that he is reminding you of his presence, letting you know he is still by your side. Even though dragonflies may fly away quickly, this Guardian Angel will always ensure you feel his presence, reassuring you that he is never far away.

The word "dragon" may sound fierce, while "fly" brings a

sense of whimsy and adventure. Like Batman and Robin, or even Superman, the idea of superpowers often feels like pure fantasy. Who wouldn't love to be like Samantha from *Bewitched*, twinkling her nose to make things happen? Not just for everyday tasks like cleaning the house or fixing the car, but for something greater — like picking the winning lottery numbers or curing cancer.

What do dragonflies have to do with any of this? For some, nothing at all. But for others, they mean everything, especially depending on when and how they appear. Our guides and Angels use signs we can relate to, helping us recognize their presence and the messages they send. In simple terms, they are just miracles. And miracles, though extraordinary, happen all the time in the lives of ordinary people.

REFLECTION 10

Faith

*Today there is a message out there for you! It may
be to protect you, or perhaps make you look in a different
direction. You may have a detour and have to drive
down a different street. Someone's watching over you
and sending a helping hand even if you are not
seeing or feeling it. Have faith.*

—Judith Turner

Needing a Little Help from Our Friends, Our Angels

S. V.

My dad needed prophylactic surgery on his femur to remove a tumor. He was very stubborn and refused to get the surgery. I was inconsolably crying and thinking catastrophic thoughts, worrying what might happen if his femur or hip were to fracture if he didn't have the surgery. Terrible thoughts preoccupied my mind, like my dad falling on concrete or the street. I started to pray and felt guided to watch the show *Friends*. I turned on an episode and one of the characters said something that resonated with me. It was something like, "Although they're your parents, after a certain point, you must let go, even if you know better. You have to let them make their own mistakes." At that moment I knew I had to let go and stop trying to control the situation by convincing my dad to have the surgery.

A year and a half later, while my dad was in a pool, his femur fractured but the water prevented him from falling. He ended up having emergency surgery, but things turned out to be okay.

Judith's Insight:

Believe it or not, Guardian Angels have unique ways of getting your attention. Messages can come through unexpected vessels—television, songs, newspaper headlines—delivering words meant to be heard. Pay attention to the ones that stand out, the ones that seem to speak directly to you. For you, these messages were especially meaningful because they helped free your soul. As much as we may want to change the minds of others, sometimes life steps in to protect us, sending signs to change our own minds instead.

Letting go of control means letting go of fear and

anxiety—feelings anyone can experience in difficult situations. In this story, it was a daughter learning to release her need for control, which in her heart was simply another form of care and protection. The tides had already turned for this young woman, much like they do for parents watching their children grow. Many parents wrestle with the same thoughts, using the same words, trying to guide their children: When do I let go? How do I let go?

Letting go is a process, and often, by the time parents reach that moment, their children are already adults. After years of stepping up, knowing the precise way to step back is where Guardian Angels come in. It takes signs, patience, understanding, and a great deal of trust in timing. It is all about the right time, the right place, and sometimes, a few lightning bolts from above to remind us that faith is stronger than fear.

Crossing Souls

Samantha D.

A week before I found out I was pregnant, I had a dream that my grandmother (who had passed away) and my husband's aunt, whom I never met and had passed away years ago, were standing next to me as I lay in a hospital bed. They looked at each other as one of them held a baby and said, "I think she's ready" and then handed me the baby. A week later we found out I was pregnant.

On Thanksgiving, we went to my husband's uncle's house (he was the husband of the aunt who passed away) and right when we announced our pregnancy the uncle said, "I had a dream you were pregnant." It was like my husband's aunt was telling him they sent our baby from Heaven.

Dreaming—a Heavenly word on its own, but when it carries a message from an Angel, it becomes a Guardian Angel story that many long for. Dreams like these are so powerful that they feel as if you have just sat down for lunch with a loved one who is no longer here.

Babies are always welcomed into this world with the presence of Angels, many of whom will follow them throughout their lives as Guardian Angels. Everyone has Angels watching over them, some they knew in life, others they have never met. Often, when someone passes around the time of a pregnancy announcement or near a child's birth, they become part of this guiding presence.

This baby is exceptionally blessed and will make their presence known in a remarkable way. While every child is special, this one will stand out. This story reveals just how extraordinary they are, already surrounded by Angels and embraced by the love of both parents. Coming into the world with strength and determination, this baby carries the spirit of an Angel. They will be cherished, supported, and enveloped in love, a living reminder of Heaven's embrace.

Vivid dreams and pregnancy go hand in hand, like peanut butter and jelly or peas and carrots. Seldom do you hear news of a pregnancy without someone saying, "I knew it," or "I had a dream." It often begins with a feeling about the baby's gender, followed by the ever-exciting name game—what should we call them? Whom do we want to honor? When a child is given a name or even a single letter from someone who has passed, it is as if that soul is being called upon to be their Guardian Angel.

Then, when the baby is born, the connections deepen—resemblances to past relatives, echoes of those who came before them. And as the baby grows, their first words and the names they give to things spark moments of recognition. It's why the saying *out of the mouths of babes* holds so much truth.

When a child enters the world, it feels as though the gates of Heaven open, filling the air with stories and memories. The significance of the birth date, the baby's weight and length, even the color of their hair—all become part of a larger story, filled with miraculous moments and whispered connections to the past. Conversations about Guardian Angels come alive, as loved ones share their own experiences of the unseen but deeply felt presence that surrounds new life.

And so, life continues, weaving together the past, present, and future. It all brings to mind a great quote from my dad: "Only God brings babies."

Angelic
Judith Turner

As I sit here with a bag of ice on my arm, I realize how important it is to have and believe in my Guardian Angels to help me get through the big and little events in life. It started last night when my brother sent a text to me and my sisters with a picture of a police car with a license plate that had my dad's badge number on it. My brother didn't know that today I was going for some important health tests early in the morning. Maybe I didn't call him because I was in a state of denial. When one doctor tells you he's getting another doctor to see you under urgent conditions, maybe it is urgent. So, I got up at the crack of dawn and headed into Columbia Presbyterian Hospital in New York to see one of my doctors. It was a smooth ride into New York, and it felt lucky when they took me into the office early. The day was heading in the right direction. That license plate picture was coming in clutch in my head because I felt my dad with me.

After four hours of testing, the doctor told me many things, but I only heard just a little of what he was saying, unable to process it all at once. He told me I needed to get two more tests across the street right now, and he was also moving up my MRI appointment. Although I was a wreck and am deathly afraid of needles, I went to get the tests done. After the first test I was sent to get blood work. As I checked in, I asked for my special blood taker named Ricky who has always been gentle and kind to me in the past. When I approached the phlebotomists' office, a woman behind the desk started asking me questions. I guess I was at my breaking point because I started crying and I didn't know why because Ricky was there and was going to take my blood. I guess I got overwhelmed with all the tests and the unknown reasons behind them. I was talking aloud about what I was actually truly going through, and as I spoke, I was hysterically crying.

Suddenly, this woman came from behind the desk and hugged me. I asked her name, but she just hugged me, and she said to me, "God is with you." I asked her name again and she said, "Angelica." I said, "You are my Angel today!" She told me that God was going to make this situation okay. She told me she was here for me, and the next time I showed up in the office, she would be here to help me through.

I was then called in to have my blood taken. When I came out, Angelica wasn't there. I went to walk away, and she came out of nowhere once again and gave me a hug. She said, "You wait and see, you are going to be fine. They will find it and fix it!"

Judith's Insight:
Sometimes even our Guardian Angels need to call in reinforcements, using Earthly Angels to step in, show up, or create what might seem like a distraction. The license plate was meant to give me confidence and support, helping me face a daunting day. That picture surely brought a smile to my face and warmth to my heart. Facing the unknown and undergoing emergency testing is beyond frightening. At that overwhelming moment, a Guardian Angel's embrace was exactly what I needed. Angelica's words—

saying that God was with me—may have been unexpected, but they were the purest and most comforting gift I could have received. If I hadn't felt such deep emotion, I might not have fully recognized how others were sending me strength, reassurance, and a much-needed hug.

In times of need, Earthly Angels step in to assist the Heavenly ones. Even for Angels, there is no "I" in team—only in time. Earthly Angels are those who appear seemingly out of nowhere, sometimes as complete strangers. Other times, they are people we know who show up at just the right moment, becoming an unexpected source of mercy and support.

I share this story to inspire others to show up for someone the way others have shown up for me. On this particular day, it was Angelica. But more importantly, I share this so you can reflect on the Earthly Angels who have touched your own heart. Angelica's unexpected hug and reassuring words left a lasting impact on me, just as I am sure there has been a moment like this in your own life.

Not all Earthly Angels perform grand gestures or save lives. Sometimes, they simply choose to be kind. Not as a random act of kindness, but as a genuine, intentional moment of compassion. And when kindness is met with strength, it becomes something even greater—the kindness of all souls, woven together in the most meaningful way.

'Tis the Season

Diane

It's the holiday season, and for the last couple of days, I've been feeling down. My husband passed away ten months ago. Today I took his truck and went in early to work for our Secret Santa exchange. I wasn't really paying attention while I was driving.

The pick-up truck in front of me was making a left-hand turn, so I came to a stop behind it. On the bottom of the tailgate were the words, "You're never alone." It took my breath away and was such a wow moment.

Judith's Insight:

This is a powerful example of hearing your Guardian Angel speak to you. These messages can come in many forms—through the words of a child, written on a sign, or even spoken aloud by a stranger. Your husband felt your loneliness and wanted to bring you comfort to help you through the holidays. You were speaking to him aloud, and he had been sending you signs for days, but your pain was so overwhelming that you weren't able to see, hear, or feel them. So, he found a way to create a message you couldn't miss—a billboard, loud and clear.

The other profound thing is that you wrote this story in a book with the exact same message: *You Are Never Alone.* That in itself is incredibly meaningful.

Santa symbolizes many things—a gift, a holiday experience, joy, and the celebration of life. The car represents moving forward, not leaving the past behind but continuing to grow and progress. Just know that when you receive these signs, they are not coincidences. They are gentle reminders from above showing you that love never fades. Just know when you see a sign like this, you are being told, "I am with you every step of the way."

Sometimes It Is All about the Outfit
Catherine DeCoite

My sister, Michelle, loved the band the Rolling Stones. I was looking for an outfit for my grandson, and I found a sweat suit that screamed out to me with the Rolling Stones, iconic tongue and lips logo. It was the only one of its kind and in his size hanging in the store. My sister passed away in September. It was definitely a message from her.

Judith's Insight:

This is a remarkable story. Many people don't consider clothing as a sign from Guardian Angels, but in this case, your sister Michelle was using it to get your attention. She wanted you to know she is at peace and comfortably home. That is just the beginning of what clothing can represent. The shirt carried more than just fabric—it brought hugs, memories, and connections to her favorite band, a reminder to listen to music when you want to feel her presence. Michelle is sending you songs that will continue to bring comfort. She knows you need a hug right now, and what better way to send one than through your grandson? I'm sure you wrapped him in countless hugs while he wore that shirt, knowing deep down that she was on the other side of every embrace. Michelle had a lot to say, and you can expect even more signs to come.

The skin you are in is what truly matters. Whenever we come across something that feels like a sign from a loved one who has passed, it brings comfort. In this story, it was clothing. But have you ever walked into a place and felt like you had been there before, even if you hadn't? It just feels like home—something about it resembles, reminds, or stirs emotions.

There are also moments when people who have passed make their presence known through their favorite everyday things, maybe a car, a restaurant, a cigar, a hammer, or a baseball cap. These were objects they loved in life, and when we see them, it's more than just a memory; it continues to give us a gentle nudge to prove over and over again to never give up looking.

Ask and You Shall Receive

Vicki D'Auria

My son Brian passed away in April. October 25 would have been his twenty-seventh birthday. We decided to celebrate his life by doing what he loved the most and that was to travel and play in the casino. We decided to take the same cruise he and I took six years ago. Well, all I can tell you was that he was on that cruise again. I asked for signs and boy did he deliver!

All I wanted was a starry night to talk to him. When I walked outside on our cruise ship, I saw a shooting star. After, I asked him to please send me another shooting star. After about an hour and not seeing one, we went back to our cabin. I stepped out to our balcony and dropped a small bear button into the ocean (my nickname for him was Baby Bear). As soon as it dropped, I told him I loved him. When I looked up, there was a shooting star! The following morning, I asked him for a heart. I didn't see a heart all day. When I went back to our cabin, I found a beautiful heart surprise. Keep talking to your loved ones. They do listen!

Judith's Insight:

Ask and you shall receive could very well be the mantra of all Guardian Angels—sending hugs, nods, winks, dreams, and messages to remind you that you are never alone. In life, we are often encouraged to manifest what we want, and the same applies to our Angels. They need to hear us ask.

Most of the time, their presence is subtle, showing up in ways we might not immediately recognize. A message falls into place, something unusual catches your eye, or a small moment stands out more than it should. Then, one day, a sign appears so vividly that it starts connecting with other moments—the object that fell from a closet, the misplaced keys, the light you were sure your partner left on. You get into your car, and suddenly, a song with deep significance plays on the radio. If you're not attuned to these signs, it might be time to start asking for them. In this story, the boy truly delivered.

Shooting stars are among the most powerful symbols—an Angel's message appearing in the blink of an eye. The name *shooting star* suggests something fleeting, but in reality, it is a message moving at the speed of light, designed to capture your attention. This Angel moved a star across the sky, ensuring it wouldn't be missed. The message was clear: *Something special is about to happen.* Keep your eyes and heart open for what's to come.

The Blind Hug
Michele Litzky

This may seem like a weird occurrence, but I'm taking it as a sign. Eight years ago, I traveled to Anguilla with my friend Kim. One afternoon we met a woman, Hattie. She was about eighty years old and the star of a reality show about cougars. We were fascinated with her and spent the afternoon together, drove her home, and continued our holiday. My friend Kim passed away in 2021. I haven't thought about Hattie since that afternoon in 2014. I also haven't heard a Heavenly peep from Kim. No signs, no visits, no dreams. Today, out of nowhere, I received a text from Hattie.

Judith's Insights:
This is a twofold Angel story. Hattie reached out to you, but it was really Kim who created the moment for that to happen. Kim reaches out to you, but you may not always notice it's her. There's no coincidence that you share her love and support; she gives it to you when you may not even know you need it. Lucky girl.

Guardian Angels have unique ways of saying hello and reminding us they are by our side. *Pulling a memory out of the closet* is one of those ways. Sometimes, it takes years for a *memory of coincidence* to find its way into our path at just the right moment. In a story like this, Kim likely reached out to Hattie as well, prompting her to connect with you. They say it takes a village, and Guardian Angels often use that village to deliver their messages to the right people.

The places we go, the meals we share, and even brief conversations with strangers become moments woven into our lives. These encounters happen for a reason. Memories are stored deep in our souls, waiting for the right time to resurface, bringing with them emotions that are meant to be felt again.

Our joy should always speak louder than our sorrows. When a joyful memory is pulled out of the cupboard, it serves a purpose—to stomp out those sorrows and remind us that love, laughter, and connection are always stronger than grief.

Michael's Story

Michael Russo

My son Michael passed away when he was twenty-nine years old, on September 25, 2021. I never thought about signs before that, even though I lost my mom at a young age, my brother, and then my dad. I have heard that feathers are signs. I had a feather on my side-view mirror of my car. I didn't think much about it. Then last week my daughter found a Saint Jude medal in the dryer in our home. No one had this medal in my house. When my son Michael was in the Intensive care unit, we prayed to Saint Jude for his intercession on Michael's behalf. We had actual relics from Saint Jude that were given to us by a friend and placed on Michael during his hospital stay. I do believe that this was a sign, but if anyone has any thoughts on this, please let me know. As I said, this is all new to me.

Judith's Insight:

I am sure Michael is reaching out in every way he can. The feather that found you is his way of letting you know he left a piece of himself behind, just as birds do when they shed a feather. It is a sign that he has not gone far and that he will continue to send reminders of his presence. Pay attention to what is happening when you find a feather—it may hold a message meant just for you.

As for St. Jude, he is often prayed to for strength in difficult times. It was no coincidence that this sign appeared. Michael's legacy is one of love, kindness, and helping others, much like the work of St. Jude. The signs we receive are never random; they are chosen with purpose, placed in our path when we need them most.

Your son Michael wants to continue spreading love and support for children, and you will find a way to keep his spirit alive. When we hold our loved ones in our hearts, they never truly leave us. That is how he will live on.

Some of us quietly recognize that something or someone is looking out for us, even if we never say it aloud. It is the inner conversation we have when we see a sign and, at first, do not even realize it is part of a bigger message. Sometimes, it takes years to connect the moments, the small miracles, until one day, we recognize them for what they are—the arms of our Angels, catching us when we need them most.

Heartache is easier to remember than the warmth of a message that arrives at the perfect milestone in our lives. But it is during times of loss and struggle that these winks and nods from beyond become part of a greater picture—one we may not fully understand but can still feel. That picture may contain words, both spoken and unspoken, moments that seem small but carry great meaning.

The things we are left with—a St. Jude medal, an urn filled

with ashes, a prayer card, an old handwritten note—once held comfort in our grief. Over time, they become something more. They transform into reminders that bring lightness, lifting our hearts like feathers when they feel weighed down by sorrow. That feather you found is not just a symbol of loss; it is a sign of love, meant to remind you that Michael's presence is still with you, giving you the strength to carry on.

This quiet but meaningful sign is meant to lift your spirits and reassure you. Think of it as a heartfelt wink or nod, a way of saying, "I see you. I'm here." It is a subtle yet powerful way of letting you know they are cheering you on and surrounding you with love and encouragement.

The timing of a feather's arrival is just as important as its presence. If you come across a feather, take note of the time on the clock; it may provide deeper insight into the message being sent. Feathers can carry many meanings, but at their core, they are a way for someone walking beside you, from beyond, to capture your attention and remind you of their unwavering support. If a feather means anything, it means that an Angel has passed by you and left you with a piece of its wing.

Still in the Game

Jan Turen

It was late at night, and I had just fallen asleep when I was suddenly jolted awake. From my bed, I saw a shadow near my bedroom window that looked just like my son, Kevin, even though he was no longer with us. As I focused, I realized it was only a six-foot houseplant. Still, I couldn't shake the feeling that Kevin's spirit was close. I spoke to the shadow and said, "I just fell asleep, and I'm really tired. Can you come back tomorrow?" Then I drifted back to sleep.

The next morning, I went about my usual routine. After getting my coffee, I started playing my standard *New York Times* word games on my iPad. These games had always been a special bond between Kevin and me. Though we lived far apart, we stayed connected through football games, word games, and Hollywood news — our top contenders for shared conversations.

I breezed through Connections and moved on to Cronos, but for some reason, the game wasn't working properly. My correct answers wouldn't register, so I gave up and switched to Wordle. On my first attempt, I got one letter right. But with each new guess, the letter "O" kept appearing first, even though I hadn't typed it. Frustrated, I set the game aside, assuming it was a glitch.

Later that night, before bed, I decided to give Wordle another try. Three rows in, I finally realized — the first letter really was "O." That was when it hit me. Kevin had been trying to give me a hint from Heaven. I wished I had noticed earlier; it would have helped my score. From now on, I promise to follow Kevin's lead.

As I write this, it happens to be Kevin's birthday. Happy Birthday, Kev!

Judith's Insight:

Your sense of Kevin's presence needed validation — something tangible, something undeniable. He knows exactly how to reach you in ways that are uniquely yours, whether it's through a Hollywood headline that suddenly catches your attention or the electrifying tension of a football game that makes you feel like he's sitting right beside you, sharing in the excitement.

This story wasn't just about feeling his presence — it was about a connection that transcended the ordinary. The soul reacts in ways that may seem incomprehensible to others but are deeply meaningful to you. The game was Kevin's way of showing you that he's still *in the game* with you, proving his presence and reminding you of the bond you still share. Even now, he finds ways to entertain you, reassuring you that love and connection remain, no matter the distance.

The letter "O" is also the chemical symbol for oxygen—a fitting representation of the life you gave Kevin and the one he now gives back to you as your Guardian Angel. His presence is the breath of life that continues to bridge the space between the physical and the spiritual, between earth and Heaven.

We all need a breath of fresh air, whether it's through a trip to Disney, sailing around an island, watching a movie, or simply taking a quiet walk in the park. Finding space in our minds and hearts allows us to reconnect with those we love, even without formal meditation. Sometimes, it happens effortlessly—during a mindless game, a stroll along the beach, or a peaceful moment when the world quiets. Those moments create the perfect opening for conversations with the ones we miss, spoken aloud or whispered softly in the heart.

My Purple Heart
Danielle Gibson

I saw this purple heart on my arm while taking a shower. I had never seen it before. This has been an emotional month for me because my mother's actual birthday and Heavenly birthday were only seven days apart. I believe this purple heart was a sign from my mother letting me know that she loves me. This may be just a bruise, but how does it come to look like a heart? No one can make that happen, so I believe it's from the spirit world. I love my mom and dad, and I know they are with me because I have them within me.

Judith's Insight:
This is so much more than you realize. Yes, your mom is send-

ing you a heart to show her love and wrap you in a hug, but she is also acknowledging the battle you are facing. She sees your struggle and wants you to know she is fighting alongside you. You are not alone in the health challenges you are facing. Even when you don't speak your fears aloud, she hears them. Even when you don't shed tears, she feels them. Even when you don't ask for help, she stands beside you. In this moment, she is handing you the Purple Heart of life—a sign of strength, resilience, and unwavering love.

The sunlight creates pictures if you take the time to look. Rainbows can appear on pillows with just the right lighting. A crumpled piece of trash can take the shape of unexpected art. The world is filled with these subtle yet powerful signs—messages meant to grab your attention at just the right moment. These glimpses of "life art or Angel art" are there for a reason, aligning with exactly what you need in that instant.

Take a moment and reflect on what is weighing on your heart. That is what they are trying to help you with. When something stands out, your instinctive reaction says it all, whether it's *Look at this, how did this happen?* Or, *I can't believe it.* These moments are not random. You wait and see, your need will be met as someone is there helping it happen. Keep the faith.

Never Doubt a Cardinal
Lisailene

I have been going through some serious health issues. Although I've had all positive outcomes, mentally it has been a roller coaster ride of emotions. Every lump, pain, or cramp sends me to the dark side. I have been asking my Guardian Angel to look after me and send me signs that he is with me during these difficult times. It seems like forever since I've had a sign. Today

I was thinking that the cardinals that always visited me in the past haven't been around, and I was sad. When I got in my car, I looked to the right and a beautiful, vibrant cardinal was sitting in the grass.

Judith's Insight:

This is a different kind of cardinal story, but still a beautiful way for you to receive a hug from above. Sometimes, our Angels change their signs based on what we are going through, which is why we may miss them at first. The proof of that is simple—you asked, and you received. The cardinal in the grass showed you that instead of looking up into the trees, you had to look down. You were feeling low, and the cardinal appeared at your level to lift you up. It was a magical response, shifting your mood from emptiness and restlessness to comfort and reassurance. This was your sign that you are being heard and held.

Every cardinal story is unique, and the way it appears adds to its meaning. Was it in a tree? At your window? On a plaque? On a Christmas card? The unifying message of a cardinal is always one of love, but the details of its appearance create a deeper personal significance. Seeing one cardinal may brighten your day. Seeing five may bring an even bigger sense of connection. If someone gifts you a piece of jewelry with a cardinal on it, it is a shared hug, a hug from the giver and another from your Guardian Angel.

After a long, difficult day, spotting a cardinal might be the reminder you need that relief is on the way. It may be telling you that your hard work is about to be recognized or that better days are just ahead. The next time you see a cardinal, take a moment to look around. Something else may be there, waiting to reveal itself—another sign of hope, a symbol of happiness, and a promise that change is right around the corner. Or perhaps across the street. Open your eyes along with your heart.

Heavenly Angel Message Day 11:11
Rhonda Charles

I saw two beautiful blue jays fly from a bush in my yard at 11:11 a.m. today. Coincidence? I think not.

Judith's Insight:
The date on the calendar or the time on the clock didn't matter—what mattered was the message coming your way. If you ask anyone about seeing certain numbers repeatedly, many will tell you they believe those numbers are trying to communicate something special. This number stood out to you, not just because it was eleven twice, but because of how many times you've seen it and felt the need to take a second look.

One reason you looked again was to confirm you saw it correctly. The other was to check if it was still there. It's funny how certain numbers seem to linger, as if they are holding on longer than a minute. The real reason for the extra glance, though, was your mind trying to decode its meaning. If you are spiritual, you may even find yourself speaking back to the number. You might say, "Okay, I know it's you," or "Oh, what a relief—you approve of that money I spent," or even "All right, I'll hang in there." Some might whisper something more personal like, "Okay, Mom, of course I'm going to do the right thing."

In this story, two blue jays appeared alongside the numbers, adding another layer to the message. You have two very special Guardian Angels reaching out to wipe away your heartache, even the pain you thought no one else knew about. Don't rush to react too quickly—stay steady, think before you take flight, and keep your focus on what truly matters. Keeping your eyes on the bigger picture will bring you more happiness in the long run.

The appearance of 11:11 is believed by many to represent the most Heavenly of numbers. Even those who don't usually believe in Guardian Angel messages tend to recognize its significance when it appears on a clock. This number doesn't represent just one Angel, it signals many lining up for you. Some might compare it to an army standing in formation or the King's Guard at the palace. Others might relate it to something personal, cultural, or religious.

These numbers are like a protective barrier, standing at the border between the seen and unseen, offering security, guidance, and reassurance. They don't just appear to warn or shield you — they also remind you that if you need protection in any way — whether in health, finances, wisdom, or clarity — help is there. They show up at just the right time, much like how we glance at a clock at the perfect moment. Like sand slipping through an hourglass, these winks and hugs from above appear as grains of reassurance beneath your feet, keeping you grounded when you need them most. And when necessary, they turn to concrete — solid, unwavering, and present in your everyday life. Guardian Angels continuously build strength like a solid foundation for you to walk on, sturdy and strong.

REFLECTION 11

Peace

*The birds may chirp as if they're speaking just to you.
A movie might stir a memory, or a picture may appear
at just the right moment.*

*Today, something will touch your heart, a small sign,
a gentle reminder, a fleeting moment of hope. It may
bring you a ray of sunshine, a warm embrace, or
the reassurance that an Angel is not only watching
over you but guiding you toward peace.*

—Judith Turner

Darling Daisies

Patricia McKenna

In our church, you can honor the memory of your beloved deceased by sponsoring announced Masses, the tabernacle candle, and the altar flowers for the week. Last year, on the one-year anniversary of my mother's death, October 7, 2021, I purchased the altar flowers in memory of Mary Sasson, with love from Patrick, Patricia, Liam, and Victoria.

That weekend, poor Father Abraham was running around trying to find flowers for the altar. He stopped me on my way into church on Sunday and apologized that he was only able to find a couple of pots of daisies. I said, "Father, you would have no way of knowing this, but my mother's favorite flower was the daisy." She even had them in her wedding bouquet! When the week was over, he gave me the two little pots, and I planted them in front of my house.

We were at Lake George, New York, for vacation this past week, and it was the second anniversary of my mother's passing. When I came home from the trip, the daisies had grown and flourished so much that I was in awe. Now, if this isn't a sign from my mother in Heaven, I don't know what is! Thank you, Father Abraham, I will always treasure your kindness.

Judith's Insight:

Your mom knows you so well. You honored her anniversary by requesting altar flowers, a gesture of love, reverence, and remembrance. In return, she made sure to send a sign back to you. Most people wouldn't have remembered the daisies in her wedding bouquet, but you did. You weren't there that day, yet you cherished every detail of her life, and she knew it. Those daisies were her way of reaching out, a symbol of her love and recognition of the deep bond you share. Just as you sent love and warmth to her, she sent it right back, reminding you that your connection is as strong as ever.

They say when you talk to plants, they grow. Maybe it's the oxygen from your breath, or maybe it's something more — someone out there helping them along. In this case, it was daisies. But it could have been any flower, a rose, a hydrangea, or even a tree that had never bloomed before suddenly bursting into flowers. Nature has a way of working magically, often with a little help from above.

You may have your own story — like being diagnosed with a health issue that suddenly disappears, thinking you failed a test only to find out you passed, or being completely broke and worried about tomorrow when you suddenly find money in a wallet you've checked a hundred times before. Or maybe you lose your car keys, for instance, and though you don't find them right away, you stumble upon a spare key you never even knew you had.

These are the mini miracles of life. Some are small and some are life-changing. We may think we know how things work, but then something happens that we can't quite explain. That's when we realize — maybe, just maybe — it's the work of Angels.

Nanny's Love!
Brianne Deptuch Kuder

Since the day my Nanny passed, I have felt her presence through signs. I could tell a million stories about the ways she has reached out, even on days when I least expect it.

I work in a very busy office, where I rarely have time to take a break, let alone eat lunch. The other day, I finally had a few free minutes and realized I was hungry, so I decided to step out for a slice of pizza. Even though it was hot and muggy outside, it felt good just to step away for a moment. Sometimes, a simple walk is all I need to reset and recalibrate.

As I walked toward the pizza parlor, I looked down and spotted a $5 bill on the street. I glanced around to see if anyone was nearby, but the street was empty. I picked up the bill, still scanning the area in case someone was looking for it. I tucked it into my pocket but didn't use it to pay for my lunch, just in case someone came back searching for it after I left the store.

The moment I saw that $5 bill, I thought of my Nanny. It was her way of buying me lunch, her reminder that I needed to take a break and take care of myself. She knows I spend more time working hard and caring for my patients than I do looking after myself, and this was her way of telling me to slow down, even if just for a meal.

Judith's Insight:

Let's start with this: It was a $5 bill. Pennies from Heaven don't always come in the form of pennies; sometimes, they come as dollars too. Nanny wasn't just sending you a sign — she was sending you comfort, nourishment, and a reminder to take care of yourself. The moment you saw that bill, you felt her energy, as if she were right there beside you. The number five seems to hold significance as well, so keep an eye out for it in the future. It may be another way she chooses to reach out.

But Nanny wasn't just helping you find money or buy lunch — she was helping you find something even more important. She was offering you peace of mind, gently guiding you toward a better balance in your life. She wanted to remind you that, as much as you dedicate yourself to others, you need to take a moment to care for yourself too.

Living life with a helping hand is far better than believing you don't have one. As every Guardian Angel might say, *It's so much easier for me to help you when you listen.* If you don't believe in Guardian Angels, think of it as the universe speaking to you. Being open-minded means being open-hearted, and those with any spiritual belief understand the comfort that comes from knowing something greater is looking out for us.

There are givers, and then there are givers. In this case, it was your Nanny, but it could be a grandmother, a loved one, or even someone unexpected sending the same message: *Pay attention to yourself.* Although you dedicate your time to caring for others, now you need to learn to care for yourself. Sometimes, it takes a grand, undeniable sign—like a billboard in Times Square—to get our attention. But Nanny's message is simple: *You are a giver who helps others but always remember to take care of yourself and I'll do what I can from the other side. I got you, Princess Me.*

A Shared Heavenly Hug
Judith Turner & Marie S.

It's November 28, and while I'm in the middle of a face-to-face meeting, my phone rings. I hesitate for a moment, caught in a deep conversation, but something about the caller's name on the screen draws me in. I glance at it again, feeling an unshakable pull to pick up. It's as if the phone itself is calling me, not just the person on the other end.

Apologizing for the interruption, I excuse myself and answer. "Marie? Is everything okay?" Marie's voice is shaky. "I don't know. I'm just driving, and I'm upset and out of sorts. I'm having a rough moment, and I had to call you."

She takes a deep breath and continues, "I was driving on the New Jersey Turnpike, feeling overwhelmed, when suddenly I felt your mom come down and wrap me in a great big hug. It was so real, like she was right there, holding me."

Marie is crying, and suddenly, so am I. Through my tears, I manage to say, "Today is her death anniversary."

We both fall silent for a moment, letting the realization sink in. Marie was meant to call at that exact moment, to deliver a message from my mom. "So, it *was* her," she whispers.

We spend the next few minutes reminiscing—talking about my mom's warmth, how she welcomed everyone into her home, and how she became a mother figure to so many without even realizing it.

Judith's Insight:

This is a story of a shared Heavenly hug—one that we both needed, for different reasons, at the same time, from the same mom. Though Marie and I didn't share the same mother by blood, the love my mom gave extended far beyond family. Her kindness, generosity, and embrace could make anyone feel at home. In that moment, her hug reached both of us, just when we needed it most.

For Marie, it was a comforting reminder of the motherly friendship they shared—proof that their bond was real and still alive. For me, November 28 is always a difficult day. I was lucky enough to call her Mommy and honored to call her my best friend. The signs I receive always tell a story straight from my heart. I was more than happy to share my mom's love with my friend who needed a hug. It was just like her to embrace more than one person at a time—she did it every day on Earth while raising five children of her own, and many others who knew her as Mama, Jud, or Clare.

Signs don't always come for just one person. Winks, nods, and waves from the beyond can touch many at once—friends, family, even strangers in the same place, all seeing something meaningful in their own way. Think of fireworks. Hundreds or even thousands of people watch them light up the sky, but maybe one particular spark means something special to someone, or to many people at once.

The message here is about *sharing*. Whether it's love, children, a job, a home, a feeling, or even a meal, sharing takes on a whole new meaning when you realize how Guardian Angels send their signs. They give us a heads-up on what's about to be shared, reminding us that we are all connected. We are all in this together, we are FAMILY!

A Bright Sign from Dad
Lizbeth Kall

My husband passed away in 2015, and yesterday my daughter got married at the same church as we did. While she was saying her vows, suddenly, the altar got bright. I thought maybe someone had turned up the lights. I looked up at the ceiling and noticed the light was coming from the windows on the roof. I think her dad was there, giving them his blessing, and I felt at peace when I saw the light.

Judith's Insight:

Of course, he had to find a way to make his presence known on this special day. Milestones in our lives often become the perfect moments for Guardian Angels to make their grand entrance. And this was no exception.

The light wasn't just a blessing for this beautiful occasion — it was his way of taking his rightful place at the altar, standing beside her, giving her away. He did it his way. You noticed. The light was his way of bringing you peace, standing beside her in spirit. It was a radiant reminder of love all around, wrapping everyone in warmth. I have no doubt it brought comfort to so many, a silent embrace from him to all of you. He was showing his best self — his love, his presence, his hug — on a day that meant so much.

Milestones often have a way of repeating history, carrying echoes of the past into the present. Weddings, graduations, birthdays, funerals, baptisms, bar mitzvahs—these are the moments when Guardian Angels show up, finding their place in the celebration however they can. And when they do, they leave the people around them with a "Was that real?" moment—an "Aha!" realization that something greater was at play.

License Plates Talking
Maria Greco Shanley

My son passed away eight and a half years ago. This morning, I visited the cemetery and asked him for a sign.

While driving later that day, something caught my eye—a license plate right in front of me. It was my son's exact birthday, April 2. I couldn't believe it. I was so happy to see it and knew instantly that it was his way of reaching out to me today.

How many of us receive signs like this? Do any of you ask for specific signs and find that they appear?

Judith's Insight:
Ask and you shall receive. Signs come in many forms, and in this story, a license plate became the perfect messenger. But this wasn't just about driving or finding your way to work or the store—it was about recognizing the path that leads to the signs your loved one is sending.

How do I know? Because you asked, and he answered, right there in front of you. It's as if license plates were designed not just to identify cars, but to carry messages for those paying attention. And at that moment, this one wasn't just for the driver, it was meant for you. A reminder, a hug, a confirmation that you are being watched over.

License plates aren't the only billboards we see on the road. Anything that catches your eye in a way that feels special could be a sign. The beauty of this story is in the simplicity of *Ask and you shall receive*. Sometimes, signs appear as clear as a bright, cloudless sky—direct, unmistakable, and just for you.

Other times, they arrive like the wind, soft and subtle, or like an airplane landing, smooth and effortless, or with a little turbulence before they settle into place. What does that mean? In this story, the message was immediate—no guessing, no searching, just a moment of clarity. But some signs take time, unfolding through small moments, little details, and unexpected connections before they fully reveal themselves.

No matter how they come, the message will always be clear in the end. Hugs from beyond are never lost in translation. Either way, hugs or messages will come across very clearly, and the message will land safely, and so will you.

Jessie's Story
Jessica

On December 3, 2022, I was called by my mom's doctor to hurry up and come to the hospital as it was only a matter of hours, maybe minutes before I would never see her again. Frantically, I called an Uber whose driver rushed me to the hospital as fast as he could. I arrived at the hospital a little before 1:00 p.m. My mom was crossing over in my arms and passed at 1:35 p.m. A week later I went to my synagogue and prayed. I asked God for a sign because I just needed to know my mom was close. I became emotional and decided to leave. I turned to my friend Audrey and said, "I'm ready, let's go." As I was walking out of the main sanctuary, there was a man who looked so familiar. I couldn't help but stare. I grabbed on to his shoulder and looked straight in his eyes. I started to cry and said, "I know you; I know you! This time last week at the exact time, I contacted you to take me to my mom. It's you! You were my Uber driver last Saturday that took me to my mom as fast as you could. It was pouring rain." He looked at me and said, "Yes, I did drive you. I remember you were crying and were so upset. Tell me, how is your mom, Sharon Siegel?" I couldn't believe he remembered my mom's name. He must have heard me talking to the doctors and the nurses. He said I kept saying "Sharon Siegel, Sharon Siegel." I then told this godly man that he was and will always be so much more than my Uber driver. He got me to my mom a half hour before she passed away.

Judith's Insight:

This story is exactly why I am writing this book—to capture these life experiences that some might call coincidences, but in reality, they are so much more. Sometimes, a single moment feels like just another slice of life, passing by without much thought. But then, in the middle of an ordinary day, something happens that turns it into something extraordinary.

Coincidences may feel magical, but in stories like this, they carry deeper meaning. They mark defining moments—proof that there is more at play than simple chance.

Your mom, Sharon, knew the journey you took to care for her. She saw your dedication, your efforts to make her happy, and most of all, she felt your love. Sending the Uber driver to the synagogue at the exact moment you were praying for her was her way of reaching back, of embracing you just as you were thinking of her. It was her undeniable sign to let you know that she heard you.

This story brings life full circle. It is her way of telling you that she is at peace—and that she wants the same for you.

If you have a synagogue like this one, or any place of worship where you find solace, know that your messages are being received loud and clear. You may have been carrying a heavy burden, feeling the weight of the world pressing down on you.

But someone—somewhere—is trying to lighten that load.

Whatever struggles you are facing, they are being answered in ways you may not yet see. Through prayer, signs, moments like this, the pressure will begin to lift. The answers are coming, and with them, the peace you are seeking. Remember, you are living this life with a new Angel now, and they were given the job to give you relief using magical memories and helping with missions impossible. You may ask, how will you know that? As problems are solved and questions are answered.

Taking Time to Smell the Roses
Barbara DiBella

My whole life, I always thought that butterflies and dragonflies were signs for me from those who have passed away. Little did I know, there were more signs to come.

As a kid you don't realize what you don't have. Losing my mom as a teenager and then my dad in my twenties shaped my life in ways I didn't fully grasp until much later. Somehow life marches on. You don't realize how young you are or how profound the absence of a parent can be until you get older. Life kept me busy, caring for my younger siblings and filling the void of not having a mom. As a kid, you don't realize what you're actually doing or what "normal" is—if there even is such a thing.

Later on, as I started my own family, becoming the proud mother of four amazing kids, my life turned into a constant whirlwind. I was always running, from one school event to the next, from wrestling matches to soccer games. Life was just so busy. But as my kids grew older, I finally found myself with moments to think and reflect. It wasn't all at once, but gradually, I started to notice things. I realized my mom dying so young made me feel like she was a stranger to me. Once she passed, I wasn't taught to look for signs to help me understand the woman she was. When grief is so painful, sometimes we block out what we know, what we feel, and what we understand. Although I didn't grow up with the memories of life flashing before my eyes from Facebook, I now reflect on the winks and nods that have started to make sense to me.

I began to realize how many times my dad's first name, Rino, came up in my life. It felt like a recurring theme woven through various events and places I visited, constantly playing a role in my story. Rino is my son's middle name. Then, I realized the significance of the name Rose — my grandmother's name. A light bulb went off when I remembered that I had given my daughter the middle name Rose. I thought about how often roses had shown up in my life, becoming a recurring symbol. Looking back, there were probably countless stories where roses appeared or were present during my struggles, whether it was sickness, death, or milestones. Roses seemed to follow me like a Guardian Angel, offering comfort and guidance. My Rose truly did — and still does.

Now, when I see the name Rino on a sign for a restaurant, on a truck passing by, the name of a tailor shop, or hear it in a country song, I know it's a sign that my family is near. When I receive a rose or see one, I know it's my mom and my grandma finding their way into my heart, healing the broken parts with their love.

As I reflected on the graduation of my son, I realized he handed me a rose. It was such an emotional day, and he was my youngest of four children going off the college in September. As I sat through the graduation feeling so sentimental, all of a sudden, a butterfly presented itself, swooping up my son's back, over his head, and down his face for all to see. Such perfection, the rose and a butterfly to let me know my family is all present and accounted for.

Judith's Insight:

It often takes a lifetime to recognize that your Guardian Angels are trying to communicate with you. Sometimes, it requires seeing the same sign repeatedly before you start to wonder why it keeps happening. When a name appears over and over again, it may be more than just coincidence—it could be a message from beyond. Once you begin to notice these patterns, they can lead to moments of reflection and an unexpected "Aha!" realization.

Roses symbolize love, affection, friendship, comfort, celebrations, and joy. You might feel drawn to a name, a place, or an image without immediately understanding why. But over time, as you look back, the reasons often become clear. Sometimes, we feel an unexplainable urge to do something, only realizing its significance later.

When a rose appears on your doorstep or during a milestone, it is a sign that your loved ones are celebrating with you. If you visit a restaurant with "Rino" in its name, it's as if your Guardian Angels have joined you for a Heavenly meal. And if you see a truck with the same name, take it as a message of strength, serenity, and comfort.

In this story, you may not have fully understood the meaning of these signs until you took the time to *smell the roses*. By reflecting on the moments of your life, you have pieced together a beautiful patchwork quilt, realizing that your loved ones have been with you all along, holding your hand from beyond. This recognition can bring a deep sense of love and reassurance.

Keep looking back at your experiences. You will likely uncover even more messages waiting to be understood. One sign does not replace another; sometimes, it takes many to tell a story. Think of the butterfly in this story and the moment of witnessing your son take a step toward manhood, feeling the excitement of what's to come. Keep looking for those dragonflies.

Keep taking the time to smell the roses. Walk with your heart knowing, even if your head questions it, it is alright. Peace was placed in your path to create new memories better than the ones you may not remember. Allow yourself to recognize the hugs from Heaven as there are plenty coming your way. Where do broken hearts go? They go everywhere but never without a flock of Guardian Angels at their side. Every sign you see is meant to be there for you to find not only your place, but your peace.

It's a Miracle!

Sharon Illson Burke

I worked in the television business, and with the strike, you can only imagine the stress it puts on a family. Buying a new house with a big mortgage, managing three kids, and having your husband in the same field only adds to the strain.

I decided to take this time to go to the doctor and get a long-overdue mammogram. Unfortunately, I received worse news than the strike; I had breast cancer. Struggling with the diagnosis, I reached out to an old friend for advice. During our conversation, she suddenly said, "Don't worry, I feel Colleen Callaghan all around this." Colleen Callaghan was a mutual friend who had introduced us many years ago. She had been a breast cancer survivor before her recent death due to a separate illness.

When my friend shared this with me, I replied, "Actually, I've been feeling Colleen myself. It's reassuring to hear you say that." My friend provided a few tips on how to expedite my care, including moving up my MRI appointment. Thanks to her advice, my MRI was rescheduled to three weeks earlier.

As time went on and I learned I needed surgery, I was overwhelmed by the additional stress of dealing with cancer during the strike. Given the timelines the doctor provided, I would have still been waiting for surgery if I hadn't been encouraged to move up my MRI appointment. By expediting the MRI, I was able to adjust the timeline for my treatment and hoped to have everything taken care of during the strike so I could return to work when it was over.

I called my friend again, hoping she might know of any plastic surgeons or ways to get an expedited appointment. She reached out to her friend Sharon for help. When Sharon heard my full name, Sharon Burke, she responded, "Did you know my maiden name is also Burke?" When my name twin referred me to a plastic surgeon named Dr. Callaghan, I felt certain that my friend Colleen was watching over me.

Judith's Insight:

Wow! It's truly remarkable how many hands came together to support you in this moment. It seems like an entire village of Angels was at work, guiding you every step of the way. From the very beginning, you felt an inner nudge to reach out to a friend introduced to you by Colleen Callaghan. That was Colleen's first gentle tap on your shoulder, nudging you in the right direction. Sometimes, we reach out to others without knowing why, only for the significance to reveal itself later when we reflect on our journey.

The power of names played a crucial role here—almost as if your Guardian Angels were orchestrating every connection. The name coincidences were no small feat; in fact, they were so precise and meaningful that they prove there is no such thing as coincidence at all.

Your willingness to seek help was instrumental in this process. The number of synchronicities and guided messages that surfaced along the way is extraordinary. It's clear that your Guardian Angels—your mom, dad, and cherished friends—came together to assist you when you needed them most.

Throughout your breast cancer journey, your Angels stood

by your side, offering their unwavering support. You reached out feeling lost and alone, unsure of where to turn. And then there was Colleen, who had faced breast cancer herself, stepping in to remind you of your strength and resilience. While it may have seemed like a series of random events, friends, family, and guiding spirits were all working in unison, leading you exactly where you needed to be. With every sign and connection, the loneliness you once felt was replaced by something much greater, a deep and undeniable sense of love.

Names, numbers, symbols, they all tell a story. Some names hold personal meaning, while others stand out unexpectedly, putting the "fort" in "comfort." A fort, like a home, is a place of shelter, protection, and safety. When we feel lost or overwhelmed, even surrounded by people who try to help, their efforts don't always reach the places where we need healing the most. But then, something happens—a familiar name appears at the right time, an appointment is rescheduled for a reason beyond our understanding, or the scent of a grandmother's perfume lingers in the air.

These moments become more than just small comforts; they are like arms wrapping around you, carrying the unmistakable touch of something greater, something only Heaven could send. Sometimes life needs more than a great makeup artist and a phenomenal hairdresser. They need a Guardian Angel to the stars.

Blue Jay Moment
Rose Ciolfi

As I was eating breakfast this morning, I heard a bird squawking on my deck. I got up and looked outside to see a beautiful blue jay. It jumped up on the back of my deck chair and was looking right at me. Another one joined it right away and just sat there gazing at me. I'm not a big fan of birds, but looking at these two beautiful blue jays, I couldn't help but wonder why this happened. I have received signs from the cardinals in my back yard in the past but wondered about the significance of the blue jays.

Judith's Insight:

Blue birds are rare, and when they appear in pairs, it is a powerful sign. Your Angels are gathering to bring you a message of joy and excitement, hinting at something wonderful on the horizon. You may soon receive news of a baby, a marriage, or something new to love—perhaps a partner, a job, or even a lifelong friend. If something has been weighing on your heart, this is their way of reassuring you that happiness and good news are on the way. Your Guardian Angels are surrounding you with love, offering warmth and encouragement.

Guides and guardians have unique ways of reaching out, sometimes changing their signals to ensure you recognize them. Some messages come from loved ones you once knew, while others may be sent by Angels you have never met. There are countless ways they try to connect, but many signs go unnoticed simply because we are not always looking for them. Their messages are often subtle yet filled with meaning. By paying attention to the signs around you—especially those that stand out—you may gain deeper insight. Watch for the clues, remain open to their guidance, and take notice of the birds, especially those that gather in groups.

Your guides and Guardian Angels may shift their usual ways of communicating to capture your attention. Sometimes, it may be a "Hidden Angel" reaching out—perhaps a great-grandparent, someone from your childhood who has passed, or even a soul you were not close to but who crosses your mind from time to time. There are endless ways for them to send messages, often changing their approach to make you reflect more deeply. The things that captivate you are often meant to keep you alert and aware.

Stay observant, and pay special attention to the birds, particularly the blue jays that flock together. Sometimes they don't want to be alone. At times you may hear them saying, "This job is going to take two."

Healing with Help

Elena Williams

My friend Rebecca just found a heart-shaped shell at St. Pete's Beach.

Judith's Insight:
Someone is sending her a message—maybe even two. Seashells are symbols of peace, often appearing when someone is struggling internally. They can be reminders to let go, signs of reassurance that better days are ahead. This particular shell carries an even deeper meaning. A heart shape is a powerful symbol of love, connection, and comfort. It may bring news of new life or a message of unconditional love from someone watching over her.

Finding a shell can also represent washing away sorrow, clearing space for renewal. While this may seem like a simple story with little context, profound messages are often hidden in the smallest moments. Just like the shortest verse in the Bible, "Jesus wept," a few words can carry immense meaning. Many people walk along the beach seeking peace, hoping to release stress, find clarity, or restore balance. A shell like this offers a quiet but powerful sign that burdens are lifting.

A solitary walk, a hand holding a shell, tears falling—and then, for a moment, a sense of comfort, as if someone unseen is wiping them away. These are the gentle ways Guardian Angels make their presence known.

Shells carry their own life force, especially those that whisper the ocean's song when held to the ear. That sound, like a heartbeat at birth, reminds us of life's rhythm and renewal. If you are searching for release, you may find yourself drawn to the beach — not necessarily to swim, but to feel the breeze, hear the waves, and let the shore work its quiet magic. The ocean has a way of washing away heartache, just as a dip in a pool, a walk along a stream, or a sail on a lake can bring a sense of peace.

The true purpose of these moments is clear — next time you hear the waves crashing on the shore or the rippling of the waters, realize that your Guardian Angels are speaking to you and helping you heal with the waters of the universe.

The Nonna Clementina Story
Massimo

Twenty-three years ago today, I opened the doors of a deli with nothing but a dream and a single dollar to my name. Named after my Nonna, this deli has been more than a business — it has been a testament to her enduring presence in my life. Nonna was, and still is, my Guardian Angel. I feel her guiding me every step of the way, always watching over me. As I reflect on this milestone, I want to say thank you, Nonna, for your endless love, wisdom, and support. I love you always.

And, of course, I cannot forget to thank the incredible community of Closter. Without your warmth and loyalty, this deli would not be what it is today. You welcomed me with open arms, embraced my dream, and helped turn it into a reality. For that, I am eternally grateful.

Judith's Insight:
Over the years, as you rang up the register, I'm sure you've come across a few special coins — maybe even a silver dollar or a rare

$2 bill. I believe each of these little treasures was a quiet nod from Nonna, a gentle reminder that she was still here, watching over you, guiding and blessing this business.

The recipes Nonna left behind were never just about Sunday Sauce and meatballs. They held the secret ingredients for life—a pinch of encouragement, a dash of determination, five generous pinches of patience, a cupful of kindness, and a pocketful of prayers, always arriving just when they were needed most. And, of course, barrels of hard work. Every one of these was stirred into the pot of success, creating not only the flavors of the deli but also the foundation of everything built here.

Nonna wanted to give you more than just a place to work—she wanted to provide security, a sense of home. Even though she may no longer be physically present, she has never truly left. The flickering lights, the spilled milk, the occasional smoky burn on the stove—these are all signs that she is still by your side.

Guardian Angels, especially this one, don't get upset when things don't go perfectly. Quite the opposite. Nonna's spirit shines through in those moments because that's when she sends her message. She wants to remind you that even in life's imperfections, she is right there, helping you grow, teaching you, and supporting you with her own brand of magical guidance. The signs are everywhere, waiting for you to notice.

Nonna's love and wisdom have been the foundation of this journey, and as you look ahead, you know her presence will continue to be felt in every step, every dish, and every smile shared over the counter. Here's to twenty-three years—and to many more—with Nonna by your side in spirit.

There's a reason we name our children after those who have passed, why we carry on their initials, their nicknames, their memory, even naming a business after them. It's our way of keeping their spirit alive, ensuring that future generations know who they were. A name is an honor, a bridge between the past and the present, binding souls together. Think about how often when a namesake is mentioned, how the stories naturally follow. It bonds souls, connects the past to the present, not just for today, but for every tomorrow and even after that.

A Deeper Understanding

Lindsay Tesher

In June 2020, my beloved grandpa, Sidney—whom I lovingly called Pop Pop—passed away at the age of ninety. He lived a full and happy life, and in his later years, I was fortunate to grow especially close to him. A deeply spiritual man, he had a way of seeing the world that I always admired. I, too, have always felt a strong connection to spirituality, particularly through my love of crystals. So when Pop Pop passed, I wanted to send him off with something meaningful—something that would carry a piece of our love with him wherever he went. I chose a small, pink rose quartz heart, a symbol of love and compassion, and buried it with him as a final gesture of our unbreakable bond.

Two years later, I traveled to Sedona, Arizona, to visit a friend, completely unaware of its reputation as a spiritual "vortex"—a place known for unexplained, powerful energy. Before my trip, I sat in my friend Judi's chair, and she looked at me knowingly. "When you see a rock," she said, "you'll know it's your grandpa." I laughed and replied, "I'm going to Sedona—there are rocks everywhere!" She just smiled and said, "You'll know." Though I didn't fully understand her words, I trusted them.

I chose to visit Sedona on the anniversary of Pop Pop's passing, feeling it would be a meaningful way to honor him. My friend suggested a prayer site with a Buddha statue in town, which seemed like the perfect place to reflect and pay my respects. While browsing a shop earlier that day, I found a small pink rose quartz crystal and decided I would leave it at the prayer site in his memory.

But something unexpected happened. As we approached the Buddha statue, I suddenly stopped in my tracks. Lying before me was a rock shaped exactly like the rose quartz heart I had buried with Pop Pop. It was no ordinary stone—it was a perfect match, an undeniable sign. In that instant, I felt his presence. I knew, without a doubt, that he was there with me. A surge of love and connection washed over me, transcending time and space. It was a moment I will cherish forever.

Judith's Insight:
Our Guardian Angels often send us messages, sometimes even before they leave this world. These moments may seem ordinary at the time—fragments of stories, shared wisdom, or simple gestures of love—but their true significance becomes clear when we need them most.

When you buried the rose quartz heart with Pop Pop, it wasn't just a symbol of love—it was a piece of your heart that you gave to him. In your grief, you may not have realized that part of you had gone with him, leaving a space that felt empty. But the heart-shaped rock you found in Sedona was not a coincidence. It was a gift. A message.

Pop Pop returned that missing piece of your heart to you at just the right moment, filling it with love, reassurance, and the promise that he is still with you. It was his way of reminding you that while he may not be here physically, his love endures—guiding you, comforting you, and walking beside you until you meet again.

Nature has a way of communicating with us through signs, rocks, rainbows, and other earthly wonders. A rainbow is a symbol of hope and promise ahead, carrying emotions that restore our spirit. A simple rock, appearing when we least expect it, can bring peace to a restless heart. These are not mere coincidences; they are divine messages.

So when you find yourself lost, doubting, or searching for meaning, remember that love always finds a way to return to us. Just like Pop Pop's heart-shaped gift in the red rocks of Sedona, the universe will always lead you back to love. Move forward with promise ahead.

REFLECTION 12

Enlightenment

Some of the most precious gifts we receive don't come wrapped in ribbons or tucked inside a box. They're often intangible, unseen, and sometimes unrecognized as gifts in the moment. It's all about opening your soul and bringing you enlightenment.

—Judith Turner

A Love That Never Leaves

Katie P.

After nearly seventy years of marriage, my father passed away in January of last year. Six months later—almost to the day—my mother followed. They were, in every way, the heart and soul of our family, guiding us with their wisdom and unwavering love. Their legacy lives on through their four children, six grandchildren, and two great-grandchildren. But for my two daughters, the bond with their grandparents was something truly special—deep, unbreakable, and filled with love.

In the days following my father's passing, I received a wind chime as a beautiful gift, inscribed with the words, "Unseen and unheard but always near." I can't say that I have seen him, but I definitely have heard him.

I hung it outside, and in my grief, I found comfort in believing that each time the wind stirred and the chimes rang, it was as if my father was there, his presence lingering in the melody, reminding me that love does not end with loss.

A week after my mother's funeral, we traveled from New York to California for my daughter's wedding, a joyous event that had been long planned. Though our hearts were heavy, we knew my parents would have wanted us to celebrate love, just as they had always done.

The ceremony was held outdoors, beneath a beautiful trellis draped in flowers, overlooking rolling pastures and lush gardens in the San Diego hills. As the justice of the peace began the ceremony, something unexpected happened; wind chimes began to play. Their melody was soft yet unmistakable, filling the air with a peaceful, soothing sound. There wasn't a single gust of wind, and yet, the chimes rang as if on cue. We couldn't see where they came from, but their presence was undeniable. My daughter turned to me, her eyes shining, and smiled. In that moment, we both understood: My father was there.

Then, just as the justice of the peace pronounced the couple husband and wife, a loud, clear rooster's crow echoed through the air. It broke the stillness with a sense of perfect timing, as if nature itself had joined in the celebration. My daughter turned to me once more, her expression filled with warmth, and mouthed, "Grandma is here too." And I knew she was right.

My mother, always vibrant and full of life, had a deep love for roosters. Our kitchen had been decorated with them for as long as I could remember. She often joked about how their boldness and energy reflected her own spirit. That rooster's call, at the exact moment of my daughter's union, was no coincidence. It was her way of making sure we knew she was watching, celebrating, and standing beside us.

Judith's Insight:

In that instant, grief, love, and joy intertwined, reminding you that those you have lost are never truly gone. They find ways—sometimes subtle, sometimes impossible to ignore—to remind you that their love endures, always walking beside you.

The chimes rang at just the right moment, their melody weaving through the air like a whisper from beyond. It was as if the universe had orchestrated the perfect harmony of love and light for your daughter's wedding day. And then, with the rooster's crow, came a final sign, bold, clear, and impossible to overlook.

Your mother always had a strong voice, a presence that commanded attention. Even in the afterlife, she made sure she was heard. That rooster's call wasn't just a sign; it was a declaration. She wanted you to know she was there, blessing this union, making sure her love remained woven into the fabric of your family's story.

There is something deeply profound about souls who share a

lifetime together, only to leave this world within months of each other. They are what we call Everlasting Soulmates—two spirits so intertwined that even death cannot separate them. Their love does not fade; it simply shifts into another form, continuing beyond the physical realm.

You may have heard the phrase *joined at the hip*—but for soulmates like your parents, their connection runs far deeper. They understood each other in a way that words could never fully capture. Their laughter, their disagreements, their unwavering devotion—all of it formed a love that could not be broken. Even in the moments when they seemed to challenge each other, their bond always led them back to love.

This is the Journey of the Known—a connection so familiar, so deeply ingrained, that even in silence, they understood each other. It's the kind of love we recognize instantly when we see it, even if we struggle to explain it. The way their eyes met, the way they could read each other without speaking—it was as if they had been together for centuries, their souls forever entwined.

The wind chimes carried a message of peace and serenity that day, like music played by the wind, or as I like to imagine, the gentle breath of an Angel guiding and comforting those they love. The rooster, in its boldness, brought strength and clarity. It set the tone for the new marriage, reminding your daughter and her husband that love requires resilience, that every challenge can be met with courage, and that their union is watched over by those who came before them.

Your mother's presence will always be there—protecting, guiding, and celebrating every milestone. Even when life feels uncertain, and the world seems out of step, her love remains steady. And just as the wind carries the sound of the chimes, just as the rooster's call rings through the air, love—true, enduring love—never fades. It simply finds new ways to be heard. *Cock-a-doodle-doo.*

Angel Luck
Snoozey

It was the first truly beautiful day in New York City. I had come to visit from another country, and I love everything about this place—there's always something exciting to do. That day, I was out exploring with my two daughters, heading to a historic bookstore on the Upper West Side.

Suddenly, I needed to find a bathroom. The bookstore, unfortunately, didn't have one available for customers. I remembered spotting a Starbucks a few buildings away and decided to hurry over—well, more of a brisk walk than a run. As soon as I stepped inside, I asked, "Do you have a ladies' room?" Without hesitation, the staff sternly replied, "No!" I walked out, not even thinking to ask if I needed to purchase something first.

In my urgency, I must have looked completely lost, my desperation probably written all over my face. Out of nowhere, a man appeared and asked, "What are you looking for?" "A bathroom," I replied. "You won't find one around here," he said. Then, without further explanation, he simply added, "Come with me."

Overwhelmed by the growing panic of not finding a restroom in time, I followed without hesitation. He led me into a building, where the first thing I noticed was a man in a uniform behind a desk. We walked past him, down a series of hallways, until we reached what looked like a storage closet. The man guiding me never said another word. I had no idea where I was going, but at that moment, all I could focus on was following him.

The "closet" seemed like an odd place to stop—until, out of the corner of my eye, I spotted an open door and caught a glimpse of a toilet. Without thinking, I darted inside and shut the door.

When I came out, the man was gone. I walked back the way we had come, looking around, but he was nowhere to be found.

Stepping outside the building, I searched the street—he had vanished.

I stood there, speechless, relieved, and deeply grateful. Looking up at the beautiful sky, I whispered, "Thank you, Dad. Thank you for my Angel luck today."

Judith's Insight:

"Angel Luck"—what a perfect name for this story. The man who appeared out of nowhere was certainly an Angel, arriving at the most profound moment. The twist of fate that led you to be turned away from Starbucks was no coincidence; it was part of the divine plan. If you hadn't been rejected, you wouldn't have this incredible story to tell.

These moments happen more often than we realize, serving as reminders that there is something greater at work. You followed a stranger into a building without hesitation, despite the fear it could have evoked. This experience is a sign of faith, perseverance, and the reassurance that, even when life feels overwhelming, you are being guided in the right direction.

Your father found a way to lead you when you needed it most. Many people have similar experiences but never share them because they seem too personal, too emotionally raw. Yet, stories like this prove that angelic forces are always at play, lending a helping hand when we least expect it.

Angel luck reveals itself in many ways. Sometimes, it's as simple as an unexplained encounter. Other times, it's a small but significant moment—a sense of comfort when you're feeling afraid. Imagine walking alone on a dark street, feeling scared, when suddenly you hear the hoot of an owl. At first, the sound startles you, but then you feel an unexpected sense of calm. Owls, with their mysterious presence, are guardians of wisdom, not creatures to be feared. Their presence serves as a reminder to pay attention to the signs around you and to trust the guidance you receive.

Every day holds the potential for an Angel luck moment—whether you recognize it or not. The next time you hear a hooting owl or tell a seemingly ordinary story about your day, take a closer look. You might just find that an Angel was with you all along.

Speaking of Dreams
Gila Seliktar

One night, I had a dream about my two sisters who have passed. Whenever I dream of them, I feel such relief just seeing them again. But when I wake up and realize it was only a dream, a wave of sadness and heartbreak often follows.

On this particular night, both sisters appeared together. We were in Israel, at our family home, and they were telling me to leave. It felt as if they were preparing something. The dream had many moving parts, but what stood out the most was how I felt when I woke up. There was an urgency in the way they pushed me to leave, as if they were trying to tell me something without saying it outright.

Two days later, I received a call that shattered me—my brother had unexpectedly passed away. The first thing that came to mind was my dream. My sisters had been preparing for him.

My family has always been my world. Losing my sisters at such a young age and so suddenly was already heartbreaking. And now, my brother was gone too.

Judith's Insight:
When tomorrow never comes for a sibling, the pain is more than a broken heart—it feels as if a piece of you has been taken away. Some describe it as losing an arm or a leg. It goes beyond losing a best friend, unless that sibling was both.

In this story, your sisters came to deliver a message, a warning of what was to come. No one can be spared from the heartbreak of losing a brother or sister, even those we weren't as close to. The bond of family runs deep—through obstacles, emotions, laughter, and pain. No other relationship can replicate the shared memories, secrets, and joys of growing up together.

In this dream, your sisters embraced you before the pain began, holding you in their arms to let you know they would not let you face this alone. More importantly, they were there to guide your brother on his journey, ensuring he would not be alone either. They had his wings ready, making his path to Heaven as smooth as possible, while leaving behind hugs from Heaven for the sister left behind.

Guardian Angels are always working behind the scenes, doing what they can to ease our journey. Of course, there is nothing easy about death—until it offers peace to those who need it most. We never truly know what battle someone was fighting, or what struggle they might have faced had they stayed longer. Sometimes, their journey ends not in defeat, but in grace.

Finding Home
Nicola Verses

I was driving down the highway on a gorgeous day when a light sun shower began. The rain glistened in the sunlight, creating a breathtaking scene. I had just gotten off the phone with my mom, who was trying to convince me to move to Florida. We were in the process of trying to purchase a house there, one I had fallen in love with, and I desperately wanted to make it happen.

As I drove, I started speaking aloud to my grandpa, telling him how much I missed him. Lost in my thoughts, I momentarily forgot about the house—until the song "Home," by Phillip

Phillips started playing on the radio. As I listened to every word in the song, I felt like it was my grandfather speaking to me through the song, trying to help me make the big decision about this move. I think it will be easier now after getting the message from my grandpa to move forward.

My mother-in-law, Jamie, always associates the song "Kars for Kids" with her father. When he was alive, he would always comment, "Jamie, how cute is this kid's voice in this song?" Now, whenever she hears it while driving, it feels like a little reminder of her dad.

In another coincidence, my mom's song has a similar connection with her father, Peter, through the song "Memories" by Maroon 5. Right after he passed, she asked him for a sign that he was still with her. The very first time the song aired, she heard the lyrics, and they were eerily fitting. Now, every time she is thinking of him, the song plays.

Judith's Insight:

Isn't it amazing how, just when we send our thoughts into the universe, someone we love answers with a message of comfort? It's like wrapping yourself in a warm blanket on a cold night, hearing the perfect words at the perfect moment—words that offer reassurance, love, and the presence of those we miss.

In this story, music becomes the bridge between worlds, delivering messages from beyond. Each song carries its own meaning, its own purpose.

For you, the song "Home" by Phillip Phillips was a push to move forward, encouraging you to take that leap of faith. Even if the first house doesn't work out, the journey itself is guiding you toward the place where you truly belong. The message isn't just about finding a home—it's about finding balance, comfort, and support in a space that brings more peace than anxiety.

For your mother-in-law, "Kars for Kids" is more than just a

nostalgic tune. It's her father's way of reminding her to listen — not just to the song, but to the voices of children around her. Whether it's her own children, grandchildren, or even a passing child on the street, the message is hidden in their words. Sometimes, our Guardian Angels speak through the innocence and wisdom of a child's voice.

For your mom, "Memories" is a direct response from her father, reminding her to reflect on the past while embracing the future. The lyrics tell her that even in the hardest moments, she is not alone. He is still guiding her, making sure she knows that life's challenges can be overcome with love and resilience.

Songs have a way of reaching us when we need them most. They aren't just background noise at weddings and funerals — they appear when we least expect them, in the car, at the gym, during a quiet moment. They are a universal language, carrying messages of hope, comfort, and reassurance.

Some songs remind us of loss — "Wind Beneath My Wings" may bring tears, yet it also brings the comforting presence of someone watching over us. "Candle in the Wind" may be about mourning, but when heard at just the right time, it can feel like a conversation with the Heavens. Songs like "Angels," "See You Again," "Somewhere Over the Rainbow," and "Life Without You" hold sorrow, yet they also bring peace. Even childhood rhymes, commercial jingles, or television show theme songs can hold special meaning when they appear unexpectedly, reminding us of those we've loved and lost.

Music holds a power beyond words. Singers are messengers, delivering the lyrics we need to hear exactly when we need them most. The right song can make our hearts skip a beat, stir our souls, and awaken memories we thought were long forgotten. Songs are one of the world's true wonders — offering unexpected hugs from Heaven.

The magic lies in the words. Words can be more than enchanting, because sometimes, Heaven is found between the notes. And when you truly listen, you just might find a piece of Heaven in every beautifully sung word.

My Dad's a Fly!
Stacy M.

No matter how old our parents get, we never truly believe they will leave us. Recently, I lost my dad—he was the heart of our family. As time has passed, I've found myself praying and speaking aloud, not always sure whom I'm talking to. Of course, I know it's God, but sometimes, I just feel someone else is there.

Ever since my dad passed, a fly keeps appearing. Yes, I know it's not the same fly, but something about it makes me believe it's him. Why do I think that? Because my dad had a unique skill—he could catch flies, even with chopsticks. He learned the technique while serving in the U.S. Army in Okinawa, Japan. Now, whenever I find myself deep in thought or silently sending my wishes out to the universe, this fly shows up.

Recently, I was on the phone with my friend from New Jersey. It was the middle of winter, and as we were talking, she said, "All of a sudden, there's a fly in my car." She had no idea about my connection between my dad and flies. I told her my story—how my dad seems to visit me in the form of a fly. I just know it's him by the way he appears and when. She paused for a moment, then said, "I guess your dad's here, looking out for you. So I won't kill it!"

Judith's Insight:
A fly's lifespan is short—only fifteen to thirty days, depending on its surroundings. So no, it's not the same fly, but it is certainly the same guide.

Flies symbolize movement, persistence, and resilience. They

are small but relentless, a reminder to keep going even when things seem tough. If at first you don't succeed, try, try again — that's your dad's message to you.

He wants you to know that although he is gone, you are never forgotten. We often try to reassure those who have passed, but sometimes, they need to remind us of the same.

Yes, flies can be a little annoying, but maybe that's the point. Your dad is saying, "I'm here. I will keep showing up until you notice me. Pay attention. Look around. Be aware of your surroundings — there is meaning in the little things."

After reading this, many of you will probably never look at flies the same way again. You may have swatted a few away, thinking they were just a nuisance, but flies are one of the most determined creatures in nature. They don't stop. They persist. And in their own way, they send messages.

Your guide might have sent you a fly — or a different kind of sign. A pocketknife, perhaps, to suggest it's time to cut ties that cause you pain. A horseshoe to remind you not to charge ahead blindly. Or even a rabbit, signaling that you're moving too fast. These subtle winks from the universe are each unique, yet they all serve the same purpose: to catch you at precisely the right moment, kind of like having the ability to catch a fly.

I Love Lucy
Ann M. Albano

I have always believed that my twin brother, John, visits me between our birthday on September 26 and the anniversary of his passing on October 25.

Today, my boyfriend, Tony, found a tattered piece of a red balloon in my yard. He picked it up before Lucy, my dog, could grab it. As he turned it over, he noticed something written on it.

We could hardly believe what it said—"I love Lucy."

Shortly after, Lucy was diagnosed with a serious illness. I searched everywhere for ways to save her, hoping for a miracle. Her sudden passing still feels unreal. She was my Angel, her white fur soft and pure like Angel wings.

At first, I thought the balloon was a message from John. But now, I wonder—was it sent by someone from Lucy's past? Or was it John, calling her home?

I can't help but think of the movie *A Dog's Purpose* and wonder if Lucy's time here was just one chapter in a much longer journey. Maybe she had already fulfilled her purpose with me, and her beautiful soul was meant to move on.

Judith's Insight:

The Heavens sent you an undeniable sign—one that recognized the depth of your love for Lucy. This message was pure affirmation, a reminder that love never fades. Your brother, your father, and even Lucy's lost brothers and sisters all came together to send you a message of comfort. They knew the pain you would soon endure and wanted to give you the reassurance you needed before facing it.

Unfortunately, Guardian Angels cannot stop pain or loss. They can't prevent the storm, but they can hold up an umbrella to shield you from its full force. In this case, they sent a balloon—a message of pure, unconditional love.

As time passes, you will reflect on that red balloon and realize it was a gift, a sign meant to remind you that love surrounds you, even in grief. Guardian Angels often send foreshadowing signals, hoping that when the moment of loss arrives, you will remember that no one ever leaves this world alone. Whether it's a pet, a loved one, or a friend, they are carried away by family—welcomed home by those who have gone before them. All dogs go to Heaven, and so do cats and turtles. Dogs come with intention and leave with a purpose. To be continued.

The Angel That Helps Me Cope
Deb Z.

It's a long story, but it started when I was driving up to visit my best friend, Marie, at her niece's house. My electric car suddenly broke down. I had been eager to see her before she returned home to Colorado, and luckily, she extended her stay, allowing us to spend the following weekend together.

That weekend was one of the best we ever had—filled with laughter and joy. We spoke daily, but after she went back home, I didn't hear from her for about a week. Then, out of the blue, I received a call from her sister, Lana, and her niece, Doreen. They wanted to visit me in Morristown, New Jersey. While I found it odd, I was thrilled that they had made the effort to see me—until I learned the real reason for their visit. They had come to tell me that Marie had suddenly passed away.

At that moment, everything became a blur. I remember dropping my bag and collapsing to the ground. They took me to my husband, Joe, at the Headquarters Plaza Hotel in Morristown. The next thing I recall, I was sitting alone on a bench in front of the hotel when a small white bird landed on my ankle. It sat there for a minute or two, unmoving. I remember thinking how unusual it was to see a white bird. When it finally flew away, I realized that, for just a brief moment, it had taken my grief with it.

In the days that followed, I would take a three-mile walk through the woods each day, my thoughts constantly drifting to Marie. Incredibly, a single white butterfly would follow me along the path. This happened so often that I started speaking to it. I would ask, "Hey, are you going to follow me the whole way today?"

In my heart, I knew it was her, letting me know she was okay and still with me. She couldn't bear to see me in such pain, so she came to me—just as she always had when she was alive.

Judith's Insight:

Messages received on walks can be truly revealing. You may walk for miles without noticing a sign from your Guardian Angel, but then, in a single moment, something catches your eye, and you just know—it's them. The presence of white was no coincidence; souls of white were trying to bring you light. Marie must have known you needed her warmth and companionship on your walks. She chose to walk beside you, to guide you, and to support you on your journey through life.

This story touches my heart deeply because the name of your best friend was also mine, my Aunt Marie, who was more like a sister to me. Our bond was woven together through love, making her my sister, my aunt, and my best friend all in one.

Marie was the kind of person who, when she loved you, she truly loved you. If you were part of her journey, she made sure you felt special. So, of course, she's showing up for you now. She understands your pain, perhaps even better than you do. Just as you knew hers, she knows yours—a sacred connection between kindred spirits. It makes perfect sense that she would visit you with multiple signs, appearing on your walks or as you sit quietly on a park bench.

The white butterflies were more than just symbols of peace; they were meant to surround you with serenity. At first, she may have come simply to ease the immediate sorrow of losing her, but she continues to walk with you to always help you cope, bringing comfort, whispering to your heart, and reminding you that she is still near. You are lucky to recognize these messages, and they will continue—just as your friendship does, stretching across worlds.

Coping messages are the ones we receive during the most painful moments of grief, but they don't fade away. They stay with us, guiding us forward through life.

Friends who have passed can become our Guardian Angels,

watching over us. Many people create families not by blood, but by choice—surrounding themselves with those who truly matter. A Guardian Angel doesn't have to be a relative; they are the souls who have touched our lives so deeply that they leave an imprint on our hearts.

Choosing an Angel is a bond between souls. True friendship leaves a mark, even in the smallest ways. Some people carve their presence so deeply into our souls that they leave us with an unspoken promise—the simple yet powerful truth: You've got a friend.

Sisters

Lil Sis

My sister, Nancy, passed away unexpectedly five years ago, just before Christmas. I was devastated. We were incredibly close.

On Christmas Eve in 2018, a bald eagle appeared in front of our house, putting on quite a show—catching and dropping its prey over and over. Then, around my birthday on January 4, something incredible happened. A very old snake plant in my family suddenly bloomed. When I looked it up, I learned that snake plants rarely bloom, and if they do, it usually happens in the spring.

This past Christmas was the first one since her passing where I actually felt excited for the holiday again. My husband made it extra special by taking me to see the Rockettes on Christmas Eve.

Then, on January 6—Little Christmas—as I was taking down the decorations, another bald eagle appeared and stayed in front of our house for an hour. Later that same day, when I went to water my snake plant, I saw that it was blooming again—once more in the middle of winter.

I love you, Nancy.

Judith's Insight:

Your sister wants you to know she is still with you. The bloom of the snake plant is a powerful symbol of new beginnings. A sudden bloom — especially in the heart of winter — isn't just rare; it's a way to catch your attention. She has likely sent other signs before, but this one was impossible to miss. She is staying close, just as she always did in life, because your bond remains unbreakable.

The bald eagle is no ordinary bird, it commands attention. It makes itself known. By appearing at significant moments in your life, it is your sister's way of reaching out, bringing the past forward, and reminding you that she is still walking beside you as your Guardian Angel.

Pay attention to the eagles that seem to follow you. They may show up in unexpected ways — in songs, images, or even during a vacation. When you recognize their presence, you will feel it in your heart. They are impossible to ignore, standing out in the crowd, just like your sister.

When you see an eagle, rise to the occasion. Sometimes, these winks from above are her way of saying, *Thank you, I love you, you're the best.* That feeling of warmth and reassurance often comes when birds become part of a Guardian Angel's message.

These signs are a two-way connection. As you wonder how she is doing, she is checking in on you. When you see an eagle soaring above, take it as a reminder to reach for the sky, to embrace the strength she is sending your way. That eagle carries a message of courage, a guiding hand as you step into something new, and a loving embrace filled with divine reassurance.

These flowers bloom for you, reminding you to celebrate life. When you see a bald eagle, remember that someone is sending you strength to help carry your burdens. It is also a gentle nudge to look up to the sky, letting the Heavens know that you hear them — just as they have heard you. Treasure these eagles, for they have landed just for you.

Tiqui's Story
Tiqui Atencio Demirdjian

All my life, I have prayed before going to sleep, and my prayers have always been directed to the Virgin Mary. Near Monaco, where I live, there is a shrine dedicated to Our Lady of Laghet. I visit often to pray and to give thanks to the Holy Mother for the many blessings in my life.

The first time I visited the shrine, a devout friend took me there, convinced of the Virgin of Laghet's miraculous power. As soon as we arrived, I felt an overwhelming spiritual energy. The shrine is renowned for its hundreds of ex-voto paintings hung on the walls—tokens of gratitude from those who have received healings, miracles, and graces from the Blessed Virgin Mary. This deeply moved me. When I walked up to the Holy Mother's statue, I was mesmerized. Looking into her eyes, I felt an incredible, almost indescribable connection with her.

One month later, I met Ago, my husband of thirty-five years—the greatest blessing of my life. Since then, I have taken six of my closest friends to visit the shrine, and incredibly, each one of them has found love and happiness, marrying soon after their visit. I discovered my Guardian Angel at the shrine, and what makes it even more extraordinary is that I now share her with my six best friends.

Judith's Insight:
Sharing the shrine is sharing the gift of belief. Like all sacred places, this shrine offers a space to place our prayers. We may also make wishes, sometimes asking for our own needs and desires, but the true message here is one of giving and sharing.

In this story, You had a profound experience—one that was then shared by friend after friend. In a way, you became an earthly guide, introducing others to the shrine much like a pastor, priest, teacher, mentor, or healer. We are all given gifts, and how we use them matters. Sometimes, we unknowingly take on the role of a Guardian Angel for others, appearing in their lives at just the right moment to offer guidance, hope, and inspiration.

Spreading the word about our personal journeys of faith and healing allows others to find their own paths to renewal. This energy creates positivity, shaping new blueprints for better, more fulfilled lives. As the saying goes, Y*you can lead a horse to water, but you cannot make it drink*. The true gift lies in the effort—in the sharing, the guiding, and the simple act of trying.

I Will Always Find You
Abigail Pall Weinshank

For many years, my parents spent three months each year in St. Moritz, Switzerland—two months skiing in the winter and one month hiking in the summer. For as long as I can remember, my mother always said she wanted to be cremated and have her ashes scattered over her favorite hiking trail.

In 1994, my mother became severely disabled by Parkinson's disease. During the last two years of her life, she was mostly bedridden. Throughout that time, I traveled at least four times a week from my home in northern New Jersey to hers on Long Island. On those long drives, I became fascinated by the variety of license plates I saw and started keeping a running list. I collected nearly all of them, including many from Canada and Mexico. The only one I never found was Wyoming.

When my mother passed away in April 1998, it was a relief for her, but a profound loss for me. That summer, my family and I traveled to Switzerland to fulfill her final wish. It was an incredible blessing to be able to honor her in the place she loved most.

After the ceremony, my husband and I were driven from our hotel in Switzerland to Milan to catch a flight to Naples. As we left, I realized I had to finally say goodbye to my mom. Though I was leaving her in the place she cherished, it was an emotional moment.

As we wound through the switchbacks of the Swiss and Italian Alps, we approached the border checkpoint between the two countries. In my memory, the building looked like a small English phone booth — quaint and unassuming. Just then, I looked ahead and saw an RV towing a car ... with a Wyoming license plate. In the middle of the Alps, in that exact moment, the one missing license plate from my list appeared. I knew then that my mother was okay, and that she was sending me a sign — her way of giving me a hug.

Years later, when my husband and I moved to a tiny town in New Jersey, I suddenly became tearful, wondering, *How will Mommy find me now that we've moved?* As I drove to our new home, just a quarter of a mile away, I stopped at a stop sign to let a car pass. And there it was. A Wyoming license plate. She had found me. She would *always* find me.

Every now and then, I see a plate from that faraway state, and I know she's still watching over me.

Judith's Insight

When we lose someone we love, we often feel lost, broken, and empty. We wonder if our loved ones can still reach us — if they can still hear us. And then, one day, it happens.

For Abigail, the missing Wyoming license plate was more than a coincidence — it was a message, a sign meant just for her. A reminder that even in a crowd, some things stand out.

What does *standing out* mean? It's about embracing the things that make life uniquely ours — the adventures we take, the friendships we cherish, the way we love, and the way we live. This story is different from other license plate stories because Abigail was already collecting them, already noticing them. And when she needed it most, that missing plate reappeared, delivering a monumental sign of love and reassurance.

Guardian Angels work with what we know, what we treasure, and what we recognize. They use what's in their divine chest of keepsakes to send us the perfect sign at just the right moment, the kind that makes your soul *feel* the presence of something greater. Perhaps your Guardian Angel was also a collector, of cars, bikes, memorabilia, baseball cards, coins, or even something else. Those items are what may be shown to you. Maybe they, too, cherished the little things that make life meaningful. A Guardian Angel doesn't just remind us of where we've been, they push us forward, urging us to keep living, keep believing, and keep searching for the treasures life still has to offer. And when the time is right, they remind us: *I am here. I have always been here. I always know where you are.*

I Give You My Permission

Joanne Kovacic

November 2023 was a whirlwind of challenges. My eighty-three-year-old father was hospitalized with pneumonia, and as his caretaker, I was by his side daily. At the same time, my eldest daughter was planning her January wedding, and I was juggling my business while trying to be the mother of the bride. Adding to it all, I was in a growing relationship with Carlo, a widower who had lost his wife, Karen, to cancer in 2018.

Karen was a beloved teacher at the high school my daughters attended, and she had taught two of them. Carlo and I originally met at a school fundraiser when Karen introduced us, urging him to buy a 50/50 ticket. Years later, after her passing, we reconnected at a soccer game, and over time, our friendship evolved into something more. Blending our lives with six children between us was no small feat, and we took our time navigating this journey.

With my father's health, my daughter's wedding preparations, and a December trip to Disney planned with Carlo's family, I prayed for strength. Thankfully, my father was improving, the wedding was coming together, and we decided to go ahead with our Disney trip, though Carlo was hesitant. His kids were excited, but he worried about how they would handle being under one roof with me for the first time.

In December 2023, we left Westchester, New York, for Florida. Carlo had attended a Christmas party the night before and was exhausted. About an hour into the flight, I woke up to check on him. His face had turned completely gray, his eyes rolled back, and he was unresponsive. I panicked, shaking his chest and yelling his name. His son jumped into action, calling for a doctor, while his youngest checked for a pulse. Thankfully, a nurse practitioner on board helped revive him, but the moment was terrifying. His children, already having lost their mother, screamed in fear, pleading, "Not you too, Dad!"

EMTs met us upon landing in Orlando. Carlo passed all their tests, and we decided to continue with the trip, though with a new perspective on how fragile life is. That night, we settled into the condo, uncertain of how the dynamics would play out. But as we ventured to Animal Kingdom and later walked through Downtown Disney, everything felt natural—right, even. We listened to music, sipped hot chocolate, and enjoyed a magical evening together.

The next day, we spent time in Magic Kingdom. Carlo's son and I arranged our Lightning Lane passes, including one for It's a Small World, one of my favorite rides. As we reached the end, where the screen usually displays "goodbye" in various languages, we saw something different—*Karen's* name appeared at least three times. The screen showed no other names.

I turned to Carlo, asking if he saw what I saw. He nodded, assuming it was a coincidence. But I had never seen names on that screen before. When I looked it up, I learned that names are only displayed when triggered by MagicBands. Yet Karen's name appeared repeatedly, and none of us had anything connected to her.

Curious, we rode It's a Small World again the next day. This time, no names appeared — just the usual farewell messages.

A month later, in January 2025, I returned to Disney with my daughter and son-in-law. I made sure to check the screen at the end of the ride once more. Again, no names, just "goodbye" in different languages.

Was Karen sending us a message? It felt like she was letting us know her children were happy and cared for — that it was okay for Carlo to keep living, to love again. Karen was definitely sending us all a message that day!

Judith's Insight:

What a trip! You experienced remarkable signs with outcomes that couldn't be ignored. It seems like Karen wanted to make sure you knew she was present the entire time.

This story is about balance. It began with a simple moment — selling 50/50 tickets — which led to an unexpected bond. Then, on the soccer field, much like in life, you faced obstacles and challenges, surrounded by family. Through it all, balance was key.

When Karen's name appeared, it was as if she was saying, "You can go the distance! You got this! And thank you for being there and for putting the glue back into my family." Here you were, at one of the biggest amusement parks in the world, living your own roller-coaster ride — one filled with ups, downs, and twists of fate. But now, it was time to create new, happy memories in a place where dreams come true, not nightmares.

Karen's message wasn't just a sign — it was an acknowledgment, an applause, a heartfelt *thank you*. Through her quiet winks and nods, she reminded you that she had been there all along. Without her unseen guidance, you may not have made it through the chaos to the happiest place on earth, and most importantly, in one piece and at peace.

Destiny has a way of unfolding in unexpected ways. Reflection helps us navigate paths that aren't always easy. We use the tools we have—one of the most powerful being the love and support of those who have passed. Karen's presence was clear. She wasn't saying Y*you are here instead of me* but rather, *I am here with you, every step of the way.*

Finding balance means holding on to the love of those we've lost while embracing new love and opening our hearts to the future. Just as life must go on, so must love.

My Nun, Sister Elizabeth: An Angel on Earth
Judith Turner

A sign from Heaven that stands out in my life is my Earthly Guardian Angel, Sister Elizabeth. She just seems to appear—right when I need her most.

Since my oldest son was five years old, Sister Elizabeth has shown up out of nowhere whenever something major is happening in my life. Most of the time, it's in person. At first, I thought seeing her around the community and hearing about the countless good deeds she had done for others was just a coincidence. Everyone who knows her feels blessed by her presence; her kindness is unmatched.

But as time went on, I realized something: There are no coincidences. It became clear—God had sent me a Guardian Angel on earth named Sister Elizabeth.

One of the first times she appeared was when my dad was in the intensive care unit. I was home, feeling unsettled, when something inside told me I needed to be at the hospital at exactly 2:00 p.m. In my world, that meant 2:17, as that's my Angel number — my dad's badge number. My mom was sick at home and wasn't planning to go, fearing she might make my dad even sicker. So, I went alone and waited in the hospital. At exactly 2:00 p.m., I was there when two monitor alarms went off — and my dad started coding. I stood there, frozen in disbelief, begging God for more time. The doctors told me I had to step out of the room. And just as I walked out, there she was. My nun, Sister Elizabeth. We sat together, we prayed, and at 2:17, they told me my dad had survived the code blue. He was given two more years of life.

The next time she appeared was when my husband had his first heart attack. I was lying on a gurney in the hospital hallway, exhausted and overwhelmed. I had just made the difficult decision to move him from a New Jersey hospital to Columbia Presbyterian Hospital in New York. I knew the move would anger the hospital staff, but something in my gut told me it was the right thing to do. And then — when I turned the corner — there she was, Sister Elizabeth. "Are you okay?" she asked. I told her about my decision and my fear of upsetting the doctors. She simply said, "Judi, you already know what to do." Her words were all the confirmation I needed. And I was right — had we not moved him, he wouldn't have survived.

Another encounter happened at a different hospital in another neighborhood. The moment I found out my mom had pancreatic cancer, I ran outside, sat on the curb, and sobbed hysterically. Then, I saw someone's feet standing in front of me. There she was. My nun, Sister Elizabeth. "Judi, what can I do? I will pray." I asked her how she knew I was there. She simply said, "I didn't." Although my mom didn't beat the cancer, she had told me she wanted one more trip around the sun. She got two more years.

When my husband had a second heart attack, I stepped out

to grab lunch after spending the morning with him. I turned around, and there she was again. We hugged, we talked, and she assured me she would pray for my husband and our family. Then she said something that brought me more comfort than she could ever know: "I always pray for you."

Last year, I was delayed getting to a funeral home for a wake. I arrived late, rushing in. And who was standing there? My Guardian Angel nun, Sister Elizabeth. "I am here for you," she said. She then told me she was supposed to arrive earlier. I smiled and said, "Me too." That delay was no accident. It was a gift. We sat together, prayed, and talked about the heartache my family was going through. I told her about my daughter's pregnancy and how the doctors had diagnosed the baby with a serious heart condition. She prayed. And through the generosity of her prayers, my granddaughter was born on Good Friday with no heart defect as the doctors had originally expected, and she came home on Easter Sunday.

Today, I was looking through some papers, and suddenly, I saw her name. And just like that, I felt hope. I have surgery coming up soon, and just seeing her name brought me comfort.

Judith's Insight:

These are just a few of my stories. Often, we expect signs to come from familiar sources or in predictable ways. Yet, they can emerge from unexpected places—a stranger's words, a chance encounter, or a friend appearing at just the right time. In my case, my nun, Sister Elizabeth, has been a constant guiding presence. Her timing has never failed. These godly moments have given me strength, hope, and comfort, reminding me that I am never truly alone.

But she is only one of my Earthly Angels. I believe we all have them. They may not always appear as a special nun, though I have been fortunate to be blessed by two nuns who have had a profound impact on my life. For someone who didn't start out as Catholic, I was blessed to have Sister Susanne as my Rite of Christian Initiation of Adults mentor, guiding me as I entered the Catholic Church.

Throughout your life, you may encounter more than one Earthly Angel—someone who helps you in ways you cannot ignore. It could be a best friend, a teacher, a rabbi, a pastor, or even a homeless person who crosses your path. No matter who they are, how they appear, or what they do for you, recognize them. Appreciate them. Let them know they matter.

If you haven't thought about it before, today is a new day—a chance to reflect, listen, and learn something about your life and yourself.

Be grateful for those who lend a hand, offer a kind word, or simply stand beside you in ways that keep you speechless even when you don't realize it. I am grateful.

The Finale
Hugs from Heaven

"Guardian Angels are there to help us and guide us,
except we don't always listen. "

—*Sister Elizabeth Holler*

"A priest once told me that an Angel was given to me at birth
and stays with me forever until death. I have a deep devotion to
my Guardian Angels and find myself constantly talking to them.
They are really there for those who believe!"

—*Sister Susanne Reynolds*

"Guardian Angels walk with you side by side, loyal and faithful,
protecting you and guiding you always and forever bringing you
closer to God."

—*Deacon John Murray*

Sources

In December 2023, Anderson Cooper's podcast with Stephen Colbert, titled "Grateful for Grief," was a profound reveal for dealing with grief and touched me personally.

Source: Cooper, Anderson. "Stephen Colbert: Grateful for Grief." *All There Is with Anderson Cooper*. Podcast Audio, December 2019.

Alan Hamel, husband of Suzanne Somers, shared with *People* magazine in January 2024 that signs and strange occurrences happened after his beloved wife passed away.

Source: https://www.facebook.com/peoplemag. "Suzanne Somers' Widower Alan Hamel Says He Can 'Feel Her in My Heart Every Night' 7 Months after Her Death (Exclusive)." People.com, 2024, people.com/suzanne-somers-widower-alan-hamel-remembers-her-7-months-after-her-death-exclusive-8649125. Accessed 17 Apr 2025.

In a May 2024 interview, Carol Burnett shared that receiving the gift of bird of paradise flowers was a loving message from her daughter.

Source: *The Late Show with Stephen Colbert*. "Carol Burnett Takes the Colbert Questionert." *YouTube*, May 2, 2024, www.youtube.com/watch?v=qzJgmc18f3I. Accessed Apr 17, 2025.

In May 2024, Courteney Cox spoke about getting a little help from her guides, meaning Matthew Perry and her parents.

Source: CBS News. "Courteney Cox: Designing Woman." Cbsnews.com, May 19, 2024, www.cbsnews.com/video/courteney-cox-designing-woman/?intcid=CNM-00-10abd1h. Accessed April 17, 2025.

List of Contributors

About the Author: Judith Turner

Author photo by
Michael Benabib

Judith Turner is an author, writer, producer, creative consultant, and has been an intuitive consultant and life coach for over forty years. She is the author of two books published by Simon and Schuster, *The Hidden World of Birthdays* (Amazon Best Seller) and *The Hidden World of Relationships* (#1 Amazon Best Seller). Judith has appeared regularly on Joan Hamburg's *Consumer Talk* radio show and has appeared on CBS News, ABC News, CNBC Live, and other television and radio programs. Judith was a contributing writer for *BC Magazine* for fifteen years and was the creative consultant of astrological and Guardian Angel compacts for Estée Lauder. She also wrote the book *Dreaming* for the Tommy Hilfiger fragrance Dreaming. Judith was born in New York and resides in New Jersey.

https://judith-turner.com/